Axminster Ecclesiastica

THE AXMINSTER ECCLESIASTICA 1660~1698

Edited
with Annotations and Appendixes
by

K. W. H. HOWARD

GOSPEL TIDINGS PUBLICATIONS

GOSPEL TIDINGS PUBLICATIONS
44 Queen's Drive, Ossett,
W. Yorks. WF5 0ND.

ISBN 0 904731 03 0

First published 1874
First annotated edition 1976

Printed in Great Britain by
Oldham & Manton Ltd., 1 Rugby Street,
Leicester LE3 5FF

CONTENTS

ILLUSTRATIONS

MAPS

INTRODUCTION

"There are certain respects in which this *Axminster Ecclesiastica* is one of the most interesting records relating to the origin and history of the Free Churches of England that has ever been printed. It is the most complete we have met with; it extends over a long period, and it is very illustrative of the history of the times. It is a narrative written at the time, of a great deal that took place connected with the Congregational Church at Axminster during a considerable portion of the latter part of the seventeenth century. By whom this narrative is written is uncertain . . . Be that, however, as it may, it is a production almost unique in value, and of the deepest interest . . . The history of this time has never been more eloquently described than it is in the simple language of these pages . . ."

So wrote a serious reviewer of the first edition of this work on its appearance in the summer of 1874. It is, I think, fair comment on what may be justly regarded as a minor classic of English evangelical Christianity. One would not too readily describe an old church record as being of both general interest and spiritual profit to all classes of christians. But this old church book is positively fascinating, instructive, and challenging. All the more so perhaps, because it sets out to be nothing of the kind. It is a simple, unaffected and honest record 'warts and all'; a mirror of its times, a microcosm of later English puritanism, and a monument of the classic Independent or Congregational churchmanship. Its motif is "tell it to the generations following", and this it does with due respect for chronology, but not too much attention to completeness. There are omissions that annoy, and silences that vex the tidy mind. But they of Axminster knew nothing of the standpoint of the twentieth century armchair onlooker. For three quarters of the period of this record they were a persecuted people.

Most of it is in effect a despatch from the beleaguered citadel of puritanism in the terrible period following the Restoration of 1660. They do not study minutiae except in matters of cardinal christian principle, and then they do it thoroughly. In general they paint on a broad canvas; they are not verbose; they tell us the great dealings of God with them as a church and leave us longing to know more. Encouragements and calamities; the heights and depths of christian experience; the privilege and the price of the 'gathered church' principle in practice, are alike recorded with a true sense of history. They saw the hand of God in everything. Concerned to learn from the past, and to "earnestly contend for the faith once delivered to the saints" in their own generation, they bequeathed a reason of the hope that was in them to those who came after.

This edition has been prepared from that of 1874 which was published from the original manuscript. In both of these latter, what now comprises Chapter 1 is headed *'Preface'*, and the remainder, headed *'Ecclesiastica'*, comprises an uninterrupted mass of page length paragraphs made up of almost interminable sentences. The work of editing has been confined strictly to reduction of sentence and paragraph length and the division into chapters, with the provision of chapter titles which are not part of the original text. The members roll has been transferred from its original position between chapters eight and nine to form the final chapter nineteen. Except for what these aids to easier reading have dictated the text remains unaltered, and in no case has its sense been changed. Obscure words, phrases and allusions are dealt with in the footnotes, together with historical and biographical outlines of persons and events incidentally or indirectly mentioned in the text. The reader may thus follow the narrative for its own sake from beginning to end, or he may satisfy his awakened curiosity as he goes along.

The first three appendixes supply from contemporary sources material which supplements the *Ecclesiastica* in various ways. The remainder are designed to help place the record in its historical setting. Those who are bibliographically curious will, I hope, find some of their questions answered in appendix F—the Story of the *Ecclesiastica.*

It should be borne in mind that the Axminster chronicler generally follows the old style of dating under which 25th of March was regarded as New Year's Day. Officially the change to January 1st began in England about the year 1580, but in legal documents and in a great deal of common usage the old form persisted until 1752. This accounts for slight discrepancies between the chronicler's dates, and those in the footnotes and appendixes.

The *Ecclesiastica* is now reissued with the conviction that "the generations to come" still need to know something of the acts of the eternal God in His church on earth in the generations past. In a day when false foundations are being both shaken and destroyed one earnestly hopes that this little work may help many to understand that—

> His love in time past forbids us to think
> He'll leave us at last in trouble to sink.

Those who are able to penetrate the historical form, and feel the eternal realities of which it speaks lay hold upon their souls, will surely join the worthies of the *Ecclesiastica* and cry—**Admired be free grace!**

K. W. H. HOWARD

Stamford, Lincs.
Summer 1975

THE AXMINSTER CHRONOLOGY

		1656	B. Ashwood admitted vicar of Axminster by Commission of Triers	Oct. 24
		1657	John Ashwood born	
Sept. 3	Oliver Cromwell died	**1658**		
Oct. 12	*Savoy Declaration of Faith & Order*			

	Convention Parliament	**1660**	B. Ashwood instituted vicar of Axminster	Feb. 13
Apr. 14	Declaration of Breda		'Gathered Church' formed in private; Ashwood appointed pastor	
May 24	Return of Charles II			
Sept. 13	Act for Confirming and Restoring Ministers			
Apr.-July	Savoy Conference	**1661**		
May 8	Cavalier Parliament			
Dec. 24	Corporation Act			
May 19	Act of Uniformity passed	**1662**		
Aug. 24	Act of Uniformity took effect		Ashwood in Exeter gaol several weeks	July/Aug.
			First elders appointed	
		1663	First deacons appointed	
July 1	1st Conventicle Act	**1664**	First losses by death	

Mar. 24	Five Mile Act	**1665**		
	Plague of London		Covenant renewed	
Sept. 2	Fire of London	**1666**	First case of discipline	
July 1	1st Conventicle Act expired	**1667**	Covenant renewed	
May 10	2nd Conventicle Act	**1670**		
May 22	Treaty of Dover			
Mar. 15	1st Declaration of Indulgence	**1672**		
			Weycroft licensed as Indep. meeting house	Apr. 11
			Ashwood licensed as Indep. teacher	Apr. 11
			Ashwood ill at Chard; his *Epistle to the Church*	Nov.
			Covenant renewed	Nov.
Mar. 8	1st Declaration of Indulgence withdrawn	**1673**		
Aug. 1	The Test Act		Covenant renewed	
		1678	Ashwood's last sermon	Oct. 20
			Ashwood died at Chard	Oct. 27
	The Popish Plot		Ashwood buried at Axminster	Nov. 6
	Cavalier Parliament dissolved	**1679**	*The Heavenly Trade* published	
			Towgood called	May 6
			Towgood ordained	Aug.
		1681	*Groans from Sion* published	Feb.
			The Best Treasure published	Nov.
			Driven out from Weycroft	

Date	Event	Year	Axminster	Date
	The Rye House Plot	**1683**		
Aug. 24	John Owen died			
Feb. 6	Chas. II died; Jas. II acceded	**1685**		
June/July	Monmouth Rebellion			
July 6	Battle of Sedgemoor		Worshipped in a cave	Aug.-Nov.
Sept. 1	Bloody Assizes			
Oct. 18	Revocation of Edict of Nantes			
	Act of Oblivion	**1686**	Discussion on occasional conformity	July 28
			Return to Weycroft	Oct. 31
Apr. 4	2nd Declaration of Indulgence	**1687**	Resolve to compile *Book of Remembrance*	Oct. 26
Apr.	2nd Declaration of Indulgence reissued	**1688**	2nd edition of *The Heavenly Trade*	
June	Trial of the seven bishops			
Nov. 5	Revolution: Jas. II fled; Wm. III landed Torbay			
	War of the Grand Alliance	**1688-97**		
Feb. 13	Declaration of Rights	**1689**	John Ashwood appointed pastor in Exeter	
May 24	Act of Toleration			
June 30	Battle of Beachy Head	**1690**		
July 1	Battle of the Boyne			
July 26	Bombardment of Teignmouth			
Apr. 6	The Happy Union	**1691**		
Oct.	Treaty of Limerick			

Month	National events	Year	Local events	Date
May	Battle of La Hogue	**1692**		
	Battle of Namur			
	Battle of Steinkerk			
July	Battle of Neerwinden	**1693**	Robt. Bryant & Matthew Towgood M.D. appointed elders	
Oct.	Battle of Marsaglia			
		1694	Conference of Indep. Churches; Exeter & Weycroft	June & Sept.
	Mary, queen of Wm. III died	**1695**		
	Assassination plot—Wm. III	**1696**		
		1696-7	Ordination controversy at Exeter	
	Treaty of Ryswick	**1697**		
		1698	Last service at Weycroft	Aug. 7
			New meeting house opened in Axminster	
			John Ashwood removed from Exeter to London	

Month	National events	Year	Local events	Date
	Wm. III died; Anne acceded	**1702**		
		1706	John Ashwood died	
		1709	B. Ashwood's widow died	

1

THAT THE GENERATION TO COME MIGHT KNOW....

It hath been the laudable practise of the saints to preserve the memory of divine dispensations. This they did sundry ways: viz., by composing Eucharistical songs (*Exod. 15, Judg. 5*), and teaching them to their children; by imposing significant names on the places where they received signal mercies; by writing them on the names of their children; by erecting memorial stones and pillars; by appointing anniversary feasts of remembrance; and by committing them to writing that they might be read by posterity. So careful were they to keep in remembrance the providences of God towards them. This practise is recommended to us also by the wisdom of God.

God would have the memory of His dispensations toward Israel to be preserved. The pot of manna was by His appointment placed in the ark as a sacred memorial of His miraculous feeding them in the wilderness.[1] The Passover was instituted in commemoration of their wonderful deliverance from the destroying angel;[2] the annual feast of tabernacles, in remembrance of their fathers dwelling in booths.[3] He also expressly commanded that His providential dispensations towards His church should be recorded and transmitted to the generations to come. (*Psa. 78.5, Psa. 102.18*). He enjoined Moses to record His gracious appearances for His people against Amalek (*Exod. 17*); to keep a journal of all Israel's travels in the wilderness (*Numb. 33.2*); to write a song and teach it to the children of Israel, expressing what God had done for them, a sinful and unworthy people (*Deut. 31.19*). Moreover the Holy Spirit hath ordered the pens of Moses, Samuel, Joshua and the rest of the prophets to record the state and condition of the church under the Old Testament, with the most remarkable occurrences that have attended the same. Yea, no small part of the Holy Scripture is an historical narrative of the church, a chronicle of the acts and monuments of the Lord's wonderful works in framing, building, preserving and ruling His church. Much of the New Testament also contains an history of the lives and acts of Christ and His apostles, together with the state of the apostolic churches.

Further, the expediency and usefulness of church registers is obvious to all. In civil concerns it is judged prudent to record things of importance; it is no less prudent in concerns of a religious and ecclesiastical nature. Shall kingdoms and commonwealths have their chronicles, civil courts their rolls and records? Shall tradesmen keep their books of accounts, lawyers their books of precedents, physicians their collections of experiments, and travellers their journals? And shall not the churches of Christ have their registers and books of remembrance wherein they may record their church transactions and the various dealings of God with them? Shall the men of this world be wiser in their generation than the children of light?

The works of God are all worthy to be remembered, but especially His work in building and preserving His churches. His providences towards them are His masterpieces which deserve to be observed most seriously and to be had in an everlasting remembrance, and there is no way so effectual to perpetuate the memory of them as to register them faithfully. Hereby not only the present but the future generation may be excited to praise the Lord when they shall see the series of His mercies in a register as so many pearls in a string, and by the frequent reading of them may keep the same fresh and green in their memories. Moreover, a church register may be singularly useful for direction, support

[1] Exod. 16. 33-34. [2] Exod. 12. 12-14. [3] Deut. 16.13

and consolation in dubious and perplexing cases in which a church may be concerned.

Upon these and the like considerations the church of Christ ordinarily assembling at Wykecroft[1] hath unanimously agreed that a church register be kept wherein the most material passages relating to them since their first incorporation might be faithfully registered, together with all things for the future appertaining to their state, rule, order, which shall be judged worthy of a particular remembrance.[2]

1 Spelled variously Wykecroft and Wickcroft in this work, the modern version is Weycroft; derived from the Anglo-Saxon Woeg or Weg, a road, and croft, denoting a home or farmstead on the road, viz the Roman Fosse Way.

2 The decision was taken on 26th October 1687, and the compilation of this record presumably began shortly after that date. (See pp. 128f, 220).

2

THE DAY OF HIS ESPOUSALS....

(1660-61)

The Lord having visited this land with the dayspring from on high, vouchsafing to its inhabitants the precious gospel of His Son, Jesus Christ, raised up many famous instruments successively that have been as burning and shining lights in their day, that have borne their testimony to the truths of Christ and many of them in the face of dangers, yea, of death itself. These received in their measure that unction from the Holy One whereby the glorious mysteries of the kingdom of God have been more fully discovered and made known than in some ages past. The same anointing having taught and led many of them more fully to understand the form and the fashion of His house, with all the ordinances thereof, the goings out thereof and the comings in thereof, all the forms thereof and all the laws thereof, the whole limit thereof to be most holy.[1] Hereby many famous churches have been planted

[1] Ezek. 43.10-12.

and the pure institutions of the Lord Jesus heedfully observed. But oh! how stately, how beautiful and glorious will Zion's assemblies be when this pattern of the Lord's house shall be more seriously weighed and carefully measured. And the churches of Christ shall be thus constituted, and all the forms, ordinances and laws thereof to the utmost bounds and limits thereof round about shall more exactly answer the rule of the great Lawgiver and the pattern shewed in the Mount.[1]

Now the churches and people of Christ in this land having had a long day of peace and tranquillity for some years together, living in the plentiful enjoyment of gospel ordinances, a great and wide door of gospel privileges having been set open before them, and no open adversary to oppose them, lo, on a sudden the scheme is changed! The infinitely wise God who changeth times and seasons (*Dan. 2.21*), was pleased to bring a black cloud over this sunny day to alter the face of the times and to cause great changes and a strange rolling of affairs to pass over these nations upon the return of an exile Prince in the year *1660*.[2]

[1] A characteristically Puritan Independent description of the development of the Protestant Reformation from its beginnings under Wyclif, Tyndale, Barnes and others, to its open establishment under the Commonwealth. Puritanism in the three counties converging near Axminster was predominantly Presbyterian though with a substantial Independent minority, notably on the Dorset side of the county boundary. Classical Presbyterianism had never covered the country as a whole, and collapsed altogether with the return of the bishops in 1660. Nevertheless on 18 October 1655 an association of Presbyterian ministers of the county of Devon had been formed at Exeter to deal with matters of doctrine and discipline. Rules drawn up agreed that none should be admitted as members that "will administer the Lord's Supper promiscuously to all sorts, good and bad"; that they are to proceed in their congregations "according to the rule of the word and the example of the best reformed churches", "to endeavour to uphold purity of doctrine and to prevent the growing and spreading errors of the time", and "that none shall wilfully contradict the confession of faith set forth by the Assembly of Divines at Westminster in his preaching". In the following year Independent ministers were also admitted, and a united Address was despatched to Oliver Cromwell seeking his favour toward their work. The gathering functioned with twice yearly meetings under the name of the Exeter Assembly until 1659, when it lapsed until conditions of toleration were introduced in 1689. An account of its work and a transcript of its earlier minutes are to be found in R. N. Worth's "Puritanism in Devon, and the Exeter Assembly". (*Transactions of the Devonshire Association,* IX. 1887).

[2] The Restoration of the Monarchy following the Commonwealth of 1649-1660 by the return of Charles II from exile in the Netherlands. The king was then thirty years of age, a clever cynic, a Roman Catholic at heart, and an absolutist in his understanding of his royal office. For reasons of expediency he had promised by the Declaration of Breda (April 1660) pardon for those who had fought against his father, the restoration of parliament, and "a liberty to tender consciences, and that no man shall be disquieted or called in question for differences of opinion in matters of religion". The promise of religious freedom was systematically broken during the next few years by the Cavalier Parliament which passed the

At which time there lived in the town of Axminster and county of Devon an able minister of the gospel, Mr. Bartholomew Ashwood,[1] who came not behind any of his predecessors in many

[1] Bartholomew Ashwood. (1622-1678). A Puritan divine. "A Warwickshire minister's son", says Anthony A. Wood, himself no friend of puritans, "became a batter or commoner of St. Albans Hall (Oxford), in the latter end of 1638, aged 16 years, but having been puritanically educated, he was translated after some continuance in the said hall to Exeter College: and there put under a tutor puritanically then esteemed, and took one degree in arts as a member of that college, and was soon after beneficed, and became a man of the times. He hath written and published, *The Heavenly Trade ... The Best Treasure ... Groans from Sion ...* and other things which I have not yet seen. He died about the year sixteen hundred and eighty. I find one Bartholomew Ashwood of Magdalen College in Oxon, to be matriculated as a Warwickshire man in 1591, aged thirteen years, and as a member of that house to have taken the degree in arts, that of master, to be completed in 1601. Which Bartholomew I take to be either father or uncle to our author before mentioned." (*Athenae Oxonienses* III. 1272).

Ashwood graduated in 1642 and is next found succeeding his father, of the same name, as rector of Bickleigh, near Tiverton, Devon, where Ashwood senior had ministered since 1610. He was admitted vicar of Axminster 24 October 1656, on the presentation of John (afterwards Sir John) Drake of Ashe House, and instituted 13 Feb. 1660; and ejected for nonconformity before August 1662. Pastor of the Independent Church of Axminster 1660-1678.

"The Reverend Mr. Bartholomew Ashwood was a judicious, godly, and laborious divine ... The son has often said of him, that if there was a good man upon earth, his father was one, being strictly pious, and much devoted to prayer. He relates this passage of his holy great-grandfather, that once being under an extraordinary solicitude about his children and posterity, those words were strangely impressed upon him by an audible voice—'I will be a God to thee, and to thy seed after thee'—and the very same thing is said to have happened to his father, when under a like concern." (Thomas Reynolds, *Sermon ... on the Death of the Revd. John Ashwood, with an account of his life and character*. London, 1707. pp.54,55.)

(See also, Appendix C; and Calamy/Palmer, *Nonconformist's Memorial;* A. G. Matthews, *Calamy Revised;* E. Windeatt, *Trans. Cong. Hist. Soc.* I.85; J. Foster, *Alumni Oxonienses,* v.I).

Clarendon Code, comprising, (i) The Corporation Act (1661), which obliged all members of municipal corporations to receive communion according to the forms of the Church of England; (ii) The Act of Uniformity (1662) (iii) The First Conventicle Act (1664); (iv) The Five Mile Act (1665); and also the Second Conventicle Act (1670). The political object of this legislation was to break the influence of Puritanism on national life by giving the Anglican Church the monopoly of higher education, so making it impossible for Puritans to reach eminence in any profession. To a great extent the aim was achieved, although Puritanism continued to exist and to comprise a vital factor in the national character. It is noteworthy that whereas many nobles and gentry had adhered to Puritanism before the Clarendon Code, very few were found in its circles thereafter.

respects as to his excellent endowments and qualifications for the ministerial work, especially as to his sweet, profitable, heavenly spirit and conversation. His parts were quick, smart and spritely. He was a man of eminent piety, mortifiedness, wisdom and gravity. He had a deep insight into the mysteries of the gospel, and was very zealous for the pure instituted worship of Christ according to gospel rule and the order of the primitive churches. His ministry was sharper than a two-edged sword, searching the very secrets of the heart. He had bowels of compassions towards perishing sinners, studying to find out the most sweet, melting, moving arguments imaginable to win souls to Jesus Christ. He was a Barnabas, a son of consolation indeed, very useful in comforting afflicted consciences. The Lord gave him the tongue of the learned to speak words in season to the weary and wounded in spirit.

Thus this faithful servant of Christ being endowed with such a spirit of wisdom gave good heed to find out acceptable words, which were as goads and nails fastened in the hearts and consciences of some poor sinners. The Lord blessed the ministry of His servant through the powerful and effectual operations of the Holy Spirit accompanying the same to the awakening, enlightening, converting and effectually drawing over some souls to close in with Jesus Christ, and whose hearts were engaged and made willing to be the Lord's covenant people. These continued waiting on his ministry in the public dispensations of the gospel, and frequently assembled themselves together with one accord in more private seasons of solemn and fervent prayer and supplication to the Lord for their mutual edification. They were waiting for an opportunity and capacity to form themselves into a church of Christ according to gospel rule and the pure institution of the Lord Jesus Christ after the order of the primitive churches at the first publication of the gospel by the apostles of our Lord Jesus Christ, as far as they apprehended the mind of the Spirit of God therein.

Now the Lord was pleased to engage the hearts of some serious pious christians of the neighbouring villages to attend frequently on the ministry of this holy man. These got into an intimate acquaintance with him, and also with those few souls in the town of Axminster whose hearts the Lord had wrought upon by His word and Spirit, who likewise resolved to join in and walk with them in the same order and fellowship of the gospel.[1] Foreseeing clouds to gather blackness over these nations and the Lord in the way of His providence to threaten His churches and interest with a flood of trouble and persecution, both Mr. Ashwood, with the

[1] The 'Axminster Circle'—the area from which the members of this church were drawn—is indicated in some detail in Chapter 19, and in Appendix D.

rest, endeavoured to incorporate themselves into one body before the storm did fall. In a short space of time after, calling in the assistance of other churches, by the hands of Mr. Benn,[1] pastor of a church of Christ at Dorchester, and Mr. Thorn,[2] pastor of a

[1] William Benn (1600-1680). A Puritan divine born at Egremont, Cumberland, and educated at Queen's College, Oxford. Called to Dorchester 1629 by the celebrated John White, 'Patriarch of Dorchester', he became rector of All Saints Church. Ministered regularly among the prisoners in the town gaol. Appointed a 'Trier' for the County of Dorset in 1646, he was ejected in 1662. Thereafter often imprisoned for preaching at conventicles. At Maiden Newton in 1665, and at Fordington in 1669. Licensed as a Congregational teacher under the Declaration of Indulgence of 1672, he became the first nonconformist minister in Dorchester. Published (in reply to Francis Bampfield, ejected from Sherborne, a Seventh Day Baptist) *A Vindication of the Christian Sabbath against the Jewish*, 1677; and *Soul Prosperity*, in several sermons on 3 John 2, 1683. (See, Palmer, *Nonconformist's Memorial*, II.126,7: W. Densham & J. Ogle, *The story of the Congregational Churches of Dorset*. 1899).

[2] George Thorne. (1624-1680) A Puritan divine born at Tiverton, Devon, and educated at Sidney Sussex College, Cambridge, graduating M.A., 1647. Rector of Radipole and Melcombe Regis, Dorset, whence he was ejected for nonconformity in 1662. In the *London Collection* of Farewell Sermons, Thorne's farewell sermon on Ps. 37,34 "Wait on the Lord and keep his way", appears:

> Not knowing whether ever I shall speak to you more from this place, being willing to leave a word in season, I shall recommend to you what, in answer to prayer, I have received of the Lord, for directing me in my course in this gloomy dark day...

He closes with this personal word:

> And here, beloved, I shall take occasion to open my heart sincerely to you. You know what is required of me, if I will continue as a minister in this kingdom. I hope no person can think me such a humorous perverse fanatic as to throw away my maintenance, much less my ministerial capacity (which is much dearer to me than livelihood, yea, than life), out of a proud humour and vain-glorious fancy. In brief, therefore, as I shall answer it before the great God, the Searcher of all hearts, and the righteous Judge, did not conscience towards God forbid me, I would willingly do all the Act requires. But seeing I cannot declare an unfeigned assent and consent, I dare not (and from your love to me, I know you would not have me) dissemble with God and man. I do therefore humbly choose to submit to the penalty rather than by a hypocritical conformity (for such it must be in me, if any) to dishonour my God, wound my own conscience, and dissemble with men; knowing assuredly that my God hath no need of my sin.

After ejection he preached secretly, fled to Holland in 1663; returned and was imprisoned several times. He was at Compton Valence in 1665, and was licensed as Congregational teacher at Weymouth under the Declaration of Indulgence of 1672. Subsequently so maliciously persecuted that he fled from place to place for safety, often returning to Compton Valence. (See, H. S. Shergold, *The Faithful of 1662. George Thorne . . . ejected minister, and the Story of Congregationalism in Weymouth* (1912); W. Densham & J. Ogle, *The story of the Congregational Churches of Dorset*. 1899).

church of Christ at Weymouth, on a solemn day of prayer and supplication, voluntarily giving up themselves to the Lord and to each other by the will of God,[1] solemnly covenanting and engaging to walk together in a due and faithful attendance upon the Lord Jesus Christ in all His ordinances and appointments, and in the faithful discharge of all those duties relating to the members of a church of Christ, so were embodied and constituted a church of Christ.

Ashwood's pulpit in Axminster Church. c.1800.[2]

1 2 Cor. 8.5.

2 "Near the middle walls of the nave and fronting the east, stand the pulpit and desk, which were erected in 1633 as appeared by a date formerly at the back of the pulpit... They were fixed originally against the south western pier of the tower, and were removed to their present situation when the south aisle was built." (James Davidson, *The History of Axminster Church,* 1835, p.68.) This change was made in 1800, in which year the organ was erected. The original 'three-decker', comprising pulpit, reading desk and clerk's desk, was dismantled in 1870 when the pulpit in its present mutilated condition was restored to its original position.

Being thus united and brought into one body, presently Mr. Bartholomew Ashwood was chosen by them to be their pastor, who immediately, by the consent of the church and his readily accepting their call, in the preference and by the assistance of those worthy pastors beforenamed, was ordained and set apart for the pastoral office in this little sister church whose foundation was now laid, the number of the names being but few, about twelve or thirteen.

Thus were a few living, lively stones that lay here and there scattered in the wilderness brought and cemented together and laid upon the foundation of the apostles and prophets, Jesus Christ Himself being the chief cornerstone,[1] and so were built up a spiritual house or temple for the Lord to dwell in, and to have pure instituted worship given unto Him.

Thus this little society continued stedfastly in a due observance of all the ordinances and institutions of the Lord Jesus Christ with gladness of heart, the Lord adding to them and increasing the number. Ah! what liveliness, what zeal and forwardness in the work and ways of God, what spiritual edifying conversations, what fervent love and warm affections, what a spirit of sympathy one with another, what tender care and watchfulness over each other! What a blessedness was there seen and found amongst them! What an eminent presence of God in the midst of them, what a resemblance of heaven upon earth! How amiable and lovely were their assemblies! How sweet, how profitable was a day spent in communion with them! Ah! these were espousal days. Now, how delightfully could they follow God in a wilderness. The blackness of the day was in no way terrifying to them. The menaces of adversaries could not daunt them. Dangers and difficulties in their way could not in the least cause them to baulk their duty, or to turn aside, or shrink from the good ways of the Lord. Days and nights spent in prayer, in an attendance upon the Lord Jesus in His sacred ordinances, in holy conferences, were sweet and refreshing notwithstanding all the inconveniences which attended the outward man. The blessing of Asher, which was frequently prayed for in their mutual assembling, evidently appeared to be granted to them (*Deut. 33.25*). "Thy shoes shall be iron and brass, and as thy days so shall thy strength be."

1 Eph. 2.20.

3

PRAYER WAS MADE ....OF THE CHURCH UNTO GOD....

(1662)

Not long after, the clouds grew blacker and the day darkened apace. In *1662* an edict was issued forth by the powers then in being that after the 24th day of the 6th month every teacher or preacher refusing to conform to those things which were to be imposed on them, part of which was a declaring their assent and consent to the Book of Common Prayer, the Book of Articles and Ceremonies of the Church of England according to the decrees and canons of the prelates &c, with other things required and enjoined by the said Act, were to be ejected. They were to be deprived of those incomes before allotted them for their temporal maintenance, and not be permitted any more to teach or preach to the people upon pain of imprisonment. So that on one day, that black and dismal day never to be forgotten, were many hundreds of eminent, pious, learned, faithful ministers of the gospel in the land put to silence, and passed under a civil death.[1]

[1] The Act of Uniformity, 1662.

> ... Every parson, vicar, or other minister whatsoever . . . shall in the church, chapel, or place of public worship belonging to his said benefice or promotion, upon some Lord's day before the feast of St. Bartholomew . . . one thousand six hundred and sixty two, openly, publicly, and solemnly read the morning and evening prayer . . . and after such reading thereof, shall openly and publicly, before the congregation there assembled, declare his unfeigned assent and consent to the use of all things in the said book contained and prescribed in these words and no other: I, A.B., do here declare my unfeigned assent and consent to all and everything contained and prescribed in and by the book entitled, *The Book of Common Prayer*...

What, then, were the things that proved to be such insuperable obstacles to this 'conformity' on the part of so many godly ministers? The reasons had been formally stated at the Savoy Conference, where twelve bishops and twelve Presbyterian ministers met from April to July 1661 to deliberate on changes in the Liturgy. The bishops would concede nothing to meet puritan wishes, whereupon the puritan representatives tabled a list of eight principal objections:

> It is contrary to the word of God, 1. That no minister is admitted to baptize without using the sign of the cross. 2. That no minister is admitted to officiate without wearing a surplice. 3. That none are admitted to the Lord's Supper without receiving it kneeling. 4. That ministers are obliged to pronounce all baptized persons regenerated by the Holy Ghost. 5. That ministers are obliged to deliver the sacrament of the body and blood of Christ to the unfit. 6. That ministers are obliged to absolve the unfit of their sins, and that in absolute expressions. 7. That ministers are forced to give thanks for all whom they bury, as persons whom God has taken to Himself. 8. That none may preach who do not subscribe that there is nothing in the Common Prayer book, Ordination Service, and Thirty Nine Articles, contrary to the word of God (Sylvester, *Reliquiae Baxterianae,* pp.341-3).

These objections were not new. They followed in the long succession of Puritan objections stemming from the *First & Second Admonitions to Parliament* of 1572, and the *Lincolnshire Ministers Apology delivered to King James, for themselves and their brethren, refusing subscription, and conformity to the book of Common-prayer and Ceremonies,* of 1605. The very threat of Uniformity following the Restoration produced a spate of pamphlets on this subject: *The Old Nonconformist, touching the Book of Common Prayer, and Ceremonies. Unto which is annexed the reasons why Scotland refused the Book of Common-Prayer* (1660); (Henry Burton) *Jesu-Worship Confuted, or Certain arguments against bowing at the Name of Jesus,* (1660); Vavasor Powell, *Common-Prayer-Book No Divine Service,* (1661); John Owen, *A Discourse Concerning Liturgies,* (1662)—(Works, Ed. Goold, XV.1).

The Act of Uniformity was also aimed at dismissing the godly ministers appointed from 1654 onward by Cromwell's 'Commission of Triers'. Such a minister (regardless of ecclesiastical order) was required to be "a person for the grace of God in him, his holy and unblamable conversation, as also for his knowledge and utterance, able and fit to preach the gospel". Schoolmasters were likewise penalised in order to make it impossible for Dissenters to have their children properly educated. The Act received royal assent on May 19th and took effect on August 24th. Ashwood's standing was evidently clearly known to the authorities who proceeded against him before the legal date. It may have been after-thoughts on this score that explain the 'two or three days' respite' he was allowed before imprisonment.

Now some weeks before this edict was to be put into execution, Mr. Bartholomew Ashwood, pastor of this church, on a Lord's day in the morning, was apprehended by soldiers, carried before a magistrate, who there refusing such oaths as were imposed on him, was sent to the common gaol in Exeter.[1] Yet such was the tender care of the Lord towards this people and so wisely and graciously did the Lord overrule the spirits of officers into whose custody he was committed that they were so favourable to him as to give him two or three days' respite to remain with his wife and family before he was conveyed to prison,[2] by which means the

[1] Indictment of the Puritans, following the Restoration and before the First Conventicle Act, was usually by resort to an old statute, the 35th of Queen Elisabeth (1593), which had been ignored during the Commonwealth but not repealed. It banned attendance at conventicles, and compelled attendance at the parish church. Under this statute Bunyan was indicted at Bedford in 1660, Ashwood at Axminster in 1662, and Francis Holcroft at Cambridge, in 1663, along with many others in all parts of the country. The oaths which Ashwood declined we may presume to have been: (i), The *Oath Ex Officio* by which a person swore to answer all questions put to him, even though it were to accuse himself; (ii) The *Etcetera Oath* which ran thus: 'I do swear that I approve the doctrine, discipline, or government established in the Church of England . . . and that I will not ever give my consent to alter the government of this church by archbishops, bishops, deans, and archdeacons, *et cetera* . . . as it now stands . . . and this I do heartily, willingly and truly upon the faith of a Christian.' Seth Ward, appointed Bishop of Exeter in 1662, made full use of these oaths in his *Articles of Visitation and Enquiry concerning matters Ecclesiastical, exhibited to the ministers, churchwardens and sidesmen of every parish within the Diocese of Exeter, in the primary Episcopal Visitation of the Right Reverend Father in God Seth, by Divine Providence Lord Bishop of Exeter*. London, 1662.

Ashwood was instituted vicar of Axminster Feb. 13, 1660, and arrested "some few weeks before" August 24, 1662. Between these dates the Independent Church was formed, Ashwood was appointed pastor, and together they "continued stedfastly". It appears that his ejectment did not await the Act of Uniformity, but followed the Act of September 1660 which restored the sequestered episcopal clergy (Kennett, *A Register and Chronicle,* p.254). Restoration rigor began immediately and the Independent incumbents were the first to feel it. Ashwood's ejectment and the formation of the Axminster Independent Church are to be dated from the latter end of 1660.

[2] This was the South Gate Prison, Exeter, taken down in 1819. A letter written by one of Ashwood's fellow prisoners, Abraham Cheare, a Baptist minister from Plymouth, suggests something of the conditions: "I received yours of the 11th of the seventh month and in it a testimony of teaching and supporting grace and presence continued to you abrode, which he is pleased not to deny his poor worms heer, in these holes of the earth, where violence hath thrust us as in so many slaughter houses of men; but overruling grace makes them as the presence-chambers of the great King, where he brings and feasts his favourites with the best things, and proclaims among them 'Thus shall it be don to them whome the King delightes to honour'... he chooseth in this furnace of affliction; a week in a *prison* giving plainer discoverie of a man's spirit, than a month in a *church* ... Our bishop, Ward, came to this citty last week, and was received in great state . . . The Deputy Lieuts. are most of them sitting, and ('tis said) we shall be brought before them, but to what end is not known . . . troops are

church had an opportunity to assemble together in his house solemnly to pour out their supplications to the Lord once more for and with their dear pastor, who then preached to them from that scripture (*Heb. 10.25*), "Not forsaking the assembling of ourselves together, as the manner of some is; but exhorting one another: and so much the more, as ye see the day approaching." And oh! what a solemn day was it. How earnestly did he caution them that they would keep at a distance from the corruptions of the times, both as to worship and conversation; that they would be as it was prophesied of Israel, "A people dwelling alone, and . . . not . . . reckoned among the nations."[1] How affectionately did he beseech and counsel them to hold fast the profession of their faith without wavering, keeping up and maintaining their communion and assembling themselves together, and in nothing to be terrified

South Gate gaol, Exeter

[1] Num. 23.9.

in town, and going forth this morning . . . to take up the non-conforming persons . . ." (Ivimey, *History of the English Baptists,* II. 105-7). Ashwood would be thankful that his detention was only "a few weeks' space."

by their adversaries but stand fast in one spirit, with one mind striving together for the faith of the gospel. With many such like exhortations that dropped from him at that time, being ready to depart from them, and, as he himself said, the Lord knowing whether it might not be his last words to them. But the time is expired, and now must this poor little flock be left without a shepherd; weak and small, and yet must take its walk into a howling wilderness, a little sister church, as it were, born out of due time, and its breasts be suddenly plucked from her. Now they "lament for the teats, for the pleasant fields, for the fruitful vine."[1] A night of darkness and dangers was come upon them, and no watchman of whom they might enquire "What of the night?"

Thus an affectionate, tender pastor and a loving people take their leave of each other, and when the prison doors should be opened again, and this skilful pilot sent back to steer their course for them through the swelling waves of trouble and persecution that began to arise amain, here sense and carnal reason was quite at a non-plus, and could see no further, but began to conclude that now the building must go down again. Yea, such were the circumstances of providence this day that faith itself was sorely tried and hard put to it. How to believe that this house of God should be built in such a troublous time was a difficult thing. Yet the Lord Jesus Christ whose house it is, and upon whose shoulders the government of Zion is laid, was graciously pleased to spirit His servants for their wilderness journey. An eminent spirit of courage and boldness was poured out upon this people, so that notwithstanding all the dangers that threatened them, when every step in the way of their duty, as to an eye of sense and carnal reason, seemed to be the way to bonds and imprisonment, yet they constantly assembled themselves together every Lord's day. They clave to the pure institutions of the Lord Jesus Christ, and improving their communion together in a mutual exhorting of one another, and praying together for their spiritual edification, and building up one another on their most holy faith, so that during the time of their pastor's imprisonment it might be said, as it was in the case of Peter (*Acts 12.5*), "Prayer was made without ceasing of the church unto God for him."

Now such ministers of Christ who refused to conform to the injunctions of authority lay dormant, being forbidden to teach and preach to the people. And men of corrupt and carnal principles, of loose, sottish, debauched conversations, many of them filled with a spirit of bitterness, enmity and persecution against the good ways of God, the power and purity of religion, and against such as did cleave to the pure institutions of the Lord Jesus Christ, such

[1] Is. 32.12.

a sort of men in many places were set up and appointed by the prelates to be preachers to the people.[1] O doleful change! Enough to cause the hearts of the Lord's faithful people in the land to ache and even break within them! The pure institutions of Jesus Christ were disregarded and laid aside. His precious ordinances were corrupted by men's devices and traditions, the pure waters of the sanctuary puddled and fouled with the feet of such as called themselves the shepherds of the flock, and the word of the Lord was now precious, there was no open vision.

In a few weeks' space, "He that hath the key of David, that opens and no man shuts, and shutteth and no man openeth"[2] was graciously pleased in the way of His providence to open the prison doors and to send back this pastor to his people again, who immediately set about his pastoral work as before. The next Lord's day after his return he began to preach to the congregation from that scripture in *Ezra 9.9,* "For we were bondmen; yet our God hath not forsaken us in our bondage, but hath extended mercy unto us in the sight of the kings of Persia, to give us a reviving, to set up the house of our God, and to repair the desolations thereof, and to give us a wall in Judah and in Jerusalem." So he continued on several Lord's days discoursing from that scripture very pertinently and profitably, fitted to the providences of the day, the state and circumstances of the Church. Then was this people greatly revived, keeping close in communion together, walking in all the ordinances and appointments of the Lord Jesus Christ, and were as a city on a hill, exemplary to all round about. Whilst darkness was covering the nation apace, here was light. Many of Zion's poor were ready to faint and swoon for bread to relieve their souls, but here was provision for Zion's children in abundance. This being known abroad what privileges this church did enjoy, many of the Lord's people began to enquire where this little flock did feed, and some from divers parts resorted to their assembly, by which means the number increased, new converts were drawn over to the Lord Jesus and more were added to the church.

The church thus increasing thought it expedient in order to its being rightly organized, to set apart two of the brethren whom they judged most fitly qualified for the work of ruling elders, to enquire after the state of the flock and be helpful to the church as to its edification, as the office of eldership required. Wherefore,

[1] An exception was Joseph Crabb (d.1699), Ashwood's parochial successor who, like the celebrated William Gurnall of Lavenham in Suffolk, was a conforming puritan. (See p.190f).

[2] Rev. 3.7.

after several days spent in solemn prayer to the Lord for His gracious presence in directing and counselling them in this case, on a day of prayer and supplication they chose Thomas Lane and James Pinson for that office, who, accepting the same, were appointed to the work and office of ruling elders in the church.

Afterwards, some space of time being passed away, the Lord was pleased to awaken up several of His messengers again, who for some time had been silent to the people, like men in their graves.[1] And who knows but that the faithfulness, zeal and forwardness of this church might provoke some of them to set about their preaching work again? Whereupon, as some of them began to be more open and public in their preaching work, the rage of the adversary increased the more, and waxed greater and greater, insomuch that several, both ministers and people, were apprehended and shut up in prison houses. Great vexations and troubles were the lot of many that dissented from the national way of worship. Notwithstanding, during this great storm of persecution, the Lord appeared in a signal manner to be a defence to this congregation, eminently preserving them from the snare of the fowler, and from those furious persecutors who hunted their steps and made it their business to search after their meeting places. The Lord gave this people prudence to appoint such seasons and places for their assembling together to worship the Lord up and down, sometimes in one obscure place, sometimes in another, in woods and solitary corners. So that the enemies which chased them sore without cause were like the men of Sodom, smitten with

1 The silence of some ejected ministers, especially in the west, was a great burden on Joseph Alleine of Taunton, who about this time wrote *A Call to Archippus; or An humble and earnest motion to some Ejected Ministers, (by way of Letter) to take heed to their Ministry, that they fulfil it. Printed in the year, 1664.*

> Your long silence (he said) hath made us speak, to utter to you our own troubles, and the sighs and groans of your helpless flocks... suffer not your worthy talents to be buried in the napkin, now the sinking church and dying religion hath such pressing need for their utmost improvement . . . Did not we reverence your parts, gifts, and graces, and esteem them every way so useful to the churches, we should contentedly see you sit still, and never be at the pains to excite you. But our high value of you hath made us humbly bold to expostulate the case a little with you, and passionately to beseech you, to remember how great a work it is that lies upon you, and to set your hands to it in this time of difficulty. ... Hath not God said, Necessity is laid on you, and WOE unto you if you preach not the Gospel? Who shall free you from that woe, or loose your bonds of that necessity, if yet you sit still in silence? ... Are you not the Shepherds of the flocks? And shall the true Shepherds flee, as soon as they see the wolves; and leave the sheep? ... (pp.3,4).

blindness and frequently wearied themselves and were quite tired to find the places of their assembling, and all in vain, for the Lord disappointed the mischievous devices of crafty adversaries so that their hands could not perform their enterprises.[1]

[1] Citing the last two sentences of this chapter, H. M. Dexter says: "...the reaction came, they were made to suffer accordingly. Independency was driven back into its old lurking places. Barns and back lanes, if not groves and gravel pits, grew shelteringly familiar with the sound of its songs, and its supplications once more." (*The Congregationalism of the last three hundred years, as seen in its Literature*. 1880. pp.668-9).

4

THE SHADOW OF THY WINGS.....

(1663)

A remarkable providence must not be omitted. On the 13th day of the 7th month *1663*, it being a sabbath day, the church had appointed that day for the celebration of the sacred ordinance of the Lord's Supper in a lonesome place near a great wood where a great number of people from divers parts were assembled together. At this time there was the pastor of another church who, through the violence of persecution was constrained frequently to be wanting from his people, and to leave his own habitation also, whose name was Mr. Henry Butler, who preached in the former part of the day from that scripture in *Psa. 17.8,* "Keep me as the apple of the eye; hide me under the shadow of thy wings." And oh! what an eminent presence of God did many of His poor people experience in that ordinance; what down-pourings of the Spirit, touching, affecting, melting, warming and enlivening the hearts of many.

Mr. Ashwood being designed to preach in the after part of the day, and though it were an obscure place and no outward glory could be seen, yet it was to many a Bethel and an emblem of heaven. But ah! how transient are the saints' tastes and enjoyments here, and how quickly doth the clouds overshadow all their mount visions, for, as soon as this first exercise was past, and the ministers being gone apart from the people into the wood to refresh themselves, some soldiers that were raging abroad like ravening wolves for the prey, observing the motions of the people, riding furiously by the place, brake in amongst the people and dispersed them. Some persons were apprehended and taken by them (whereof some of them were members of this church) and carried them away. Several persons as they could have opportunity hastened to their habitations, others tarried some space of time in the wood and secretly in corners to escape the hands of the enemy. Towards the close of the day Mr. Ashwood and Mr. Butler[1]with several of the members of the church, drawing out of the wood and hiding places, providentially meeting each other, resolved to spend the night solemnly together, and accordingly hasted away with as much prudence as possible to a private house about two miles distant from that place, where the night was spent in fervent and solemn prayer to the Lord, sympathizing with those poor brethren which were carried from them and, as was feared, might be laid up in bonds. And oh! what a mighty spirit of prayer was poured out. What strong supplications and cries to the Lord for them! And what expectations were raised in the hearts of some that they should be returned again, which accordingly it came to pass. For the Lord so overruled the spirits of the soldiers that they, beholding the courage and undauntedness of their prisoners, let them go back again, who in the morning came to their brethren who had been wrestling with the Lord for them.

[1] Henry Butler (1624-1696). A Puritan divine, born at Ashford, Kent; emigrated with his parents to New England where he was educated. M.A. Harvard 1651, after which he taught school at Dorchester, Mass. till 1656, when he returned to England. Settled briefly at Dorchester, then as vicar of Yeovil, whence he was ejected for nonconformity in 1660. After ejection fined and imprisoned several times for conventicling in Yeovil and elsewhere in Somerset. Invited to succeed Richard Mather at Dorchester, Mass, in 1670, but declined. Under Declaration of Indulgence 1672, he was licensed as a Congregational teacher at Yeovil and Maiden Bradley; and as Presbyterian at Lavington. Settled finally as pastor of Independent Church at Witham Friary, Somerset, 1690, also preaching at Frome, and founding a congregation at Truddoxhill, Somerset.

Thus, though weeping continued for a night, yet joy came in the morning. Then was that word accomplished in the experience of a praying people, *Isa. 65.24,* "Before they call, I will answer; and while they are yet speaking, I will hear." Though the Lord permitted the wrath of the enemy to break forth, yet He overruled it to His own glory, and the remainder of their wrath He did restrain. Considering the publicness of this assembly and the great company of people many times that resorted to them, it was marvellous that the eyes of the adversaries had not been more frequently upon them to espy their meeting places, to interrupt their communion and to bring them under bonds, as was the lot of many of the people of God in many places. But this was the Lord's doing, who was as a cloud by day and a pillar of fire by night betwixt this people and their enemies in all their movings up and down. So evidently did the Lord fulfil that word in their experience: *Zech. 9.8,* "I will encamp about mine house because of the army;" and in *Zech. 2.5,* "I, saith the LORD, will be unto her a wall of fire round about, and will be the glory in the midst of her."

Now, at the next general assizes, those ministers of Christ and others of the Lord's people who were in bonds for the sake of Christ, His gospel and worship, were brought forth before that Judge Foster[1] who came the circuits into those western parts at that time. He was a man of violence and cruelty to the poor people of God, an enemy to the good ways of God, who sentenced them to be kept in their prison house until they had paid such fines or sums of money as he then imposed on each of them to pay, and which was more than some of them had ability to pay. Now the Lord stirred up the hearts of their christian friends to disburse the money for several of them, whereby their liberty was granted to them. The rest, some few of them, not accepting deliverance upon such terms, could not consent that their liberty should be purchased with the price of money. They judged it to be more for

1 The assizes of 1663. Sir Robert Foster (1589-1663), appointed Lord Chief Justice at the Restoration as a reward for his zeal at the trial of the regicides. He had also brought about the execution of Sir Henry Vane (1613-1662), had treated the Quakers with the fiercest cruelty, and was now bent on prosecuting the Act of Uniformity with a view to exterminating all Nonconformity. Accounts of Foster's handling of the cases of Joseph Alleine, ejected from Taunton and John Norman, ejected from Bridgwater, are to be found in Charles Stanford, *Joseph Alleine: His Companions and Times*, 1861, pp.223-247; and in Palmer, *Nonconformist's Memorial,* III. 169,70. To Foster's invective, Norman replied, "Sir, you must ere long appear before a greater Judge to give an account of your actions, and for your railing on me, the servant of that great Judge." Within a month Foster died suddenly on circuit, and the country people recalled John Norman's words and regarded them as prophetic.

the honour of their Lord and of His gospel, whose prisoners they were, to continue in bonds till He should open the prison doors for them and bring them forth with greater glory to His Name and with more satisfaction to their own souls. Wherefore their imprisonment was continued during the space of five years and some months. Afterwards, the Lord in the way of His providence, opened the prison doors and brought them forth out of their prison house without paying so much as one farthing, nay, even the keeper of the prison house was constrained to let them go free without paying the least mite or farthing of what was his usual fee. So wonderfully did the Lord contradict the cruel sentence of that unjust judge, nay, the hand of God was evidently seen in the speedy cutting off of that cruel persecutor, for ere he could return back again to London, that grim serjeant, death, met him with the summons to appear before the great Judge of all the earth, who judgeth most righteously. So suddenly the Lord can, and many times doth cut off the proud foes of His church and people, and cause their violent dealing to come down upon their own heads. Now one of those sufferers that remained so long in the prison, whose name was Thomas Marther, after his liberty was given him, joined himself unto this church and walked in fellowship with this people.

Afterwards, the number of members increasing, the church thought it meet that some of the brethren might be chosen for the office of deacons, to take care of the poor, and to minister in all other parts of the work belonging to the office of deacons, according to the institution in that primitive church, (*Acts ch. 6*). Wherefore, after solemn days of prayer and supplication to the Lord for direction and counsel in this weighty case, by the joint consent of the church, Robert Bryant and Robert Batt were chosen and appointed for the work and office of deacons.

5

THOU HAST AVOUCHED THE LORD..... TO BE THY GOD.....

(1664-69)

The year 1664. The persecution waxed hotter, and greater bonds were prepared for the people of God, such as kept themselves faithful and separated from the corruptions of the day in matters of God's worship, both ministers and people. Another edict was issued forth by King and Parliament that where any were found convened together above the number of four to worship God contrary to the national way of worship established by authority, each person so offending, if taken and convicted, for the first offence, as it was termed, was to pay the sum of five pounds, or suffer imprisonment three months; afterwards, if offending so again the second time, the penalty was ten pounds or six months' imprisonment.[1] Nevertheless this church resolved to stand their ground, having taken the Lord Jesus Christ, Zion's King, for their only Lord and Lawgiver, so to adhere to His laws and institutions notwithstanding the menaces or edicts of men.

Accordingly, the Lord's day before this decree was to be put into execution, which was in the third month of this year, Mr. Ashwood began to preach to the congregation from that Scripture, *Haggai 2.4,* "Yet now be strong, O Zerubbabel, saith the LORD; and be strong, O Joshua, son of Josedech, the high priest; and be strong, all ye people of the land, saith the LORD, and work: for I am with you, saith the LORD of hosts." In the close of the Sabbath, when the public worship was finished, it was determined by the church that the congregation meet together again the next Lord's day, as they had done, so continuing their assembling themselves together from Sabbath to Sabbath, as the Lord should direct them to the most convenient places for worship, during the time the Lord should grant them liberty so to do.

Now where ministers were most public in their preaching work, there the adversary was most raging, endeavouring to suppress the preaching of the gospel and to hinder its progress. But ah! how vain were all their attempts. The Lord raised up the hearts of a people to bear their testimony to His truth and gospel in the face of dangers, insomuch that the prisons were filled apace both with ministers and people. Yet the Lord most wonderfully appeared to be a protection to this church all along whilst the blast of the terrible ones was as a storm against the wall; for there was only one member related to this church that was called forth to suffer imprisonment, whose name was Thomas Dean. He on a Lord's day had been attending upon the ministry of the word in some other place, and himself and several other persons falling under the cognizance of the enemy were convicted, and refusing to

[1] The First Conventicle Act, 1664. Came into effect on July 1, for three years. A third offence required the offender to "be transported beyond the seas to any of his majesty's foreign plantations (Virginia and New England only excepted) there to remain seven years." Transportation might be avoided by payment of a fine of one hundred pounds. Escape and return from transportation without the king's licence adjudged the person a felon and, as such, carried the penalty of death. The act was enforced by troops under the direction of county lieutenants and justices of the peace whose ears were readily given to any malicious informer. Whereas the Act of Uniformity had been directed primarily against ministers, the Conventicle Act was aimed against freedom of religious assembly on the part of the laity.

gratify the covetous lusts of the adversaries by paying the money required in this case, were all committed to prison. And the Lord made that faithful brother eminently useful in the prison house for the encouraging of those his fellow-prisoners in bonds with him, and in preserving the savour of religion amongst them during their three months' imprisonment; who then was returned to his brethren again, to the joy and consolation of the church.

In the 11th month of this year *1664*, the Lord was pleased to make a breach upon this congregation, by sending an arrow of death amongst them. A steady, pious, faithful brother in this fellowship of the gospel was cut down, named William Tucker. And oh! what sympathy appeared at the solemnizing of his funeral. As at the removal of a member or limb the whole body is pained, such a fellow-feeling was there at the removal of this dear brother, all the members being grieved at it. If ever there was a house of mourning that was. It is said of Stephen that "devout men carried him to his burial, and made great lamentation over him." It might be truly said so of this deceased brother, though he died not an actual martyr as Stephen did. Yet was there such solemnity at his burial whilst Mr. Ashwood preached before they carried him to the grave, discoursing to the church from that scripture *Eccles. 7.2,* "It is better to go to the house of mourning, than to go to the house of feasting: for that is the end of all men; and the living will lay it to his heart." There was such a mourning and lamentation that very few persons, if any were present, were without tears in their eyes and sadness and sorrow in their hearts for this sore loss; so near a union and so great a sympathy was yet remaining in this body.

Afterwards, the infinitely wise God removed another by death, a woman, named Margery Whitty, one of a gracious spirit that had much of heaven in her soul before her soul was carried up into heaven.

Afterwards, Agnes, wife of the aforesaid William Tucker, one of the firstripe fruits in this garden of the Lord.

In the 11th month of the year *1665*, that faithful and useful brother, James Pinson, died. He had for some time before served the church in the office of eldership, and in his day hastened to dispatch his work and ripened apace for glory.[1]

Now the church thought it expedient to make up this gap and repair this loss again by electing another brother for his place

[1] 1665. In this year of the Plague of London, Parliament met at Oxford and passed the Five Mile Act. Ministers who had not subscribed the Act of Uniformity, 1662, were required to make on oath a declaration abhorring

and office. Wherefore, after solemn prayer to the Lord for direction in this case, the Lord disposed the hearts of the congregation as one man that they unanimously agreed in choosing James Hawker, a man eminently qualified with gifts and graces for so great a work, who, accepting the same, was set apart for that office of eldership in this church.

Not long after other members were taken away by death, persons of no mean size or stature for piety and holiness, shining stars greatly adorning the firmament of this church. Amongst these was John Martine, and his wife Elizabeth, a couple eminent for piety

---

armed resistance to the king as it stood in the Act of Uniformity, but with this additional clause—'I will not at any time endeavour any alteration of government, either in church or state.' This was known as the 'Oxford Oath', and those who refused to take it were forbidden from 24 March 1665 "to come or be within five miles of any city, town, or borough . . . or within five miles of any parish, town, or place wherein he or they have been parson . . ." Such persons were also forbidden to "teach any private or public school, or take any boarders that are instructed by him." The penalty of disobedience was £40. Ejectment had reduced the ejected ministers to poverty; the Five Mile Act was designed to drive them out of the reach of neighbours who could help them. Hence the readiness with which Bartholomew Ashwood received hospitality from time to time in the homes of Robert Batt and Roger Hoor in Chard, which was some seven miles from Axminster. (See pp. 42, 60).

Another development in 1665 was the attempt of Gilbert Sheldon (Archbishop of Canterbury 1663-77) to obtain precise information as to the whereabouts and activities of the ejected ministers of 1662. In a letter of July 7th to Humphrey Henchman, Bishop of London, Sheldon wrote—"Having heard frequent complaints from many parts of my province . . . of great disorders and disturbances caused by ye crafty insinuations & turbulent factions of Inconformist ministers . . . I have thought good . . . to recommend to your Lordship & ye rest of . . . ye Bishops . . . ye orders and Instructions herewith all sent . . ." The enquiries concerned Ordinations, Pluralists, Lectures and Lecturers, Schoolmasters and Instructors of Youth, Practisers of Physicke, and Nonconformist Ministers—all which categories had relevance to the nonconformists. The Returns, preserved at Lambeth Palace (*Cod. Tenison* Vol. 639; and printed by G. Lyon Turner, in his *Original Records of Early Nonconformity in Persecution and Indulgence*, I.178-191), are incomplete, but include those of the dioceses of Exeter and Bristol. Seth Ward, Bishop of Exeter, reported sixty four ejected ministers in his diocese, and among them, "Mr. Bartholomew Ashwood sometymes minister of Axminster, now living in Axminster." (*Cod. Tenison*. 639.402b). At the same time Gilbert Ironside, Bishop of Bristol, reported:

> There are many non Conformist Ministers in the County of Dorset within my dioces, who neither hath nor will take the oath enjoyned them by the late act of parliament, but have gotten them private habitations 5 miles from any Corporate towne, where they often meet together (about what, noe man knowes) And holds Conventicles frequently in divers places, viz. Mr. Benn, late Rector of Alsaints in the towne of Dorchester, is now Resident at Maiden Newton. Mr. Thorne, late Rector of Radipole, is now Resident at Compton Valence. (*Cod. Tenison*, 639.315).

and holiness, of whom it might be said, as of Zacharias and Elisabeth, "They were both righteous before God, walking in all the commandments and ordinances of the Lord blameless."[1] Thus several green, flourishing, fruitful branches that had been planted in this garden of the Lord here below were cropped off and transplanted into the paradise of God above. They had a shorter walk and less way through this howling wilderness and encountered not with such difficulties, met not with such fiery serpents and scorpions as many of their brethren afterwards did. Neither did they see the great temptations and signs and miracles, and those great acts of the Lord which He did before the eyes of many of them. The Lord saw it meet to remove them betimes from His church militant here below and to place them in His church triumphant above in glory.

The form of the covenant that this church assented and subscribed unto at their first embodiment is as follows:

The Lord having called us into fellowship with His Son, and convinced us of the necessity of church fellowship we do solemnly profess in the strength of Christ, the accepting of the Lord for our God, and the giving up ourselves to Him to walk, through the strength of Christ, together in all His holy commandments and ordinances according to the rule of His word. And we do likewise give up ourselves to one another in the Lord, to walk together in the exercise of all those graces and discharging all those duties that are required of us as a church of Christ.

This covenant was afterwards on special occasions and seasons several times renewed.

Now though this church appeared as the morning, fair as the moon, yet as it increased spots appeared in it. Churches whilst in their militant state are in an imperfect state. 'Tis the glory and happiness of the church triumphant in heaven above to be without spot or wrinkle or any such thing. On earth here is still work for the church's Redeemer to do in them and for them, to sanctify and cleanse them with the washing of water by the word. Here are mixtures in the purest churches. These golden candlesticks are often sullied and become dim. Whilst the pastor of this church, like a painful labourer or husbandman, was diligent in sowing good seed, preaching sound doctrine and instilling pure gospel notions and principles into His people, labouring to keep this vineyard of the Lord clean and fertile, the devil, the great adversary and enemy of souls and churches, sowed tares. Discords and dissensions began sometimes to arise amongst the brethren which

[1] Luke 1.6.

occasioned debates, strifes, envyings, sharp contentions, strange heats of spirit in some, backbitings, whisperings, swellings, and the breaking forth of ungoverned passions to the defiling of the church, staining its glory and darkening its shining lustre. This was matter of mourning and humiliation before the Lord and hath occasioned the pastor many times to come with sharp rebuking messages, to call a solemn assembly to bewail these disorders before the Lord; to call upon the pastors of other sister churches for their aid and advice in weighty cases, and those messengers of the churches have been useful in composing of differences, repairing of breaches and setting things in order again. And the Prince of Peace Himself, who hath made peace through the blood of His cross, hath assuaged the swellings of pride and passion, and allayed those tumours that have been in the spirits of His poor people and hath caused them to be at peace amongst themselves, so that the adversary by all his designs has not been able to break the staff of bands, that firm union of this people in the fellowship of the gospel, but there has been a re-giving up of themselves to the Lord and to one another again and again.

The form of the covenant when renewed by this church:

O Thou most holy God, and Searcher of all hearts; we, Thy poor people, unworthy to be called Thy children by reason of our manifold backslidings and violations of Thy holy covenant, are emboldened through Thy goodness, promise, and covenant mercy in Thy Son, to prostrate our souls at the feet of grace, confessing from our hearts all our transgressions against Thy holy law and gospel, with our breaches of covenant with Thee and our great unfaithfulness, desiring to be ashamed in Thy sight, to abhor ourselves in dust and ashes for them, humbly begging Thy pardon in the blood of Thy dear Son, and desiring and professing from our hearts our willingness to return unto Thee, and to walk more closely with Thee in Thy covenant for the time to come. And therefore do we this day re-give up our souls, bodies and all that is ours to Thee, to be more entirely thine for ever; and do, in the strength of Christ, resolve and bind our souls by solemn vow and covenant to Thee and one another in Thee, to walk with Thee in all Thy holy will, and with one another in the fellowship of the gospel, as Thou hast required of us in Thy Word, solemnly covenanting in Thy presence and through Thy Son, to take Thy Word for our rule and to endeavour the ordering of our conversations according to it, and to be more careful in attending on Thy holy ordinances and keeping up our communion in the duties of Thy worship according to our capacity; to love and watch over one another; to endeavour the building up and saving each other's souls; to be governed in all things by Thy holy will and to persevere with Thee too through good report and bad report, through life and death, through Thy grace strengthening us. So help us, O God.

The manner of this church's covenanting, and in all after renewals of covenant, was observed to be on solemn days of humiliation and prayer. And after the reading the covenant deliberately and distinctly in the audience of the congregation, each and every individual member subscribed, or by their voluntary consent had their names subscribed to the covenant; or, which was most usually practised, solemnly lifted up their right hand to heaven in testification of their real assenting to this covenant, and then subscribed with the hand.

Notwithstanding all the care and means that was used to keep this church pure and clean, yet some dust and filth was sometimes arising. Churches will find there is reason and cause enough for that counsel and exhortation in *Heb. 12.15,* "Looking diligently . . . lest any root of bitterness springing up trouble you, and thereby many be defiled."

A sister in fellowship with this church was charged with the sin of lying, a breach of that holy precept, *Eph. 4.25,* "Wherefore putting away lying, speak every man truth with his neighbour: for we are members one of another." She being discoursed with about it, endeavoured to vindicate and clear herself as guilty of no such evil. Whereupon some members of the church were acquainted with it, who in a regular way more privately counselled and admonished her and endeavoured to convince her of her evil, but she justified herself as being in no way guilty. It being likely to become a public scandal and to reflect upon the church, they judged it expedient to declare it to the church, and having appointed a season for the church to assemble together, notice was given to this sister to be present in the church assembly. In order to the bringing her to a confession and acknowledgment of her evil, after some time had been spent in prayer, Mr. Ashwood, the pastor, preached from that scripture, *Josh. 7.19,* "My son, give, I pray thee, glory to the LORD God of Israel, and make confession unto Him; and tell me now what thou hast done; hide it not from me." After sermon was ended, the matter of fact was examined, plainly proved before her, the church being present, who heard the evidences, and called upon her by the ministry of the elders to make an acknowledgment of her evil. She remaining still impenitent, without the least remorse or acknowledgment of her sin, but endeavouring to hide and cover it, passed under the censure of church admonition, the pastor opening to her from the word of God the heinous nature of the sin of lying, the dangerous and dreadful effects of it, how she stood guilty of this sin, wherefore, in the name of Christ, solemnly admonished, charged and warned her to repent.

Now the Lord was pleased to bless this censure of admonition, for no long space of time afterwards the church being assembled together, she came publicly before the church with much brokenness and many tears and manifested her repentance by an ingenuous, free and full acknowledgment and confession of her evil, and of this her sin of lying, particularly to the satisfaction of the church, who then re-admitted her into fellowship and communion with them again in all the ordinances and privileges of the gospel.

Time passing on, the Lord being graciously pleased to keep up the hedge of protection about this congregation in a day of distraction and persecution, continuing to this people a fulness and frequency of gospel privileges when many others were denied, and no reason could be given of this difference but the sovereign pleasure of God who worketh according to the counsel of His own will. Now the pastor, like a faithful, heedful watchman, had a quick eye to espy danger, internal soul dangers and external dangers also. He was a man of a discerning spirit, and being filled with godly jealousy over his people, lest they should begin in the spirit and end in the flesh, and lest he should labour in vain amongst them, and fearing, or at least foreseeing that the plenty and commonness of gospel ordinances and privileges might occasion an abatement of their zeal and affection to them, and that liveliness and vigour of spirit that appeared at first might languish and decay, therefore, he soon gave warning. O the calls, O the counsels and arguments he used to prevent their declensions and backslidings. Alarms were often sounded in their ears, to prevent if possible, a dull, drowsy, sleepy posture and temper of soul, the common distemper of professors and churches in these latter days of the gospel. Oh how prone are churches and professors, like children, to sleep at the breasts, under a fulness of gospel provisions. This servant of the Lord, like a good shepherd, gave diligent heed to know the state of his flock, and oh the endeavours he used to keep them from wandering and going astray.

A day being appointed for a solemn assembly, and the church being gathered together, he preached from that scripture, *Psa. 85.6,* "Wilt thou not revive us again: that thy people may rejoice in thee?" Oh what a rousing, awakening message did the Lord send by him; how affectionately did he plead and reason with his people that day. What moving, melting arguments did he lay before them, if possible, to awaken and beget a sense of danger. What rubbings and chafings, as it were, to get in the word upon hearts, if by any means to get life, heat and warmth again where it seemed to be dwindling away. Oh what a heart-breaking, heart-melting day was it! A little sense seemed to be left in some, and some hopes of a recovery and of strengthening the things that remain and were ready to die.[1] Then was there an addition of members to the church that day. In the close of the day the church solemnly renewed the covenant with the Lord and one another.

The form of the covenant once more renewed:

We having, through grace, been made sensible of our breach of covenant with God, and many neglects of duty, soul decays and backslidings from God, great coldness of love to one another, with many provocations against the Lord, whereby we have deserved His displeasure and given Him just cause to take His candlestick from us and blast our present privileges; and being liable to temptations and dangers from our present liberty to neglect our relation duty[2] *to God and each other in this fellowship of the gospel wherein we stand, do this day confess and desire to bewail all our sins and backslidings from God, and omissions of duty to one another, humbly begging mercy, pardon and re-acceptance in the favour of our God, through the blood of Christ; and do again re-give up ourselves unto the Lord in*

[1] The least easing of outward persecution and oppression being regarded as a potential spiritual danger. Writing from prison in Cambridge Castle, 27 December 1667, six months after the First Conventicle Act expired, Francis Holcroft addressed a similar warning to "the faithful brethren in Christ in London":

> Beware of false mistaken prophets that say the bitterness of death in these things is over, lest you find at last they bite with their teeth, though you now love to hear them cry to you peace, peace. There has been too much of this daubing with untempered mortar already. The Lord spare us. Here is more than two years and an half, twice told, since our affliction began, and yet I think we hardly judge the witnesses are yet risen. (*A Word to the Saints from the Watch Tower* ... 1667. p.20).

[2] i.e. the obligations of covenanted membership.

covenant to be more entirely His, and to walk together in all His holy commandments and ordinances, in maintaining our fellowship, and in exercising our graces, and discharging those duties toward God and one another as is required of us by the Lord in this state of fellowship in Christ. And we do solemnly profess we shall, through the strength of Christ, own and cleave to one another and walk together in the mutual performance of all those duties that are commanded us as a Church of Christ unto the end.

6

AND TOOK JOYFULLY THE SPOILING OF YOUR GOODS....

(1670-72)

After some time another mischievous device was framed against the people of God in the land, the old and usual practice of a popish brood, and of a malignant generation of men of near affinity with them to be plotting and endeavouring how to bring persons into their way of religion and worship by imprisonments, deprivations, fines, confiscation of goods and other cruelties used by them. Former weapons framed and formed against Zion have not prospered to accomplish the designs of Zion's adversaries. Rulers and governers have been plotting and consulting against Zion and her King, but all in vain. By all their edicts they could not break the assemblies of the people of God in many places, but like the Israelites of old the more they were afflicted the more they multiplied and increased. Wherefore, now new methods are fixed upon. They take crafty counsel once more and are confederate together with one consent if possible to root out religion, the gospel, and professors of it out of the land, that the name thereof might be no more in remembrance.

It was now enacted by law that where any were convened together to worship God contrary to the worship of the nation established by authority, if exceeding the number of four persons, for every such offence, the sum of twenty pounds was to be levied for the house, out-house, orchard, field, &c., where such a convention was held; and twenty pounds was to be levied for the preacher, teacher, or any person so officiating in any such religious worship, five shillings for each particular person so convicted; and the money to be levied on any of the persons present at such an assembly not exceeding the sum of ten pounds a person. And upon the refusal of paying the money when demanded, the goods or cattle of such persons to be taken and sold for the payment thereof. Every magistrate, justice of the peace, or any inferior officer whatsoever refusing to discharge their office what was required in this case, were to pay five pounds, and for the encouragement of such as should inform against such conventions, one third part of the money so raised was to be paid to the informers, &c. (This being the substance of this Act).[1] So that now magistrates and other inferior officers were subject to every such informer, who were certain lewd and wicked persons of the baser sort that afterwards hunted up and down, assaulted houses and sought out where such assemblies were.

[1] The Second Conventicle Act, 10 May 1670, mitigated somewhat the penalties of its predecessor but gave wider powers to those enforcing the Act. Its significance is that it followed swiftly on the second set of Episcopal Returns demanded by Gilbert Sheldon, Archbishop of Canterbury. In a letter of June 8, 1689 to his Commissary and to the Dean of St. Pauls, Sheldon said:

> ... You cannot ... but be alarmed on all hands with continual reports of the frequency of Conventicles and unlawful meetings of those who, under a pretence of religion and the worship of God, separate from the unity and uniformity of God's service, to the great offence of all ... What and how many Conventicles and unlawful assemblies and church meetings are held, in every town and parish? What are the numbers that usually meet at them, and of what condition or sort of people they consist ... ? Whether you do not think they might easily be suppressed by the assistance of the civil magistrate ... ? (Wilkins, *Concilia Magnae* IV.588).

The Returns, though much fuller than those of 1665, are incomplete. Gilbert Ironside, still Bishop of Bristol, sent none at all. Seth Ward had been succeeded at Exeter by Anthony Sparrow who sent only a fragmentary

Now what might not such a device as this do to overturn all religion and to root out the pure institutions of the Lord Jesus? Especially in such a day when so many, even of a professing people, were so staked down to the world and looked like so many Demas's, lovers of this present world, this being the epidemical distemper of these latter days. And indeed it proved a great trial. Now several ministers withdrew from their public preachings as before and resolved to preach only to four persons at a time besides those of the family, according to the tenor of the Act. But blessed be God that so many were found in this land to witness to the kingly government of the Lord Jesus in His churches, such as were redeemed from the earth, pure, chaste virgin professors that were not defiled with the abominations of that mother of harlots, nor bowed down to the image of the beast that supported her, but were followers of the Lamb whithersoever He goeth.

Now on the Sabbath day before this Act was to be put into execution, this congregation being assembled together, Mr. Ashwood preached from that scripture, *Heb. 10.34,* "And took joyfully the spoiling of your goods, knowing in yourselves that ye have in heaven a better and an enduring substance." He endeavoured to fortify the people against the fear of losing earthly interests in the way of duty and obedience. Then the church unanimously agreed to keep up their assembling together, as they had done, and resolved the next Lord's day, the Lord permitting, to retire into a

---

account of South East Devon, making mention of Colyton, Thorncombe and (by inference) Ford Abbey, but no mention of Axminster. The continued activity of ejected ministers is displayed, with indications that many of them with missionary zeal travelled far and wide in their conventicling ministrations. From the neighbouring diocese of Bath & Wells, Bishop William Piers reported that Richard Alleine ejected from Batcombe, Thomas Creese from Combe Hay, John Turner from North Cricket, Timothy Batt from Riston, and Henry Butler from Yeovil were all regularly engaged in a circuit of five places. John Baker ejected from Currey Mallett regularly visited nine places, while John Galpin ejected from Ashpriors had a circuit of no less than fifteen places. It was to halt all this that the Second Conventicle Act became law, and Sheldon became its chief executive, in letters urging the bishops to see it carried out. "It becomes us, the Bishops", he said, "to endeavour as much as in us lies, the promoting of so blessed a work". The Bishops were to "take notice of all Nonconformists, holders, frequenters, and maintainers of conventicles; especially of the preachers and teachers in them, and of the places where the same were held", and to call in the aid of the justices concerned. The justices in turn were empowered "with what aid, force, and assistance they shall think necessary, (to) break open and enter into, any house or place where they shall be informed of the conventicle, and take the person into custody"; all which may be seen in practice against Stephen Towgood, pp. 84, 86f, 89f, 91.

solitary wood,[1] only judging it prudent to change the hour of the day. And through the good hand of God towards this people they assembled together every Lord's day, and very frequently on other days of the week also, and never met with any conviction by informers. Only some few persons sustained a little loss several years after as may be recorded in its place.

Cloakham Wood

O how much of God has been seen, wonderfully hiding and preserving a poor unworthy people all along in a dangerous day in one howling wilderness and another, in the midst of lions, wolves and wild beasts that have gaped to devour them and subtle foxes that would have spoiled this vine. How has this church been fed and nourished in the wilderness! Sometimes the rage of the enemy and the fury of the oppressor have been so restrained that they have assembled peaceably together for a considerable space of time in one place, sometimes many Sabbath days successively in a wood, sometimes several Lord's days in the pastor's own hired house, and none to interrupt them. Sometimes again, the rage of

[1] Longstanding local tradition says that the usual place for these secret gatherings was the Great Wood at Cloakham, to the West of Weycroft, although some hold that it was in woods then existing to the East of Weycroft in the direction of Hawkchurch.

the enemy has been somewhat let out against them and they have been constrained to retire into more solitary places, and to change the place of their assembling up and down in woods, in fields, in obscure desert places. Sometimes through the violence and fury of the adversary they have been constrained to take the solitary night watches to assemble together to worship the Lord, but still their church communion and their fellowship in the gospel have been continued, and members have been added to this church in the worst of times.[1]

After some time another stratagem was devised by the counsellors of the nation, which was to give some tolerance to the dissenting party. For a small sum of money license and liberty might be obtained for persons to assemble together to worship the Lord, and penal laws enacted by authority in this case were suspended, but this not being enacted legally by Parliament continued not long.[2] And still the design was the same, whether by fury or flattery, by laying on heavy yokes, or granting liberty, all was to

1 John Ashwood, the pastor's son, became a member about this time, following the experience described in Appendix C.

2 The Declaration of Indulgence, 15th March 1672, was issued as the outcome of a policy to which Charles II was committed by the secret treaty of Dover of May 22, 1670. War with Holland having broken out abroad, and the Clarendon Code having produced nothing but strife at home, it appeared that the King had a desire to conciliate the Dissenters while he was preoccupied with the war. But his real aim was to liberate Roman Catholics. Accordingly, by royal prerogative in face of parliamentary opposition, Charles issued his "Declaration of Indulgence for Tender Consciences", suspending "all manner of penal laws in matters ecclesiastical against whatever sort of Nonconformists or recusants". Although many were uneasy about sharing a liberty on equal terms with Roman Catholics, the Nonconformists generally received the Declaration with heartfelt relief and at once embraced its provision for licences for places of worship for their use, and also for their teachers or pastors. "Under its authorization" says A. G. Matthews, "1,434 'teachers' were licenced in England . . . their number was largely made up . . . of the men who had been ejected or silenced ten years before." (*Calamy Revised,* Intro. p.9).

One week after the issue of the Indulgence a joint address of thanks and application was signed by seventy two Devon ministers, as follows:

To the Kings Most Excellent Majesty

The grateful acknowledgement of several Ministers in the City of Exon & County of Devon, who do not conforme to ye Established Discipline and Lyturgie of ye Church of England.

May it please your most Excellent Majesty

We your most Loyall and Faithful subjects, being deeply sensible of that full and clear demonstration you have given of your Royall Favour & abundant clemency towards us, by vertue of your late most gracious Declaration of Indulgence Dated March 15 167½; Do (as we are obliged) make a most humble and thankfull acknowledgement

promote a popish interest and to overturn the protestant interest. But whatever men's designs and intentions were, the Lord had a hand in it, and His thoughts are not as man's thoughts, nor His ways as man's ways. He knew how to overrule all for the advancement of His Name, interest and glory, and for the propagation of the gospel. And who knows but that the gospel and the pure institutions of Jesus Christ gained such regard and esteem in the judgments and consciences of many, in this time of peace and liberty, that the enemies thereof by all their after persecutions could never rase out again.

Now when this indulgence was granted to such as dissented from the worship of the nation, then this church thought it meet to procure a convenient place for the worship of God, and accordingly hired a house at WYKECROFT in the parish of Axminster, which hath ever since been ordinarily the place for their assembling

---

thereof; and being confident of your Majesties most gracious purposes and resolutions to continue to us this your most princely Indulgence, and that we shall reap the benefit and advantage thereof, so long as we deport ourselves as becomes your Loyal Subjects peaceably under your Majesties Government. We do hereby promise all due Allegiance & faithful subjection to your Majesties person and Government, humbly desiring that we may be approved and places allowed for the publique exercise of our Ministry, & as our bounden duty is, we shall pray for your Majesties long and most prosperous Reigne.
March 22, 167½.

... John Hodder William Sampson John Eaton
John Wakely Bartho Ashwood Tho Mall
John Flavell Lewis Hatch Francis Whidden
Richard Buckley.

(*SPD. Chas.* II.320.2).

The address was carried to London and, on April 6th, presented to the king by two of the signatories, John Hickes ejected from Stoke Damerel, and Thomas Martin ejected from Plymouth. Licences were granted only by the king in person and in response to an express desire notified to the Court by the applicant. Since all Indulgence business was transacted from an office in Whitehall, presided over by Sir Joseph Williamson, country ministers were glad of the services of licence agents to secure their licences for them and save them the trouble and danger of a journey to the metropolis. John Hickes, James Innes (ejected from St. Breock, Cornwall), and James Innes junior, the last two actually residing in London, were very active in this capacity. Between the presentation of the Devon *Address* on April 6 and April 11, Hickes had made one, and James Innes junior, two representations at Court on behalf of Ashwood. The following entries in the State Papers (Chas. II, *Domestic Entry Book No. 38A pp.10,13*), show the outcome:

Mr. Barth. Ashwoods howse in Axminster licensed to be a Place of Meeting of the Independent way. 11.Apr.1672.

Like (licence) to Bartholomew Ashwood of Axminster to be a Ind: Teacher in any allowed Place. 11.Apr.1672.

together to worship the Lord,[1] unless when persecution has been so hot and violent that they have been constrained to withdraw for a season and retire into more private and solitary places as the Lord hath directed them, and upon the abatement of the storm have returned to that place again. Yea, many times the Lord hath signally preserved them in that public and open place, when the solemn assemblies of the people of God have been broken in many other places. This is the Lord's own doing, and it hath been marvellous in the eyes of many to behold it.

Weycroft Manor House
c.1900

[1] This is believed to have been an older portion of Weycroft manor house which is about a mile and a quarter from Axminster, on high ground some sixty feet above the river. It is said to occupy the site of an old Roman fort which commanded the Fosse Way. The estate was purchased in 1385 by Sir Thomas Brooke of Holditch, and the mansion was erected soon after 1400.

> Attached to it was an oratory or chapel, for which a licence was granted to Thomas Brook, Esq., and Joan his wife, on November 29, 1417. Traces of the chapel and of the spacious hall still exist . . . the Brookes became Lord Cobham, and the family removing to Kent, in time let down their establishment at . . . Weycroft . . . and perhaps the mansion became ruinous . . . On the attainder of Henry Lord Cobham in 1603 . . . the manor and mansion were forfeited to the crown, and in the following year were bestowed by the king on the Earl of Devon . . . in 1611 it was sold to Sir Thomas Bennett, sheriff of London, whose son dismembered the manor and sold the estate piecemeal. (G. P. R. Pulman, *Book of the Axe,* 1875, pp.579-80).

Whoever was owner or tenant in 1672 was a sympathizer with, if not actually a member of the Independent Church of Axminster; for this person may have been the "William Bennett, Esq., of Gabriels", whose name appears on the membership roll in 1687. In 1875 Pulman notes that, "the principal portion of the estate is now the property of Henry Bilke, Esq., of the Stock Exchange", and James Davidson's particular noting (in 1834) of the name of Edward Bilck in the members roll, in his *MS Collections for Axminster* (East Devon Record Office), suggests a connection there. At the end of the nineteenth century Weycroft manor was a farmhouse, and today it is a private residence. (See also p.81).

In this time of liberty in the year *1672,* about the beginning of the 9th month, the Lord was pleased to visit Mr. Ashwood, pastor of this church with much weakness. He being at that time in the town of Chard, where several members of this church then lived, was confined to a bed of sickness in the house of Robert Batt,

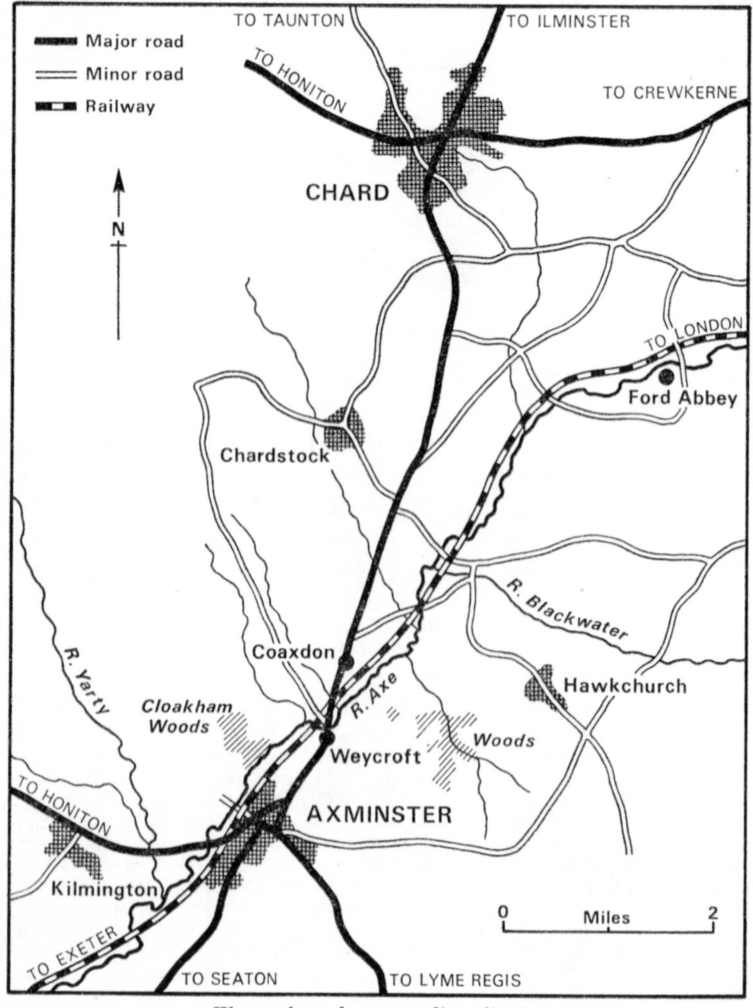

Weycroft and surrounding district

one of the deacons of this church,[1] where he lay some weeks under great distempers and weakness of body. It was very dark and dubious what the issue of the providence might be, the Lord threatening to put out this burning, shining light, to remove this labouring servant by death. The providence looked with a black and gloomy aspect upon the church, so that there were great thoughts of heart about it. Wherefore some of the brethren appointed to meet together in the same house on the 13th day of this 9th month, solemnly to seek to the Lord by prayer and supplication on his behalf.

The day being come, very early in the morning as soon as it began to be light, he sent for a brother in fellowship that came into the town the night before in order to the carrying on the work of prayer appointed for that day, one who used frequently to write for him. When he was come to him, Mr. Ashwood acquainted him what the frame and posture of his spirit had been the night past, what he had communicated to him from the Lord, and how full his heart was of some things he would have imparted to the church, being greatly concerned in his spirit about it, for he was like a vessel full, ready to vent itself. Wherefore he desired him speedily to take his pen in hand and to write down from his mouth such things as he would dictate to him, which was as followeth:

For the Church of Christ in Axminster, and every member thereof.

My brethren and friends in the fellowship of the Gospel,

I have received a message from the Lord this morning to be imparted to you, which if you hear and obey your souls shall live, your prayers shall be answered, your temple state continued; but if you refuse and rebel you shall surely perish, the candle and candlestick taken from you and the indignation of the Lord will scatter you that not a stone shall be left upon a stone in His habitation amongst you. The Lord hath often spoken out of my mouth to you, but you have not obeyed. Now He speaks to you out of the seeming mouth of my grave. O hear, hear this one voice, that your souls may live. The glory is upon the threshold of the house. The gospel seems

[1] Under the Indulgence of 1672, Walter Payne an eager nonconformist layman and a minor licence-agent residing in London, applied for 'A Lycence for the Howse of Robert Batt in the Towne of Chard in the County of Somerset to be a place for Worshipp for the Nonconformitie of the Presbeterian Judgement to meet in.' The licence was issued on July 25, 1672. (*SPD. Chas. II: 321.39; EB38A.208*).

to be fetching its last breath amongst you. If ever you will return, return; make haste, repent. I am commanded to offer these counsels from God to you as the last and only way of your health and cure.

First, confess your own and your brethren's sins before the Lord, that have caused this threatening of His departure from you. Be serious, solemn, particular and thorough in this work. Open your plague sores to this great Physician; your falseness, hypocrisy, covenant breaking with God; your coldness, decays of love to God and one another; your great forsaking of His habitation and neglect of solemn assemblies; your wretched earthly spirits by which you have departed from God, and loved this present world; your great barrenness and unprofitableness under the gospel; your sensible decays and witherings of soul uncured to this day by all the remedies God hath given you; with all those other abominations you know yourselves and brethren guilty of.

Secondly, get a deep sense of these evils upon your hearts. Let the iron enter into your souls. Let your sweetmeats be turned in your stomachs, and your pleasant idols be wormwood and gall in your bowels. Your sins have struck God at the heart. O let them smite through yours, lest God smite you, and break you in pieces, as a potter's vessel. See what your sins have been all this while a doing, undermining your temple mercies, and driving God to a final departure from you.

Thirdly, mourn bitterly over all your provocations. Weep, O weep for yourselves, ye sons and daughters of Jerusalem. Your house is like to be left desolate. The dying peal of gospel ordinances is ringing in your ears. God is preparing for the funeral of His church in Axminster, and will you not yet lay it to heart? O sow in tears if you will not reap in terrors.

Fourthly, Fly, make haste to Christ for pardon. Run for your lives to the City of Refuge. Take every one his censer and offer the incense of Christ's intercession. Stand between the living and the dead, for wrath is gone forth from the God of Zion. The plague is begun. You have but this one Friend left. Your profession will serve no longer. Your prayers will not do. See you not how the Lord turns them all as dung upon your faces? O make haste to Christ to stand in this gap, and dry up this flood that is coming on.

Fifthly, cast away all your idols from you. Confessions and promises will no longer serve your turn. God will be no longer mocked with. He is now resolved to reform or ruin you. Nothing but a separation from sin will divert God's separation from you. O bury under the oak all your idols this day; wash you, make you clean, put away the evil of your doings. The Lord of hosts is besieging you, and sends you this last offer. Throw over the heads of your Shebas, or He is resolved to pull your habitation to the ground.

Sixthly, renew your covenant with God in Christ, and bind yourselves to Him again by a curse. You have broken the everlasting covenant, and God will smite you with breach on breach till that be made up. Make vows to God and perform them. Solemnly, sincerely, sensibly renew your engagements to the Lord, to be no more your own, nor the world's slaves; to be entirely His, to walk with Him in all His ordinances and holy commandments faithfully; to cleave to the Lord and one another fully; to endeavour the furtherance of your own and your brethren's salvation; to pursue all those duties that lie before you towards the reviving of one another, and keeping the temple of the Lord holy. Vow faithfulness to one another towards the recovering and preserving each other unblamable to the day of Christ. Do this in the shame of your former treacheries and perfidious dealing with God hitherto. Do it in the sense of your own weakness and inability to fulfil it. Do it in all truth and sincerity, for God will shortly take away the covering from all flesh, and then shall the secrets of all hearts be laid open. Subscribe it considerately and unreservedly; and then lift it up with your hand to the most high God, calling heaven and earth to witness to the truth of your resolutions through grace in this matter. Get Christ to be your Surety and to sign with you, and to give security to the Father for the performance of those vows of God upon you. Go over to Christ by faith daily for a heart and strength to keep up with God in this covenant.

Seventhly, give God the glory for former prayer mercies which you have abused. How oft hath God returned a departing gospel upon your cries and importunity! But alas! how soon hath all this been forgotten, and all your goodness been as the morning cloud and early dew. Bewail this vile and unworthy carriage, and renew the memory of these former mercies.

Eighthly, pour out your souls to God for His returning grace and sparing mercy. Take unto you words and turn unto the Lord. Urge God with all those arguments that He Himself hath put into the mouths of His people. Plead His omnipotency. He can do all things. Is anything too hard for God? Was there never a mercy brought back from the grave's mouth before? Our impossibilities are no difficulties as to God. Remember what great things your eyes have seen, and from what sentences of death I have been restored to you, and roll upon this mighty arm of God. Plead former experiences, both your own and others, what great things God hath done upon the cries of His returning people. He hath delivered, and doth deliver; plead this with God for present deliverance. Plead the mercifulness of His nature, how loath He is to grieve the children of men; what pleasure He takes in the prosperity of His people. In their afflictions He is afflicted; their troubles reach His heart.

Urge with God the discovery of His own bowels. Plead His promises; the word is gone out of His mouth and cannot return to Him void; that He never said to the seed of Jacob, 'Seek ye My face in vain'. Muster up those multitude of promises that hath passed from the sacred mouth of God for the fulfilling the desires of them that fear Him; 'Whatever you ask in my Name, believing, you shall receive'. Stand this ground; be not so easily baffled from these firm foundations; God cannot deny Himself. Is not this mercy you beg for, for His glory, and the furtherance of salvation? Why then should you doubt, O ye of little faith, if you seek it with all your heart? Plead the present change of His countenance towards His people. He hath smiled on His interest, and will He frown on you? He hath turned the captivity of Zion, and will He return you into worse than captivity? O urge the gracious carriage of God to those that are not His people, and will He cast you off who have chosen Him for your God? Plead His glory, His great Name. Will the pulling down the walls of His house advance His Name? Is not God glorified when His house is built? What will the heathen say, or how will the enemy reproach thy Name?

Lastly, plead the sad and doleful effects of such a departure. Who can bear an 'Anathema Maranatha'?[1] Who can endure

[1] 1 Cor. 16.22 Literally, "accursed; our Lord cometh"; i.e. those who love not the Lord Jesus Christ are already accursed for their response to His first advent, and will suffer still further vengeance at His second advent.

to see God write 'Lo-ammi'?[1] O the troops of terrors that come in the room of Gospel mercies departed. Weep out this to God and lay it before His tender bowels.

Ninthly, be faithful in all your subservient duties to this great end. O flatter God with your lips no more. Can you endure to hear the bills of those treacheries read against you at the bar of God? Set about your newly covenanted duties and resolve upon fidelity to God however He deals with you.

Tenthly, wait patiently. Hearken what God will say. Be not hasty in spirit in going out of His presence. Say not He doth not hear because He doth not answer you. God will be waited on in the way of His judgments. Limit not the Holy One of Israel to your time and way. The vision is for an appointed time. It will speak. Tarry for it.

Eleventhly, cherish hopes. Who can tell but He may return and have mercy? What though sin abounds, grace abounds much more. What great things hath God done for the elect's sake, and upon the account of a few sincere ones in evil times. God takes notice of a few names in Sardis, a dying church, that had not defiled their garments. Ten righteous persons had more potency with God for Sodom's preservation than a whole city of sinners for its destruction. Though we are a corrupt people, yet I am persuaded several corns of salt are mingled amongst us to keep us from destruction, and I am encouraged to assure you from the Lord that if this message of God be received and obeyed by you I shall be again restored to you. If not, I fear the next place where I shall see some of your faces may be at the judgment seat of Christ, which that it may be diverted is the fervent prayer of,

Your affectionate though afflicted pastor

BARTHOL: ASHWOOD.

Chard, 9th month, 13th day, 1672.

Written from my mouth in much weakness.

Brethren, pray for me, that the Lord would accomplish in me the design of His grace in this providence. That He would make me a partaker of His holiness, sanctifying me throughout in spirit, soul and body. That He would give me the spirit of wisdom and understanding in the mysteries of the Gospel,

[1] Hos. 1.9. Literally, "Not my people".

with all those pure anointings that are needful for my work. That He would give me a body and strength suited to all the employments He hath called me unto. That He would abundantly pour out His Spirit upon my ministration of His gospel, for the conversion and building up of those that hear it.[1]

Here followeth a form of the covenant, which was renewed on this occasion, which was written from his mouth the same time:

Most glorious Jehovah, Thine eyes are upon the truth, who wilt have all the churches know that Thou searchest hearts and reins, and abhorrest all unrighteousness and violations of Thy holy will. We, Thy poor creatures, are ashamed and confounded in the sense of our manifold transgressions, and breaches of Thy holy covenant, and cannot but tremble at the thoughts of opening our mouths again unto Thee, and any more taking Thy holy covenant into our lips. But being convinced of our duty and necessity to return unto Thee from whom we are fallen, do again prostrate our souls at Thy feet, confessing our unfaithfulness unto Thy majesty, to one another, and to our own souls, our unbelief, apostasy, coldness of love to Thy Name, ways and people; our neglect of Thy service, our unsoundness, formality, unthankfulness, barrenness, earthly-mindedness, with our manifold omissions of duty, and transgressions of Thy will; desiring to bear our shame, and to be for ever vile and loathsome in our own sight. And we do open our hearts to Thee this day, to be searched, pierced, and broken for all our whoredoms, humbly begging the multitude of Thy tender mercies to blot out all our transgressions, to take away Thy present wrath that lies hard upon us, and to restore again Thy gospel and presence, which we confess we have by our manifold sins justly forfeited. And do roll ourselves upon Thy covenant, grace, and faithfulness for the retaking us into Thy favour. And we do once more from the bottom of our hearts, desire, purpose, and resolve, and covenant with Thee, through Thy Son and grace assisting us, to be henceforward Thy devoted subjects, to be governed by Thy laws, to walk in all Thy known ways, to preserve our attendance on Thy service and fellowship in the gospel at all times as Thou

[1] The same affectionate pastoral concern expressed in this *Epistle to the Church of Axminster* is found in Ashwood's preface to his *The Heavenly Trade*, 1679. (See Appendix B).

shalt give us opportunity; to endeavour a return to our first love unto, and care of one another; to watch over and admonish our falling brethren, and to do our utmost to recover and promote the welfare of this Thy body, of which we are members, and do resign up ourselves and interests to Thy disposal, to bring them into a subserviency to Thy Name, interest and glory; to observe and do all Thy will that Thou shalt make known unto us, through Thy grace assisting us. In witness whereof we have hereunto subscribed our hands. So help us, O God.

Now, as soon as this epistle was written from his mouth he desired that brother to go and read it to the brethren who were already met together in another chamber and had begun the great work of prayer appointed for that day, and such as were then and there present to renew the covenant. Afterwards he desired this epistle might be sent to Axminster, that a solemn day be set apart in which the elders, with the rest of the church, might assemble together to afflict their souls before the Lord, and pour out their supplications to Him; that this epistle be read in the audience of all the members, and the covenant solemnly renewed by them. All which was performed accordingly, and managed with great solemnity, in the meeting house at WYKECROFT.

Afterwards, it pleased the Lord to renew his strength, and to raise him up again, so he returned to his ministerial work as before, the Lord leading him into the great and glorious mysteries of the gospel, and enabling him by His Spirit to preach to the congregation the unsearchable riches of Christ.

THE LOVE OF MANY SHALL WAX COLD...

(1673-78)

But the day of liberty and indulgence is now expired. The infinitely wise God saw it meet to lead His people back again into the wilderness. Further trials must attend them. The state of the churches and people of God is much like that of the Israelites whilst marching through the wilderness. Sometimes they came where were wells of water and palm trees. At other times they came where was no water, but ready to faint for thirst, and no bread, ready to die with hunger; to encounter with many difficulties, and to face the sons of Anak.[1] But still the Lord is leading His churches in the right way towards their promised enlargements and amplitude, stability and settlement, peace and safety, beauty and glory. Whilst they are in the wilderness they are liable to manifold temptations. A wilderness state is a temptation state. How many and great were their temptations in the wilderness. How did they tempt and grieve the Spirit of the Lord forty years in the

[1] Num. 13.33.

wilderness! Gospel churches are very prone to lust after evil things, as they also lusted. The blessed apostle cautions the churches and the people of God against it. "Neither be ye idolaters, as were some of them . . . Neither let us commit fornication, as some of them committed, and fell in one day three and twenty thousand. Neither let us tempt Christ, as some of them also tempted, and were destroyed of serpents. Neither murmur ye, as some of them also murmured, and were destroyed of the destroyer. Now (says he) all these things happened unto them for ensamples: and they are written for our admonition."[1]

Sad instances there have been of the scandalous practices and irregular walking of many professing godliness, yea, amongst church members, even in such a day when sore troubles, persecutions, and great afflictions have been the lot of the churches and people of God, by reason of the fury of oppressing adversaries. What staggering, what stumblings, and falls have there been amongst many, which occasioned the pastor, whilst preaching to the congregation, and showing what great danger there was of apostasy in these evil times, by reason of the great shakings that were like to attend us, to deliver these words.

> Surely, said he, If God should leave His rod upon us, who may not put forth his hand to folly? Sad instances are before us, how far persons that seem to be christians indeed, may go and yet fall. Judgment begins at the house of God. Pursuers rise out of ambush against us. Hunters are upon the fresh scent after us and who can tell what the end will be?

A sad instance must here be remarked of a sore rebuking, humbling providence which at this time befell this church, by means of the scandalous fall of one of its members, which was as follows.

R—— B——[2] most grievously sinned and trespassed against the Lord, by stealing a sheep from his neighbour, violating the express law of God, "Thou shalt not steal." And being accused for this wicked fact, he denied it. To conceal, or cover his theft he added that abominable sin of lying, and said it was a sheep of one that owed him money for some time. Now this caused great grief and trouble to this church. And this thing being noised abroad, the church fell under great reproach and calumny, but they

[1] 1 Cor. 10.7-11.

[2] Identified as Robert Bull, by G. P. R. Pulman, *Book of the Axe*, 1875, p.680.

endeavoured with all speed to clear themselves of the guilt of this man's sin, and, if possible, to stop the mouths of the reproachful adversaries. Wherefore they delayed not to appoint a day for a solemn church assembly in that public and open place at WYKECROFT, where as many as were desirous might be present to behold the order and transactions of the church in this case.

The day being come, the church, with others not in fellowship, being assembled and the offending brother being present, the pastor preached from that scripture, *Josh. 7.25,* "And Joshua said, Why hast thou troubled us? the LORD shall trouble thee this day. And all Israel stoned him with stones." And it was a day of trembling of soul, trouble and heaviness indeed to many. The pastor, having despatched the doctrinal part of his sermon, and proved how the scandalous sins of professors do draw much trouble upon those they are related unto, and will at last on their own heads. He called forth this guilty brother, who stood before him in the midst of the congregation, and told him he must apply it to his own soul, being the occasion of this sad meeting that had brought trouble upon the church of God by his scandalous sin of theft, charged upon him. Then he opened and shewed to him from the scriptures what an abominable sin it is, that it brings judgment upon the sinner, for which God threatens a curse upon a person's estate, that it cuts off persons from the kingdom of God, the church of God, yea, without repentance it will cut off a soul from eternal salvation, and shut him out of the kingdom of heaven itself. Wherefore he called upon him to manifest his repentance by making an acknowledgment of his sin, and by his deep sorrow for it. But he, standing in the midst, struck into silence, and made not the least acknowledgment of his evil. Whereupon the pastor proceeded to that terrible sentence of excommunication, whilst many of the congregation were in a trembling posture, deeply affected with this sore stroke. Take the pastor's own words as he delivered them in passing this church censure upon the offending brother. His words were these:

> It is, I suppose, a great grief to all your friends in Christ that we have such an occasion thus to deal with you this day and, oh, if it had been the will of God that you had foreseen the snare and pit and had escaped it! But we are servants entrusted with the laws of our Lord, and desire to be faithful. You have heard with us our duty; you have heard also the desert of your sin. And we do now in the Name of the Lord Jesus Christ, and by that authority He hath committed to us according to our knowledge of His will, we do this day for

this great offence of yours of stealing, and lying proved against you—we do in the Name of Christ, and by the authority of the Lord Jesus, declare you to be this day excommunicated from the table of the Lord, deprived of your right to the blessed feast of the body and blood of Christ, and feast of fat things. You have lost your right and title by reason of this offence to glorious privileges. You are an offender. You dare not, you cannot come to the altar of the Lord without great repentance. And we do declare you in the Name of Christ disprivileged from a right to all the privileges of members of a church of Christ; and you have lost your right also to a comfortable communion with your brethren, who must put a mark upon you, and cannot maintain that intimate sweet converse with you whilst you stand off from us. And this is your punishment till you repent. Therefore we do in the Name of Christ call upon you to repent. We must tell you there is hope for your poor soul. There is the blood of Christ to wash away your sins. Though you have fallen foully, yet if you return to the Lord, He will bind up your wounds and heal your soul. Having such encouragement we charge you in the Name of Christ. O look to Him for repentance, for a broken heart. We charge you in the Name of Christ, that you give glory to God by making confession of your sins, evidence your repentance in your conversation by abhorring those persons that had confederacy with you, and this is that sentence pronounced upon you. The Lord bless it to you.

Turning his speech to such as were not of the church he said—

Let all strangers report we abhor such sins.

And directing his discourse to the brethren in fellowship he said,

Brethren, know your duty, to admonish him, and call upon him to repentance; know your duty, to abstain from affectionate communion with him till he doth repent, but still to pray for him and put on bowels for him. The Lord give a blessing to this institution of His for the saving benefit of the whole body.

The covenant was again renewed in the following form:

Being convinced this day by the word and our own consciences that we have dealt falsely in covenant with God time after time, and have fallen short of our duties towards God and one another, which we have frequently engaged to before the God of truth, at sacraments and other seasons; and being sensible that we have hereby provoked the Lord to anger, and have justly procured those breaches that have been made upon us, and that cutting off of a member of this body, we do desire to bear our shame before the Lord, and do from the bottom of our hearts confess our sins, and bewail our souls, humbly desiring to return to the Lord from whom we have fallen, begging His pardon through the blood of Christ, and purposing through His grace more watchfulness against our backslidings for the time to come. In order thereunto that we may obtain mercy and grace to help in time of need, we do again this day re-give up ourselves to the Lord, to be more entirely His and do purpose and promise through His grace assisting us to cleave to Him with full purpose of heart; to keep more close to God in all His holy commandments; to labour after more sincerity and universal holiness in His sight; to attend more constantly according to our ability, and the liberty God shall give us on His holy ordinances and church assemblies together; to love one another more fervently and to discharge our duties towards each other more faithfully; to renounce the world, Satan, the flesh more fully, and to abide with God in all known duty, and in the fellowship of the gospel to the end. So help us, O Lord.

Afterwards, there were other members belonging to this church, for their disorderly and scandalous practices, and neglecting or refusing to hear the church, continuing impenitent after due admonition, passed under the sentence of excommunication, namely, J—— T—— for his fraudulent dealing in a certain bargain with another. Also A—— B—— for the sin of drunkenness, or frequently drinking to excess. And S—— W—— who, for her disorderly walking, caused great offence to the church, and passed under this church censure.

Thus, the privileges of this church were continued, their fellowship in the gospel, and frequent communion and assembling together maintained. The times that passed over them[1] were sometimes calm and sometimes stormy, yet, through all the rollings and changes of times and providences, salvation did the Lord still

1 When Parliament reassembled in 1673 the Declaration of Indulgence was withdrawn (March 8th). There was a general fear both in Parliament and in the Church of England that the policy of general toleration had been a move in a serious Roman Catholic intrigue. The Test Act of 1673, though primarily designed against Roman Catholics, imposed on Non-

appoint for walls and bulwarks round about them. Several members successively dropping into their graves, and were removed into the church triumphant above. Several others were placed in their room and added to this church to help in labours, conflicts, and trials in bearing the burden with those that yet survived, whose warfare was not yet fully accomplished.

Now, after all counsels, warnings, prayers, studies and the most sedulous endeavours of this careful, painful watchman, a strange change began to appear in this church. The quickening, enlivening, warming, comforting influences of the Spirit of God seemed to be greatly withdrawn. A strange abatement of former affections; membership love much decayed; a dull, slothful, drowsy temper, and lameness in attending on church assemblies on week-day seasons, which was no small grief to this tender hearted pastor, as appeared by his frequent bewailing it before the Lord, together with a zealous reprehending the same, if possible these evils might be cured. Great decays and soul languishings there were in many. Others, and that not a few, were under sad clouds and darkness in their souls, full of complaints and soul trouble. Whereupon this faithful and wise steward endeavoured to give to each one his portion of meat in due season and, like a skilful physician, sometimes he prepared corrosives and sometimes cordials. The welfare of this whole body was much upon his heart, so that it might be truly said of him as the apostle Paul said of Timotheus, "I have no man likeminded, who will naturally care for your estate."[1] So full was he of tender pity and sympathy, that the various cases, trials, burdens, afflictions and troubles of each individual member were, as it were, his own, and he carried a feeling sense of it before the Lord, and his great study was how to apply himself, and

[1] Phil. 2.20.

---

conformists the further disability of exclusion from State service, whether civil or military, by its requirement that all such persons must receive the sacrament according to the rites of the Church of England. The combined Test (1673) and Corporation (1661) Acts thus kept Nonconformists out of national and municipal government until their joint repeal in 1828. Licences issued under the Indulgence were withdrawn by proclamation in 1675, and Archbishop Sheldon again took the lead in reintroducing the Clarendon policy. In 1676 he required, for the third time, a full census of Nonconformists from the diocesan bishops. Only two made full returns on the model of 1669 (*Cod. Tenison* vol. 639); the remainder returned statistics only (MS. Wm. Salt Library, Stafford). These colourless statistics disrobed of names and personalities were however impressive enough to the Nonconformists' persecutors, and the reign of intolerance returned with vigour.

speak a word seasonably and suitably unto all; and after all would lamentingly say, "O how hard is it to reach hearts this day!" To a brother in fellowship, a few weeks before his dissolution, he said, "I believe my work is almost done," which words proved to be true indeed, as a little time after made it evident.

8

THE PROPHETS, DO THEY LIVE FOR EVER ?.....

(1678)

In the year *1678,* on the 20th day of the 8th month, it being the Sabbath day, the church being then assembled in the public meeting house at WYKECROFT, Mr. Ashwood preached from that scripture, *Acts 5.30,31,* "The God of our fathers raised up Jesus, whom ye slew and hanged on a tree. Him hath God exalted with his right hand to be a Prince and a Saviour, for to give repentance to Israel, and forgiveness of sins." From thence he observed, that the foundation of salvation mercies and the whole of redemption work is laid upon the death of Christ. In which discourse, he vindicated some of the great foundation truths of the gospel, against the corrupt and erroneous assertions of papists, arminians and socinians, who becloud and darken the glorious mysteries of the gospel by their false and mistaken notions. Afterwards he answered several doubts and objections of disconsolate dejected souls and endeavoured to satisfy and encourage the scrupulous and doubting christians. And so with advice and counsel he concluded his discourse, and with it he finished his testimony as to preaching work, it being the last sermon that he ever preached. And after the administration of that blessed ordinance of the Lord's Supper in the close of the day, having recommended His people to the Lord by fervent prayer for them he dismissed the congregation, and very few of them that ever saw his face any more, it being the last work that ever he did publicly in and for the church.

On the 23rd day of the month he rode some miles from his own home to visit a religious gentlewoman, and the next day being the 24th day of the month, a messenger was sent to Roger Hoor, a member of this church living in the town of Chard, to acquaint him that there was danger for Mr. Ashwood to return home, by reason of adversaries that laid wait to take him. On the same day, returning into Chard, he was way-laid by this brother, who acquainting him with the danger, desired him to tarry at Chard, offering him the liberty of his house for his entertainment, or leaving him to his liberty at any other house where he listed. Whereupon Mr. Ashwood voluntarily chose his house to tarry there.

The next day, being the 25th day, finding himself somewhat indisposed as to his bodily health, he sent to an apothecary for a vomit, such as he used to take. Some friends advised him not to take it, but he being otherwise inclined, towards the close of that day took the vomit. But the effects of it proved quite otherwise than formerly it had been. His countenance was quickly changed. His fair, ruddy complexion turned blackish and swarthy, his body swollen, a violent and unusual sweat seized upon him, which much surprised those friends that were with him to behold it, himself also being much concerned about it.

The next day being the 26th day of the month, his violent sweat was abated and he seemed a little more revived, which put a little life into the hopes of friends that yet he might recover. Notwithstanding, he remained very ill, wherefore they sent to a physician for advice, but all in vain. Death's harbingers came on amain. At the close of that day he grew worse and worse. His last encounters were at hand. Death had its commission to remove him. The Lord

Jesus Christ, his Master whom he faithfully served, would now call home this His ambassador, his work being done, and the time of his departure being at hand. The fathers, where are they? And the prophets don't live for ever. Ministers must die even as others.

A sister in fellowship with this church, who waited on him at that time, and watched with him, perceiving him near death said unto him, "Sir, you seem to be near eternity, and going from us." He looking earnestly upon her, said, "Do you think so? For me 'tis best of all, but for you if I so abide. I have been struggling all this night with death and did not know it." Being asked whether he would speak with any of the friends (i.e. those in church fellowship), he answered he would gladly, for he had something to impart to every one of them. And indeed it was the welfare of his people, the prosperity of this church of Christ that was on his heart, both living and dying.

Something he dropped by way of advice to the church, which were some of his last words, and the last words of dying friends, especially of such an eminent and holy servant of Christ, what a deep and lasting impression should it have upon the hearts of such especially whom it most nearly concerns! His words were these:

> I had hopes that the Lord would have continued me longer amongst you that I might have been more serviceable for Him and you; but I think the Lord had somewhat against you because of your barrenness under ordinances, and lameness in coming to week-day meetings.

Then, breathing forth some requests to the Lord, he added,

> If I am going from you, then labour to know your places, and agree together as one, and choose you a faithful pastor after God's own heart that may feed you with knowledge and understanding. Keep together in the same judgment, and the Lord bless you.

Now some of those christian friends which lived in that town being called, were come about him; to whom he spake further by way of advice relating to the whole church in those following words written from his mouth by John Smith, a brother then present. He said:

> O keep close to God and then He will abide with you and will feed His flock as a shepherd doth. As for me, I have declared unto you the whole counsel of God, but I fear too many are fallen off to an earthly spirit. O return unto the Lord. Rest not till matters be throughly made up betwixt God and you, and keep close together and live in love. I fear many will fall away, or sit still in their places, or fall out by the

> way. O live in love, live in love, and the God of love and peace will be with you. Consider God's works. Consider His wonders what He hath wrought for you; what great things He hath done for you, how He hath hid you and how He hath fed you many a time and many a year.

The morning he died he said to that brother,

> O Brother Smith, keep on in the way of God. Follow Him fully. The Lord will strengthen and help you and O pray, pray, pray.

Being asked what they should beg of God for him, he said,

> Not that the guilt of any one sin be removed, for it was all abundantly done away in the blood of Christ, and I have laboured in some measure to be faithful both to saints and sinners.

He said also,

> Pray for me that an abundant entrance be administered unto me into the kingdom of our dear Lord and Saviour.

A little before he died the same brother said unto him, "Sir, you are now going to receive the reward of all your labours." He answered, "Yea, and I wish I may not be deceived." This brother said again to him, "Sir, you are now going to your Lord on your Lord's day with Him to begin and keep an everlasting Sabbath." He answered, "I confess this is a peculiar privilege." Thus on the 27th of this 8th month, it being the Lord's day, about 6 o'clock in the morning, yielding up his spirit, he slept in Jesus. Ah! blessed exchange to this precious servant of Christ, mortality for immortality; society with imperfect saints in the church militant here below, for the blessed fellowship with an innumerable company of glorious angels, and the spirits of just men made perfect in the church triumphant in heaven; dark, transient, mediate sights of God in His sanctuary in duties and ordinances, for clear and immediate visions, full and complete fruition and enjoyment of God, Father, Son and Spirit, ever, ever.

Now the church had procured a minister to preach at Wykecroft that day, and about the middle of the day when the first public exercise in the worship of God was ended, tidings was brought that Mr. Ashwood was dead. O what a change was presently seen and heard amongst the people. What weeping and wailing, what sighs and tears! What wringing of hands and lamentable outcries. It was a Bochim,[1] a place of weeping indeed. And the more amazing and dismal was this providence in that it was a surprising

[1] Judges 2.4,5.

stroke. He was taken away suddenly when very few of the congregation had any knowledge of his weakness that they might lift up a prayer for him. He had frequently been under great weakness before, but the Church had knowledge of it, and so an opportunity, either singly, members apart, or jointly together, to pour out supplications to the Lord for him, and by means of prayer, through the intercession of a blessed Advocate, he had from many sentences of death been restored again to them. But the Lord was now resolved to remove him and therefore He would have few or none to stand in the gap to stay His hand, or seek to turn away the stroke. It is observed by a reverend divine, that when God intends not to hear He lays the key of prayer out of the way, as being loath that such precious breath as that of prayer is, should be without its full and dearest success.

On the 6th day of the 9th month was the day of his interment when Mr. Robert Bartlett[1] preached from that scripture, *2 Tim. 4.7,8,* "I have fought a good fight, I have finished my course, I have kept the faith: Henceforth there is laid up for me a crown of righteousness, which the Lord, the righteous judge, shall give me at that day: and not to me only, but unto all them also that love His appearing". This was a place of scripture which in his lifetime he desired might be insisted upon at his funeral. He was accompanied by many ministers, and a great concourse of people from several parts to his bed of rest. As his life was very desirable, so his death was greatly lamented, he having been such a

[1] Robert Bartlett, (1632-1710) was born at Frampton, Dorset, where he was educated. He became a lecturer at Salisbury, 1652-54, and was appointed rector of Over Compton, Dorset, being one of "the faithful ministers whom the Triers let in, for whom many thousands of souls blessed God," and was ordained by presbyters among whom was Henry Butler. Ejected for Nonconformity in 1662, he afterwards ministered in conventicles at Over Compton, Yeovil, and North Cadbury. He was frequently prosecuted but appears to have escaped imprisonment though numbers of his people suffered in Ilchester gaol. The Episcopal Returns of 1669 report that at "Over Compton at the house of Henry Beaton" a sect of Presbyterians numbering "70 or 80 constantly" are ministered to by "M Robert Bartlet late minister there". Under the Declaration of Indulgence of 1672, Bartlett received licence to preach at Warminster, Kingsbury, North Cheriton, Holton, North Cadbury, and Over Compton.

Calamy says Bartlett "was a judicious and learned man . . . of a very healing spirit. He was humble in his deportment; a plain, affectionate and popular preacher . . . and took great pains to speak to the capacities of his hearers. He appeared to have a great awe of the Divine Majesty upon his spirit when he was in the pulpit, and always behaved with great gravity out of it . . ." After the Toleration Act of 1689 Bartlett ministered regularly to congregations at Yeovil and Lower Compton. "He was of the Congregational persuasion, but very moderate". (S. Palmer, *Nonconformist's Memorial,* II.142-45).

famous instrument in his day for the conversion, edification and consolation of many souls.[1]

It was not only this church sustained a great loss, but his removal was a public loss to the interest of Christ, he being, as it were, the chariots of Israel and the horsemen thereof; one that stood in the gap, and had the holy skill indeed of wrestling with the Lord for poor Zion in this day of her sore distress and calamity. He would often call the church to observe solemn days of prayer and humiliation, and was much delighted in such work. But now he is gone from the society of mourners to a company of harpers harping with their harps, singing the song of Moses and of the Lamb. He had gone in and out before this people, and been as a tender nurse or father to them for several years past, in weariness and painfulness, in frequent watchings for them, through many straits and temptations that befell him, and was willing to spend himself and be spent for them. But lo! now he is gone, he is gone, and left this poor church like a broken ship in the midst

[1] Bartholomew Ashwood was buried at Axminster 6th November 1678. His widow, Elizabeth, outlived him by thirty years, and was buried at Axminster on 10 March 1709. Her will describes her as late of Hawkchurch, and refers to property at Claypole, Lincs. As well as a son, John, there was a daughter, Anna. (A. G. Matthews, *Calamy Revised*). It is strange that the name of Elizabeth Ashwood does not appear on the members roll.

In this last year of his life Ashwood prepared for the press his work, *The Heavenly Trade*, an extended exposition of Proverbs 3.14, first published in May 1679, and then later, in 1688. The "Epistle to the Readers, especially those who are the more peculiar objects of my care, love, and labours", in which the author speaks of his twenty years' service in the Gospel among them (which he dates from his pre-ejection days) will be found in Appendix B. The work indicates incidentally something of Ashwood's wider contacts in its dedication to "my honoured friend, Mr. Jeremy Holwey, merchant in Bristol", in whose home and fellowship the idea of working out the merchandise theme had been conceived. Jeremiah Holwey was a Puritan layman of stature and earnest purpose, who felt so strongly on religious matters as to travel all the way from Bristol to London to secure a licence under the Indulgence of 1672 authorizing the use of his house for public worship. He was one of only thirty eight who came to Whitehall in person for this purpose, and his licence was issued within a week—'The howse of Jeremy Holwey in Cornestreet, Bristoll Congr. Meeting Place. 16 May'. (*SPD. Chas. II. EB 38A.117*). The minister for whose services this licence was obtained was almost certainly John Thompson ejected from Christ Church, Oxford, but Ashwood and others who held general preaching licences were obviously welcome visitors. Holwey was a wealthy and respected citizen, elected to the Common Council of Bristol in 1656, withdrawing from civic affairs in 1661 following the resurgence of royalist power. (See *Broadmead Records*, 213,221,224; G. Lyon Turner, *Original Records of Early Nonconformity under Persecution and Indulgence, III. 290-293*). The merchandise theme was taken up later by William Bagshaw (1628-1702), ejected from Glossop, Derbys, in his *Trading Spiritualised or, Certain Heads, Points, or Positions, on which Tradesmen (and others) may (O that they would) enlarge in their Meditations*, 1694-96.

THE

Heavenly Trade,

OR THE

Beſt Merchandizing:

The only way to live well in
IMPOVERISHING TIMES.

A Diſcourſe occaſioned from the decay of Earthly Trades, and viſible waſtes of Practical Piety in the day we live in, offering Arguments and Counſels to all, towards a ſpeedy revival of dying Godlineſs and timely prevention of the dangerous iſſues thereof impending on us.

Neceſſary for all Families.

By *BARTHOLOMEW ASHWOOD*
Miniſter of the Goſpel.

Labour not for the meat that periſheth, but for that meat which endureth unto everlaſting life, Joh. 6.27.
Seek ye firſt the Kingdom of God, and his righteouſneſs, and all theſe things ſhall be added to you, Matth. 6.33.

Ne nimium operæ conſumas in rebus leviſſimis, fugax ætas, & vitrea res valetudo, non quibuſlibet eſt impendenda: quædam deſpicienda ſunt, & animus ad magna eſt erigendus, Eraſ.

Αὐτοὺς δὲ μετ' εὐσεβείας ϗ δικαιοσύνης ζῶντας ἔντε τοῖς πᾶσι χρόνοις ἀσφαλῶς διάγοντας ϗ περὶ τοῦ σύμπαντος αἰῶνος ἡδίους τὰς ἐλπίδας ἔχοντας. Iſocrat.

London, Printed for *Samuel Lee* near *Pope's Head Alley,* over againſt the *Poſt-houſe* in *Lombard-ſtreet,* 1679.

of swelling, boisterous waves, and furious, violent storms, surrounded with dangers. Dangers from without of being made a prey by cruel persecutors; dangers from within amongst themselves lest the adversary, the devil, should get an advantage by this sore providence to alienate their affections each from other, to break their union, cause fractions, and divide them into parties.

But oh the wonderful goodness of the Lord to a poor unworthy people. Though He cast them down, yet He hath not cast them away. Though He hath sorely rebuked them, yet He hath not destroyed them. Though He hath written bitter things against them, yet He hath not written a 'Lo-ammi'[1] upon them. Though He hath put out a burning, shining light, yet He hath not removed the candlestick, but by His almighty power and infinite wisdom overruled this sore rebuking providence to His own glory and caused light to arise out of this dark and obscure dispensation. And in His abundant goodness and manifold mercies did not utterly forsake them in this wilderness, but returned again to a poor, desolate congregation, and after some time provided another shining light to be set up in this candlestick, as may further be recorded in its place. Admired be free grace!

All the glory to Jehovah, Father, Son and Spirit![2]

[1] Hos. 1.9. Literally, "Not my people".

[2] In the MS, a roll of members follows at this point. In this edition this roll is placed at the end as Chapter 19 in order to allow the unimpeded flow of the narrative.

9

AND I WILL GIVE YOU PASTORS.....

(1678-79)

Now, after the death of Mr. Bartholomew Ashwood, late pastor of the congregation, the church being now left in a desolate condition, like sheep having no shepherd, in great danger of being broken and scattered, great thoughts of heart, and sad fears in many of the members what the issue of this sad providence might be, the breach the Lord had made amongst them was judged by many professors, who were not of them, to be incurable. Yet the Lord was graciously pleased so to overrule and sanctify this sore stroke as that it proved of wonderful advantage to the awakening of them, for the members were abundantly quickened and stirred up to a more full assembling together in their communion seasons on weekdays for solemn prayer and mutual conference together.

The Lord stirred up the spirits of Thomas Lane and James Hawker, ruling elders in this church, who endeavoured to the utmost of their care and prudence to preserve this body entire, and to that end laboured to promote their communion together as frequently as when their pastor was amongst them. Also that the bond of union in this church might be preserved and kept entire and unbroken, they judged it expedient that the covenant be again renewed in this sad juncture of time. And accordingly, Thomas Lane having drawn up a form of the covenant, the church being assembled on a solemn day for prayer and humiliation, it was publicly read in the congregation and assented unto by the members. At which time the church did renew their covenant with the Lord and each other, re-giving up themselves to the Lord and each other afresh, and engaging to maintain their fellowship and communion in the gospel.

Now, immediately after the death of Mr. Ashwood, they invited and called upon several ministers for their help and assistance in this their distressed state, to preach amongst them Sabbath days, that the congregation might be preserved and kept entire. Accordingly those ministers did consent thereto, and readily gave in their assistance, by which means this congregation constantly enjoyed this great privilege of sitting under the ministry of the word and preaching of the gospel from Sabbath to Sabbath. Also, they began to look abroad, and to make enquiry if there might be a man found out whom the Lord might raise up and direct them unto, that might be set over them in the room and place of their deceased pastor. For this they prayed, and for this they waited.

Not long after, there was an able minister of the gospel sent to preach amongst this people, named Mr. Stephen Towgood, being recommended to this church by Mr. Henry Butler and Mr. Robert Bartlett, he being a member of a church of Christ at Maiden-Crawley,[1] Mr. Henry Butler being pastor of that church. This Mr. Stephen Towgood had the office of a deacon amongst them. On certain sabbaths appointed him he came and preached to this congregation, and, though he was but young in years, yet such were his ministerial gifts and abilities as did render him more like an old disciple and an aged minister of Christ. The Apostle Paul exhorts Titus: In all things to shew himself a pattern of good works: in doctrine shewing uncorruptness, gravity, sincerity, sound speech, not to be condemned.[2] These and many more such like eminent gifts and graces adorning a minister of Jesus Christ did evidently appear in him. He had indeed those qualifications, as the same apostle acquaints Timothy, that the servants of the Lord ought to have; to be gentle unto all men, apt to teach, patient, in meekness instructing those that oppose themselves. When Elijah was carried up into heaven his mantle fell from him, which Elisha

[1] This is in error for Maiden Bradley, Wilts, where Henry Butler ministered.
[2] Titus 2.7,8.

took up and the spirit of Elijah did rest on Elisha that succeeded him. The Lord having taken home His servant, the former pastor of this church, to heaven, a large measure of the same spirit, gifts, graces, excellent endowments, which were found in him, did eminently appear and shine forth to the adorning of this young man, whom the Lord was raising up to succeed him.

The church having had a taste of his spirit, his gifts and graces, the hearts of the people were soon knit to him, and the major part of this congregation were inclined to give him a call to the pastoral office amongst them. Many times did they confer together about it. Some few were not presently so fully satisfied about it, and the only argument or reason assigned by them was his being so young, and the church having been near twenty years since its first constitution. Yet it pleased the Lord so to bias the spirits of those brethren that they resolved not to oppose the church in this choice so as to cause any rents or fractions amongst them, but were resolved to submit unto the determination of the church in this matter.

On the 6th day of the third month, *1679,* the church solemnly assembled together in prayer and supplication to the Lord for counsel and direction in this weighty case. Towards the close of the day Mr. Henry Butler came amongst them to give his advice and counsel in this case, that if possible all might be fully satisfied, and after conference with him, and at other times with Mr. Robert Bartlett, the brethren were more generally satisfied, and more unanimous as to their consent and choice in this matter, only three or four members that dissented.

Mr. Stephen Towgood having received a call from this church to the pastoral office amongst them and likewise accepting and embracing the same, in the 6th month of this year of *1679,* a day was appointed on which the church solemnly assembled together in their public meeting house at Wykecroft, by fasting and prayer for the setting apart and ordaining of him to the office and work of a pastor amongst them. There were also present Mr. Henry Butler, pastor of that church whereof Mr. Towgood was a member, Mr. Robert Bartlett, pastor of a church of Christ at Compton,[1] and Mr. Down,[2] then pastor of the church that is at Bridport, whom this church had called in for their assistance to transact the

1 Over Compton, Dorset; between Yeovil and Sherborne.

2 Richard Downe. (*fl.* 1658-1692). Admitted to the ministry by Cromwell's 'Triers', ordained by presbyters, and appointed rector of Winterbourne Monkton, Dorset. Ejected for nonconformity 1662, whence he removed to Bridport and ministered in secret. Licensed under the Declaration of

great work of this day. In the management whereof, Mr. Robert Bartlett began in solemn prayer and supplication to the Lord, and afterwards discoursed to the congregation from that Scripture, *Col. 4.17,* "Take heed to the ministry which thou hast received in the Lord, that thou fulfil it". Next, Mr. Down succeeded in supplication and prayer. Afterwards Mr. Henry Butler assumed the pulpit and despatched the remaining work of the day.

All was performed with much seriousness and reverence. Take Mr. Butler's own words as he delivered them in managing this work. His words were these:

> We are before the Lord Jesus Christ, and are upon some of the greatest work in all the world; I begin to tremble in it! There are two or three things remain yet behind.

Then he began first to give him a dismission from his membership, place and office in that church to which he was related, and to pass him over, or give him up as a member unto this church in these following words:

> This beloved brother of ours, Mr. Towgood, has been conversant among our society, over which the Lord hath been pleased to place me for some time. We have heard and seen both his expressions and life and conversation, both which, excepting deep hypocrisy, do argue him to be one of the Lord's own planting. There is no breach of charity to presume so, to conclude so, and had it been the good pleasure of God, for his advantage as well as ours, we could have been glad to have enjoyed more of his fellowship and company. But now

---

Indulgence 1672 as 'Congregational teacher in the house of John Golding in Bridport' where he had 100 hearers. Further persecution drove his church into the woods and fields and increased it to 500 hearers, some of whom, along with Downe, were imprisoned in 1680 for their continuing nonconformity, "the government being become more jealous than ever of all who dissented in the slightest degree from the Church of England". As a result of this fierce persecution the dissenters of Bridport were induced to favour the claims of the Duke of Monmouth when he landed at Lyme Regis in 1685. Following the Bloody Assizes twelve men of Bridport were sentenced to be publicly hanged, drawn and quartered. It is not certain, though it is possible, that these were members of Downe's congregation. In his later years, Downe ran into other troubles. An MS countrywide review of Nonconformist Churches and ministers in 1690, compiled to help the administration of a Common Fund for the support of ministers, reports: 'Mr. Downe at Bridport, an ejected minister, has but a small maintenance"; and, "proposall: to consider Mr. Downe, the people not liking", but nothing more is heard of his case. (A. Gordon, *Freedom After Ejection,* 1917, 34,35). His immediate successor in office was Samuel Baker of Axminster, (see p.167).

> seeing that the providence of God hath for a time left you desolate and destitute, and your eyes and hearts have been on him thus far to bring him hither, we have concluded to give him up unto you. Time doth not give leave, nor is it convenient, to make a relation of that gracious work God hath wrought upon his soul.

So, passing him over into a union with this church, he added these words:

> Dear christians, I hope it is a blessed addition to your number. I would to God that we did abound with such mercies, for they are precious things, vessels of the sanctuary, and especially such as I hope you may comfortably drink of without offence; bowls of the sanctuary that will afford precious wine of Christ's preparing to refresh your souls with.

Next, he demanded the church's satisfaction and cordial consent as to the separating of Mr. Towgood amongst them for the office of a pastor, which assent was signified by their silence, a usual note or sign in this church of their satisfaction in all public cases relating to the church, at any time transacted amongst themselves.

Then he called upon Mr. Towgood to make a confession of his faith, which when Mr. Towgood had so done, to the great satisfaction of all, Mr. Butler further directed his speech to him in these words following:

> Sir, you are entering upon a most awful, tremendous work, and I say, though princes have great solemnities at their coronations, yet it hath not that dread and awe that this great and solemn work hath. Let me tell you with trembling that you are entering into such an office as were angels called to do it, they would even tremble to take it upon their shoulders. And I say, as upon one hand you ought to fear with an awful reverent fear of entering into such a solemn work, so, on the other hand, be not afraid to engage yourself for Christ, to put yourself amongst the servants of the highest order that He hath in this world. Be not afraid to engage in so good a work, for he that desireth the office of a bishop desireth a worthy work.

Thus he continued his discourse for some time, with particular counsels and instructions, both to the minister, and also to the congregation; and after he had finished his discourse, he entered upon the work of prayer, each of them laying their hands upon

Mr. Towgood, with fervent prayer and supplication they recommended him to the grace of God. Thus was the work of this day managed, and this was the day in which Mr. Stephen Towgood[1] was added to this church and with all solemnity invested into that great and weighty office of a pastor or overseer over this flock of God, having the keys of this church of Christ committed to him by the joint consent of the church. And oh! what a refreshing, reviving day was it to this poor, desolate congregation. The Lord seems to be returning again to a poor destitute people, raising up their hopes that He would repair the breaches and build them up again. It hath been the sad lot of many once famous churches and congregations, falling under such sore providences as the removal or taking away of their pastors, they have been broken with an incurable breach, or have strangely receded from their principles, and their beauty and glory have been much eclipsed. That the Lord should so wonderfully overrule and sweetly dispose the spirits of this people, by His good Spirit, that of all their number that had ordinarily kept up in communion together, being about one hundred persons, so very few should now desert their places. This was the Lord's doings and marvellous in the eyes of all wise observers. Surely the works of the Lord in and for this church are great and to be sought out of all them that have pleasure therein.

There was only one brother, named Robert Batt, being one of the deacons in this church, he being dissatisfied with the proceedings of the church in this election, because they would not comply with the dictates of his judgment and reason, broke off from communion with them. Albeit he could urge nothing of reason against the choice of his pastor, and, after all endeavours, both by the eldership of this church and others of the brethren, to convince him of his duty, and to persuade him to return to his place, persisting in his opinion and, as was too evident, supposing by the death of the former pastor he was now loosed from those bonds which engaged him to maintain fellowship with this church and take his liberty to go where he list, so quitted his station in this house of God.

[1] Stephen Towgood (?-1722). Member of a notable west country family of this name, in whom the general transition from Puritanism's golden age in the earlier seventeenth century, through the decline that followed toleration in 1689, to the fall that largely swept it away in the Arianism of the early eighteenth century, is vividly portrayed in a ministerial succession. Stephen Towgood of Axminster was both orthodox in doctrine and godly in his life. His father was the ejected rector of Semly, Wilts, who in 1662 exchanged his £600 per annum living for a good conscience towards God. (For the Towgood family, see Appendix F).

10

ZEAL..... NOT ACCORDING TO KNOWLEDGE.....

(1679-81)

There was a sister named Carrettis Wyatt that had walked in fellowship with this church for some years, who presently after the death of the former pastor left her place and returned no more. Another sister named Hannah Parker that discovered too much heat of spirit with respect to this new pastor, but her case was different from the other. This Hannah had been a member of this church for some space of time, zealous and forward with respect to religion and the things of God, and much respected by religious people. Some time before the death of the former pastor she began to be somewhat leavened with enthusiasm, giving too much heed to voices, visions and revelations, principles and notions whereby even gracious souls are greatly in danger of being led aside from a more sure word of prophecy. Now there was a brother of this society had intimate familiarity with her on the account of her piety, zeal and forwardness in the ways and worship of God, and by frequent conversations with her his feet had well nigh slipped and he was greatly in danger of receiving in such notions as might have tended to cause schism in this body. But their intimate and frequent conversations together being observed began to be offensive to many of the brethren and gave too much occasion of discourse to some that were without and were not of them. And fearing lest some erroneous principles might spread and any of the members should be leavened therewith, endeavours were used to prevent it.

The former pastor prepared a word that might be seasonable, and preached to the congregation from that scripture, *2 Cor. 11.3,* "But I fear lest by any means, as the serpent beguiled Eve through his subtilty, so your minds should be corrupted from the simplicity that is in Christ". Also advice was given to this brother to withdraw himself from that intimate society with this sister, especially in such seasons when none besides were present. Whereupon he endeavoured to satisfy the church in this thing, and after occasions of this nature were removed, and the minds and tongues of persons much quieted and allayed, on a certain time there arose a sharp contention betwixt this brother's wife and this sister, both members of this church. In the heat of their passions such words were dropped, and such discourses passed betwixt them, as were overheard by a very evil neighbour, a scoffer at religion, who presently spread abroad the same to the defaming of those members, so that both this brother and sister were taken up in the lips of talkers round about, and grievous things laid to their charge of which there was not the least shadow or appearance. Yea, the whole church fell under obloquy by the reproachful adversary. Whereupon, the church being assembled made enquiry into this matter and H—— P—— through her too haughty carriage before the congregation passed under public admonition by the church. The former pastor in a short time after being removed by death, she was left as a member out of joint, so that her assenting or dissenting as to this choice signified nothing in the church.

It was now the work of this new pastor to endeavour to restore her again, and to reduce her to her place, which accordingly he did, and had discourses with her. For some time she stood off from communion with this church, yet afterwards falling under great trouble of spirit, made her application to the church and was re-admitted into communion with them again. Some time after, she fell under great weakness and languishing as to her body, and so continuing for some considerable space of time had not a capacity of waiting upon God in public ordinances. On her death bed she acknowledged she had been very guilty of many irregular carriages, and too harsh censorious speeches concerning Mr. Towgood and, as she said, much through the instigation of others, which she bewailed. However she said she did own and acknowledge Mr. Towgood to be a faithful minister of Jesus Christ.

There was also one sister more, named M—— M—— being warned by the church to withdraw from intimate familiarity with this H—— P—— she also behaving herself so high and arrogant before the church, passed under admonition, and after the election of Mr. Towgood, refused any further communion with this church, and would not accept and own him for her pastor. These were the most considerable rents and breaches in this church under this change and turn of providence upon the election of this new pastor.

Now did this pastor and people walk together in all mutual love and affection, and in the due observation of all the laws and ordinances of the Lord Jesus Christ, the Lord further adding to them such of whom there was ground of hope they should be saved. The Lord also poured out from time to time fresh and choice anointings of His Spirit upon this pastor, eminently furnishing him with suitable gifts and endowments for his ministerial function. And during the space of about two whole years an open door was continued to them in their public meeting house at Wickcroft, with much peace and liberty, the Lord binding up the hands of adversaries.

Whilst this calm continued, the church on a day being assembled together, information was given to the church by some of the brethren concerning the immodest, obscene carriage and behaviour of a member of this congregation named J—— D——. And, for her impudent actions frequently repeated by her, and the matter of fact evidently proved by some of the brethren before the church, she passed under the censure of excommunication, and was wholly cut off from communion with the church. The Pastor, by joint consent of the church, in the Name of the Lord Jesus Christ, by power received from Him, delivered her over to Satan for the destruction of the flesh.[1] She, understanding what the church had done, sought to join herself unto another congregation not far distant, who readily received her into fellowship. But in a few weeks such irregularities were discovered in her conversation, that they as speedily cut her off from communion with them again.

[1] I Cor. 5.5.

11 A DAY OF CLOUDS AND OF THICK DARKNESS...

(1681-84)

Towards the latter end of this year *1681,* the clouds returned again and gathered blackness apace. A dreadful storm of persecution began to fall and it proved to be a violent storm, and of some continuance. The Lord stirring up adversaries again to afflict the professors of religion and to break the assemblies of the people of God, ranging up and down like roaring and ravening lions, with fierceness and rage in many places, and about this time was this congregation constrained to leave their public meeting house at Wickcroft.[1] The violence of the adversary was so great that they could not assemble together in that place with any quietness or safety for a considerable space of time, but wandered up and down, sometimes in one place, or wood, sometimes in another, as in former days. And thus they continued stedfastly in their

[1] They did not return until October 1686.

assembling together, the Lord being as a shadow of a great Rock to them in a weary land, as a refuge from the storm, even whilst the blast of the terrible one was as a storm against the wall.[1]

In *1682* great confederacies and combinations were amongst magistrates and officers of divers sorts, to suppress religion, and to break the assemblies of the people of God, the day growing darker and darker. There were sore arbitrary actings amongst many men, their wills and lusts were a law, overturning lawful rights and privileges; great injustice and wrong judgment going forth from the place of judicature, cruel oppressions and persecutions in many places. Now was that cruel Act called the Twenty-pound Act that was made against Conventicles, more thoroughly prosecuted than it had been hitherto. Also those penal laws, edicts, statutes, acts of Parliaments formerly made with a design to suppress the growth and increase of papists and popery, were formed as weapons and

[1] Isaiah 32.2; 25.4. During this year of violence two further works from the pen of Bartholomew Ashwood were published in London:

(1) In February 1681 there appeared: *Groans from Sion, or a Sermon preached at the solemnization of the Funeral of A.C.* By Bartholomew Ashwood, late minister of the Gospel, Author of *The Heavenly Trade.* Twelves. Price bound 6d. Both printed for W. Marshall at the Bible in Newgate Street. (*Term Catalogues* I.427; Wood, *Athenae Oxonienses* III. 1272; D. Wing, *Gallery of Ghosts,* No. A3999A. A. B. Grosart, *DNB,* mistakenly calls it *Groans for Sin*). This work has not been traced, and so the identity of "A.C." must remain in some doubt, though Ambrose Clare, M.A. is a likely candidate. When Ashwood ministered at Bickleigh (1650-56), Clare was his neighbour in the nearby rectory of Poltimore, whence he was ejected in 1662. He had signed the 1648 *Testimony* of the Devon ministers supporting the Westminster Assembly, and was a founder member, along with John Flavel and others, of the Exeter Assembly in 1656. When Seth Ward made his Episcopal Returns for the diocese of Exeter in 1665 he reported "Mr. Ambrose Clare sometymes rector of Poltimore lives in (Ottery St. Mary) still upon his own meanes and carryes himself peaceably as farre as I can learn." Under the Declaration of Indulgence of 1672 Clare was given a general preaching licence, being then described as of Beaminster, and the licence was applied for and received by the same licence-agent who acted for Ashwood—James Innes, junior.

(2). In November 1681, *The Best Treasure, or the way to be Truly Rich.* Founded on Ephesians 3.8, "Unto me, who am less than the least of all saints, is this grace given, that I should preach among the gentiles the unsearchable riches of Christ." It expounds the riches of Christ's person, and of His redemptive purchase for His Church. Chapter heads, abbreviated, include: (2) Personal riches of Christ in His divine nature. (3) The Human Nature of Christ. (4) Christ as Mediator. (5) Advocateship of Christ. (7) Intercession of Christ. (9) Dispositions of Christ. (10) The Love of Christ. (11) Christ's Tender Pity opened and displayed. (13) Transcendent Humility of Christ. (15) The Infinite Bounty of Christ. (16) The Faithfulness of Christ. (17) Christ and His Purchase. (18) Holiness purchased. (19) Adoption grace purchased. (20) Confirmation of the New Covenant purchased. (22) Treasures of Christ in the Gospel. (25) Christ set forth to sinners. (28-30) Use of reprehension, examination, and exhortation. The work has an Epistle to the Reader by John Owen. (See Appendix A).

THE

BEST TREASURE,

Or, THE WAY to be

Truly Rich.

BEING

A Diſcourſe on EPHES. 3. 8.

Wherein is opened and commended to Saints and Sinners the Perſonal and Purchaſed Riches of Chriſt,as the beſt Treaſure,to be purſu'd, and enſur'd by all that would be happy here and hereafter.

By *Bartholomew Aſhwood*, Late Miniſter of the Goſpel; Author of *The Heavenly Trade.*

Riches and Honour are with me, yea, durable Riches and Righteouſneſs. Prov. 8. 18.
For ye know the Grace of our Lord Jeſus Chriſt, that though he was Rich, yet for your ſakes he became Poor; *that ye through his Poverty might be Rich.* 2 Cor. 8. 9.

In Chriſto igitur ſitæ ſunt omnes noſtræ Divitiæ.
In Chriſto ſita ſpes noſtræ gloriæ. Daven.

LONDON,

Printed for *William Marſhal*, at the Bible in *Newgate-Street*, at the corner of *Ivy Lane.* 1681.

by the malice and enmity of a malignant generation of men were sharpened, and the edge of them turned directly against the dissenting protestants, such as kept close to the institutions of the Lord Jesus Christ. So that now lewd and base fellows were encouraged to assault houses, to hunt up and down to give information against the assemblies of the people of God, the adversaries of Zion encouraging each other as the Moabites of old when they thought the victory was theirs; Up Moab to the spoil![1] Hence, great wastes and spoils were made and great losses several persons sustained for the sake of Christ and religion, and on the account of conscience; their houses and shops were rifled, their goods and cattle violently taken away and sold at a small price.

Hereupon grew lamentable sad decays of religion amongst many professors, woeful compliances, and great apostasies. O what a staggering time it was, some turning to profaneness, as the dog that turns to his own vomit again, and as the sow that was washed to her wallowing in the mire,[2] others falling in with the worship of the nations. O what an heart breaking sight was it to behold many that had stood firm and kept themselves clean from the corruptions of the times for many years past, now to turn and warp and let go their profession, conform unto and fall in with the corruptions of the times, both as to worship and conversation.

About the latter end of this year, or in the year *1683*, the Lord was pleased to remove by death, James Hawker, one of the ruling elders of this congregation.

Those high winds of persecution continued to blow, and were fanning to purpose in some places, this storm ushering in the year 1683. The rage of adversaries increasing more and more, and the hearts of a professing people ready to faint. On one Sabbath the tidings was that such a congregation was broken and scattered, and another time, such or such a congregation was broken and scattered. Thus the assemblies of the people of God were broken almost in all places, so that about the 4th month of this year there was no other congregation round about that could keep up their open constant assembling together on Lord's days, except at uncertain times and places, only this congregation whom the Lord wonderfully preserved and helped to maintain their constant assembling together every Sabbath, openly in woods and retired places. Yea, about this time the congregation assembled constantly every Sabbath day for several weeks successively in one certain

[1] 2 Kings 3.22-24.
[2] 2 Peter 2.22.

place with much peace and liberty.[1] And O what flocking was there of many persons to this assembly. It was an affecting sight to behold such numbers of people from divers parts and quarters, in such a stormy day as this was, to assemble together to worship God. As yet this people could go up with a multitude, with the voice of joy and praise, to keep holy days before the Lord. And oh! how great was the mercy of this congregation, that the Lord, the God of the spirits of all flesh, should set such a man over this congregation, to go in and out before this people, to lead them out, and to bring them in; one whom the blessed God had raised up for such a time as this, being filled with a wonderful spirit of courage and magnanimity, whom no danger by reason of enraged adversaries did so far terrify as to cause him to omit any part of his work in his place and station in this church of God. And oh what suitable and seasonable messages did the Spirit of the Lord help him to bring forth to the congregation! What discoveries and unveilings of a blessed Jesus, and of the great and glorious mysteries of the gospel from Sabbath to Sabbath! And whence

[1] The several allusions to the security in which the church often met in times of persecution, and their ability to obtain so convenient a meeting place as Weycroft manor, may be explained by the following:

(1). Joseph Crabb, the rector of Axminster, was himself a conforming puritan with much sympathy to the Nonconformists. He would certainly befriend them. (see p.190f).

(2). Nearby was Ford Abbey, home of the Prideaux family. Sir Edmund Prideaux (d.1659) had been appointed a commoner member of the Westminster Assembly 1643-48, and was attorney general to Oliver Cromwell. His son and successor in the estate, also Edmund (d.1702), had been tutored by John Tillotson fresh from his graduation at Cambridge, and inherited his father's affection for the dissenters. The Abbey was frequently the scene of conventicles during times of persecution when ejected ministers oppressed by the Five Mile Act were especially befriended. John Hodder of Hawkchurch, John Wakely of Thorncombe, John Turner of North Cricket, and Henry Backaller of Combe St. Nicholas, among others frequently preached there, the last-named being chaplain to Mr. Prideaux. Services were sometimes held in the cellar for greater safety. The Episcopal Returns of 1669, stated that "about one hundred, sometimes more, vulgar sort," attended. Any possible help to the Weycroft Church would be forthcoming from the Prideaux's.

(3). One of the church members was William Bennett, Esq., of Gabriels, the only 'Esquire' on the roll. He may well have been related to the Bennetts of London who owned Weycroft manor house, and had the task of breaking up the estate shortly after the time of the ejectment.

(4). Richard Cogan, a strong dissenter, though not a member of the church, resided just across the river Axe at Coaxdon Hall. Weycroft and Coaxdon are on high ground, and the wood behind Weycroft had plenty of combes and other suitable hiding places. Cogan could easily signal across the valley when danger approached along the Fosse Way from Chard; the worshippers then had only to make for the wood and continue their service, which they doubtless often did. See map p.42.

was all this distinguishing grace and mercy? Surely these were the motions of sovereign pleasure, of Him that causeth the rain to fall on one city and not on another, and on one piece of ground and not on another; that the gospel dew and rain should descend on this congregation when other congregations were even parched with drought. O how free, how admirable was this grace to an undeserving people!

In the 5th month of this year several persons of public note and quality that had stood as a bank or bulwark against the flood of popery were seized and imprisoned.[1] The face of the times grew worse and worse, the adversaries of Zion rampant and full of rage, dangers still increasing, great contempt cast upon the poor people of God, religion going down and dwindling away apace, the interest of Christ very low. Some of the Lord's messengers were apprehended, many imprisoned, very few that could openly appear, but were constrained to wander from their habitations. Now in this sad juncture of time the church set apart the 12th day of this month for a solemn assembly to humble their souls before the Lord, and the day was spent in solemn prayer and supplication to the Lord, in which the Lord did graciously own His poor people, lengthening out their gospel privileges. And now when so many of the Lord's people had their teachers driven into corners, yet the eyes of this people could see their teacher.

On the 5th day of the sixth month, it being the Sabbath day, the church had appointed to celebrate that blessed ordinance of the Lord's supper. The place where they were assembled for the public worship of God being in a solitary wood, near a way where it was supposed adversaries might pass.

Some therefore doubted it might not be so convenient to tarry in that place in regard to credible information which was given them of several soldiers and informers were abroad, hunting for their prey, with a design to break this assembly, as they had several others already. Yet the blessed God wonderfully overruled their rage and malice, and set bounds to those raging waves of the sea,

[1] July 1683. On June 12 there was divulged the Rye House Plot, by which the king was to have been killed near Rye House in Hertfordshire some three months before. The plot had failed, but in the aftermath of its disclosure many eminent men known to be strongly opposed to Charles' pro-Roman Catholic policies were harried under pretext of complicity in the affair. Robert Baillie of Jerviswood, William Carstares, John Hampden jun. and Arthur Capel first Earl of Essex were imprisoned. London ministers including Matthew Mead, John Owen, and George Griffiths were falsely implicated. Then, after scandalously unfair trials before Judge Jeffreys, Lord William Russell and Sir Algernon Sidney were executed. The Duke of Monmouth sought exile in Holland.

Ford Abbey

and said, "Hitherto shall you come, but no further, and here shall thy proud waves be stayed"; they being not far from the place where this congregation were assembled. Yet the Lord was pleased signally to hide and protect this church, that with peace and quietness they passed through all the duties and enjoyed all the privileges and ordinances of this sabbath. And that scripture was verified to the experience of this people which was this day the subject of Mr. Towgood's discourse to the congregation in *Psa. 23.5,* "Thou preparest a table before me in the presence of mine enemies". O how greatly doth it behove a people of such signal salvations[1] and privileges to mention the lovingkindness of the Lord, and the praises of the Lord according to the multitude of His lovingkindness, and to make His Name to be remembered in all generations.

On the 28th day of the 8th month, being the Sabbath day, a very great concourse of people were assembled together from divers parts and quarters. All other public assemblies of the people of God round about being broken by enraged adversaries, who had made great waste and havoc, and eaten up the poor people of God as bread, and were still wandering up and down, making a noise

[1] i.e. deliverances.

like dogs, and grudge because they were not satisfied. Now they belch and breathe out threatenings against this congregation also, gaping upon them with open mouth, as if they had one morsel to swallow down more, and then they should devour up all. Now this sabbath there was a subtle enemy like a fox privily conveyed himself in amongst the crowd of people with a mischievous design to betray at least some of them into the hands of oppressors. Also at the same time were adversaries lying in wait in the town of Axminster where Mr. Towgood lived, watchers to observe the motions of some that were going to the assembly, by reason whereto it was judged prudent that Mr. Towgood should tarry somewhat beyond the usual hour of the day before he did go forth. And whilst the people that assembled waited for the coming of Mr. Towgood, by the good hand of God's providence, this secret underminer of the interest of Christ was discovered, and thrust out from amongst the people. Now the people thought it meet to disperse themselves before the pastor came, so that great assembly was dismissed for that season. Notwithstanding, towards the close of the day many of the church, with others that tarried, met again in a solitary place, at which time Mr. Towgood preached from that scripture, *Lk. 22.53,* "When I was daily with you in the temple, ye stretched forth no hands against me: but this is your hour, and the power of darkness".

Now it is worthy of observation that this adversary and enemy that so wickedly devised the overthrow of this people's privileges, was some time after by one of his own companions, who had been confederate with him in informing against and persecuting of the people of God, whilst they were in their profanity together, mortally wounded in a quarrel, and in a few days after he died of the wound. His wicked companion also that had killed him, privily conveyed himself away from the hands of justice, so that both these troublers of the poor people of God, their iniquity being come to the full, were cut off in one day; so terrible is the Lord out of His holy places, that He ordaineth His arrows against the persecutors.

Now did the clouds gather blackness, hovering over this congregation also, threatening it with a little storm; the mighty Nimrods[1] being greatly enraged, and were resolved personally to

[1] "Nimrod the mighty hunter"—Gen. 10.9. An allusion to local magistrates and pro-royalist gentry emboldened against the Nonconformists in the wake of the Rye House Plot.

hunt the steps of the people of God, and if possible to break this assembly. Accordingly on the 11th day of this month, it being the sabbath day, as soon as the congregation was assembled together, with a great concourse of people from divers parts, tidings was brought of a company of horsemen riding towards them. These were some of the grandees of the time, some of them having the titles of justices of the peace, who yet were the great disturbers of the peace of the people of God, and with them several gentlemen, so termed. Upon this their approaching, the congregation dispersed themselves; and Mr. Towgood, wth several others, removed to a place somewhat remote from thence, and spent the day in prayer and preaching the word.

It was now a time of great fear and distraction with the people of God. This church also was sorely tried, not knowing what to do to keep up their communion together on sabbath days. The enemy being so enraged, it was extremely difficult to assemble together in any wood or field, as before, without interruption. Moreover, the winter season drawing on apace, it was also unseasonable in respect of the weather to assemble in the open air as they had done. Wherefore in this perplexing case the church set apart the 23rd day of this month for solemn prayer and supplication to the Lord for direction and conduct in this critical day. At which time, the congregation being assembled, an eminent presence of God was experienced amongst them, and a mighty spirit of prayer and supplication was poured out upon them. Choice and fresh anointings upon the pastor, both in prayer and preaching; solemn and fervent supplications poured out to the Lord against the designs of the adversaries who were high in their resolutions to break this assembly. And the Lord was entreated at this time, for at the close of the day the Lord engaged the heart of Joseph Harvey, a faithful brother of this society, that he freely offered the liberty of his house for the congregation to assemble together on the next sabbath, and so on any future seasons as was judged expedient, provided the people came together early in the morning before their motions might be observed by the adversaries. This was agreed upon, and by this means the designs of the adversary were greatly baffled and the church had a peaceable and comfortable sabbath. Mr. Towgood then began his discourse to the congregation from that scripture *Zepha. 3.18*, "I will gather them that are sorrowful for the solemn assembly, who are of thee, to whom the reproach of it was a burden".

The flood of persecution did yet swell higher and higher. It was now dangerous for Mr. Towgood to continue in the town of

Axminster as he had formerly, and after this sabbath was past, riding a journey some miles distant, whilst he was absent, a warrant came from the Justice of the Peace to the officers of the town to apprehend him. But it being known, this snare was broken and this design of the enemy frustrated, so that notwithstanding all the rage and fury, subtilty and policy of the adversaries, both pastor and people were preserved throughout the winter season. The Lord inclined the heart of that brother, Joseph Harvey, as also of another brother in fellowship, Benjamin Shute, that as the ark of God remained in the house of Obed-Edom three months,[1] so had this church liberty and freedom to assemble in their houses on all seasons as the church judged it expedient to the end of this year.[2] During this space for the most part, the pastor continued his discourse to the congregation from that scripture in *Zepha. 3.18,* during which time, though the number of people was much abated, this church enjoyed choice sabbaths, with suitable and seasonable provisions. The Lord sent them by the hand of their faithful steward an open door to assemble together, sometimes in one house and then in another, with much peace and safety, the Lord being still a guard and a wall about them.

In the year *1684,* on the 22nd day of the 4th month, it being the sabbath day, the church had appointed to celebrate that sacred ordinance of the Lord's Supper. The congregation assembled in a place remote from the usual meeting places, if possible to avoid disturbance by reason of persecutors, a great concourse of people being convened together. Mr. Towgood having dispatched the work of preaching for that day without any interruption, a little stop or interval was allowed whilst the people that attended the preaching of the word dismissed themselves. In the meanwhile the members of this congregation were withdrawn into an house, for the breaking of bread and prayers together. But while they were preparing and setting all things in order hereunto, before the pastor and people were sat down together at the table, an officer with an informer came suddenly at the door. Whereupon the doors were immediately shut against those adversaries, so that they had not the least advantage to understand what persons were in the house, nor what was designed to be done by them. Those adversaries presently withdrew from the house and called some other officer, but before they returned again all the members were withdrawn,

[1] 2 Sam. 6.11.

[2] At Winsham, if Susannah Harvey (p.166) was Joseph Harvey's widow, and at Chard where Benjamin Shute resided.

carrying the elements of bread and wine with them. So escaping into a wood about two or three miles distant from that place, where they sat down together with much peace and safety, the Lord manifesting His gracious presence in the administration of that sacred ordinance. O how wonderfully did the Lord frustrate and disappoint the devices of ungodly men at this time!

Notwithstanding, some days after, both those officers and informers made information before a Justice of the Peace of what they saw and found, so that there were great thoughts of heart in several what the issue might be. Divers persons supposed they would make a conviction of that meeting to the great damage of some persons, but the Lord so wonderfully appeared in restraining the wrath of those adversaries that they could not, nor did not positively sware or affirm of any meeting that was there. Yea, the Lord so wonderfully overruled that magistrate that though he had been at all times, and still was forward enough upon the least and far more dubious evidence to convict such religious assemblies, yet now he was not at all inclined to make inquisition into this matter. And so all was hushed and still. O how long hath the Lord caused this people to abide under the shadow of His spread wings! Who hath an arm like Jehovah? O the wonders of grace that in such a day of scattering this flock should have such peaceable foldings, and that in a day of great scarcity of gospel provisions the Lord should vouchsafe to them such rich feastings! How was this church left as a cottage in a vineyard, as a lodge in a garden of cucumbers, as a beseiged city,[1] environed with dangers, yet preserved; threatened and hunted after, yet hid and secured. Surely it might be said of them, as Moses once said of the children of Israel, 'O people, saved by the LORD, the shield of thy help.'[2]

After this the Lord was graciously pleased to stay these rough winds, and to give to this church a little breathing. And though those lions were as mad and furious as before, yet the Lord plucked in their chain, and held them back from ranging after this people for the space of two or three months, so that they assembled with a little more quiet, yet not without fear of oppressors. The bitterness of death was not past, nor the storm of persecution over and gone, but greater calamities were at the door. On the 12th day of the 8th month, being the sabbath day, the Lord permitted

1 Is. 1.8.
2 Deut. 33.29.

ungodly men to range up and down again hunting the steps of this people. It being a very rainy day, yet did the congregation continue in the public duties of God's worship throughout the day in the open air, exposed to the violence of the weather. Those hunters came not at the place where the people were assembled by a considerable space, only meeting some persons of the town of Axminster, as they returned home. Notwithstanding the next day information was made against them before a magistrate, and the enemies resolution being very high to hold on in their persecuting work, some persons whom they had sworn against were convicted by the magistrate, and in a few weeks after their houses were rifled and their goods violently taken away. Those of this congregation that shared in this trouble were Samuel Rampson, Nicholas Marder, Emmet Lucas, and also a serious pious christian named Edward Slade, as also Richard Oliver of the town of Axminster. These having been waiting on the Lord in this assembly this day had the honour to share with them in their losses for Christ's sake.

Now it is worthy of remark that one of those informers which swore against those persons, some few months after made an attempt to hang himself, but being seen by his wife, when he was almost dead, she cut the cord and so his fearful ruin was prevented at that time.

12

TREASURES OF DARKNESS

(1684-85)

The external glory of this assembly began now to be somewhat more eclipsed, and they were made to drink somewhat deeper of the cup of affliction. Instead of going up with the multitude to keep holy day before the Lord, now were their seasons for waiting upon the Lord in His public ordinances turned into the silent night watches. Yet many times were there a considerable number of people that resorted to their assembly, the Lord still pouring out eminent anointings of His Spirit upon the pastor, who cheerfully waded through many hardships and difficulties to serve the Lord Jesus Christ amongst His people.

On the last day of the 9th month, it being the sabbath day, the congregation had determined to assemble together in the evening or close of the day about a mile and a half from the town of Chard, Mr. Towgood that day being in that town with as much privacy as possible, the rage of adversaries being so hot against him. However, the magistrates of the town had knowledge of it, and whilst he was in the house of Roger Hoor, both the magistrates and other inferior officers beset the house and made search for him in the house. But he being privily conveyed into a room they least suspected, was from thence let out at a door into the street where they little thought of, and though he was met there by the town clerk who had a mind to apprehend him, yet he escaped their hands and hasted immediately to the place where the congregation was assembled, where they had a peaceable and refreshing season together in the worship of God. The Apostle Paul in one of his Epistles to the Corinthians[1] relates such an experience he had when he was in Damascus, how the governor under Aretas, the king that kept the city of the Damascenes, was desirous to apprehend him, and how he was let down through a window by the wall in a basket and escaped his hands. And though here was not the same way or manner of escape as the Apostle had, yet much of the infinite wisdom, marvellous care, and protecting power of a gracious God appeared in his escape from this danger; and such a providence as this ought not to be buried in oblivion.

On the third day after, the church met together again in a neighbourhood appertaining to this town of Chard, where the Lord signally favoured His servants whilst waiting on Him, eminently assisting this pastor in the work of prayer and preaching whilst he discoursed to them from that scripture, *Psa. 59.9*, "Because of his strength will I wait upon thee: for God is my defence". The Lord made it an heart reviving season to His poor people.

Now the persecution growing so hot, and the difficulties for this congregation to assemble together being so great by reason the solemn meetings were in the night season, several members especially of the weaker sex could not travel by night to the meeting places, who lived at some distance. It was therefore determined by the church that Mr. Towgood should preach in the evenings of the Sabbaths, or fore part of the night,[2] near the town of Axminster, that the members of the parts thereabouts might have the benefit of the ordinance. And towards the morning of the sabbath to be about Chard-Land that the members of those parts might have the benefit of the ordinance, so that the pastor's hardship and burdens were now increased to ride from place to place. However, he willingly consented thereto, and was diligent and constant in his work, approving himself as a minister of Christ, in labours abundant, in journeying often, in weariness, and painfulness, in watchings often.

1 2 Cor. 11. 32,33.
2 i.e. the Eve of the Sabbath, or late on Saturday night.

On the 15th day of the 12th month, on the sabbath day in the evening, when he was come to the house appointed for the meeting near the town of Axminster, the people being assembled together, through the indiscretion of some persons the adversaries had knowledge of it, and before the duty was begun the officers of the town with several other persons were come to the house, and brake in like lions amongst them to the surprising and disturbance of the congregation. A great stir was made, and some persons seized, supposing they had apprehended Mr. Towgood, but were greatly mistaken and disappointed, for through the wonderful care and good providence of God he was slipped out at the door, where some persons were set by the constable as a guard to secure the door that none might escape, yet did he pass through the midst of them, and not one of them did open the mouth or lift up a hand; so he was marvellously delivered this time also, and escaped that danger. Blessed be God who hath delivered and doth deliver.[1]

In this twelfth month the Lord, who changeth times and seasons, who removeth kings and setteth up kings, was pleased to remove and take away King Charles by death, which caused great thoughts of heart in many what the event might be. For now his brother James, a professed papist, was proclaimed king, invested with the crown, and got into the throne, though it proved uneasy to him. And what could the poor people of God now expect but as his

[1] The Axminster experience conformed to the general pattern of the times, described by Neal thus:

> The dissenters continued to take the most prudent measures to cover their private meetings from their adversaries. They assembled in small numbers; they frequently shifted their places of worship, and met together late in the evenings, or early in the mornings. There were friends within doors, always on the watch to give notice of approaching danger. When the dwellings of the dissenters joined, they made windows or holes in the walls, that the preacher's voice might be heard in two or three houses. They had sometimes private passages from one house to another, and trap doors for the escape of the minister, who went always in disguise, except when he was discharging his office. In country towns and villages they were admitted through back yards and gardens into the house, to avoid the observation of neighbours and passengers. For the same reason they never sang psalms, and the minister was placed in such an inward part of the house, that his voice might not be heard in the streets. The doors were always locked, and a sentinel placed near them to give the alarm, that the preacher might escape by some private passage with as many of the congregation as could avoid the informers. But notwithstanding all their precautions, spies and false brethren crept in among them in disguise, their assemblies were frequently interrupted, and great sums of money raised by fines . . .". (Daniel Neal, *History of the Puritans*. Ed. J. Toulmin 1797. V.13).

brother, the former king, had made their yokes heavy, so this man[1] would add to their yokes; as his brother had chastised them with whips, so he would now chastise them with scorpions.[2] And indeed these were the sad fears and apprehensions which many wise and judicious persons were filled with, all by reason of the present face of times and changes. However, 'The LORD reigneth', and that is matter of great joy and consolation to all true lovers of Zion. "The LORD sitteth upon the flood; yea the LORD sitteth King for ever."[3]

It was now an amazing time with many. The popish party began to win the day apace in England. This new king publicly and constantly resorted to the mass, or popish worship, to the great encouragement of papists and growth of popery. And now was that remarkable year for gloominess and bloodiness ushered in, *1685*. Still endeavours were carried on amain to suppress the power and purity of religion; the penal laws executed with great severity in many places, and many pious christians sorely oppressed on the account of religion; yet in this evening time there was light in this sanctuary, or church. The Lord was pleased to favour this people with many choice sabbaths and other seasons for the worship of God, without the least interruption in their assembling together, frequently meeting in the woods by day as formerly they had done.

On the 3rd day of the third month in this year, *1685*, the Lord eminently protected this congregation. It being on a sabbath day a very great number of people were assembled together to wait on the Lord in His pure institutions. It was wonderful to behold it, that in such an evil and distressing day so great a company of people could assemble together in the worship of God in peace, without the least annoyance. Choice anointings were poured out on the pastor, especially in the close of the day, whilst that sacred Ordinance of the Supper was administered to this church. O how much of the gracious presence of God did they enjoy! How was it the experience of many of the congregation that their cup was filled up even to an overflowing! Surely the Lord manifested Himself to them and was known of them in breaking of bread.

[1] James II (1633-1701). King of England 1685-88. Second son of Charles I; engaged in the civil war as Duke of York; escaped to France and served with the French army. Returned at the Restoration. Received into the Roman Catholic Church about 1670. Bill of Exclusion from succession to the throne rejected by House of Lords, and on accession he appointed many R.C.s to office in the State.

[2] 1 Kings 12.11.

[3] Ps. 29.10.

But this was but an hansell[1] or pledge, a sip of the brook in the way, or as a cordial to strengthen them for greater troubles and wilderness journeys.

It hath been the experience of the saints of God all along that usually the Lord doth vouchsafe more than ordinary manifestations of Himself to His people, either before some great work He hath for them to do, or some more than ordinary trials they are to pass through. Such was this season at least to many of this church, much like to that of Elijah when he fled for his life, and lay and slept under a juniper tree. The Angel of the Lord touched him, and said unto him the second time, Arise and eat; for the journey is too great for thee: and he went in the strength of that meat forty days and forty nights unto the mount of God.[2] Thus it was with this church. After this feasting season they passed through a black and howling wilderness indeed, and for some space of time had not the privilege of enjoying such an ordinance again. Yea, the refreshing tastes of this day were prelibations and foretastes of heaven to several members of this congregation, who fell in the wilderness, and never enjoyed the privilege of sitting at the table of the Lord any more, it being the last feasting season of this nature to them. Great troubles the people of God have passed through, but far greater troubles were now just at the door.

Now the Lord stirred up James, Duke of Monmouth, reputed son of the former King Charles II, who had been in an exile state for some time. And on the 11th day of the 4th month of this year, *1685,* he safely and peaceably landed at the haven belonging to Lyme Regis, with a small number of men, about eighty, having their ship laden with armour and ammunition; who, immediately upon his landing, gave forth his declaration to restore liberty to the people of God for the worship of God, to preserve the rights and privileges of the nation, etc. Tidings of his landing was spread abroad far and near very speedily, and divers persons from several quarters hasted to resort to him. Now were the hearts of the people of God gladdened, and their hopes and expectations raised that this man might be a deliverer for the nation, and the interest of Christ in it, who had been even harassed out with trouble and persecution, and even broken with the weight of oppression under which they had long groaned. Now also they hoped that the day was come in which the good old cause of God and religion that

1 Hansell, or Handsell: to inaugurate with a ceremony or observance of an auspicious nature. (*OED*).

2 1 Kings 19.4-8.

had lain as dead and buried for a long time would revive again; and now was the sounding of trumpets and alarm for wars heard.[1]

On the 15th day of the month they began their march from the town of Lyme, with much dread and terror, to the amazement and wonder of many what the Lord had wrought. A great number of sober and pious men marched forth with the army.

The first day of their march they came into the town of Axminster, where some companies of soldiers came towards them on each side of the town, so that it was supposed by some there might be a battle. But the Lord eminently appeared, filling this new army with wonderful courage, and sending an hornet of fear amongst those that came to oppose them, so that a dreadful consternation of spirit seized on them, that in some places they fell one upon another. In other places some ran away with amazement, some were so stricken with terror that they were even bereft of their reason, and like distracted persons. Others threw away their weapons of war, and would take them up no more; and many watched opportunities to leave their colours and old officers and came and joined with this new company; and as they marched on from town to town the army increased daily. In a few days the

[1] Having endured so much under the Roman Catholics, Charles II and James II, many of the dissenters of the West responded eagerly, if unwisely, to the Duke of Monmouth in his pose as the champion of Protestantism. They regarded him as a hero who would deliver them from the Clarendon Code and give liberty of public worship to Nonconformists at a stroke. In his march from Lyme Regis through Axminster to Taunton, Monmouth gathered an army of five thousand undisciplined and ill-armed men. Among them were members of Presbyterian and Independent Churches of Dorset, Devon and Somerset, and including the pastor and ruling elder and at least six other members of the Independent Church of Axminster. Many, however, held back from supporting so ill-organised a venture which, after three week's manouvering against the formidable and well-trained royalist army, was routed at the Battle of Sedgemoor.

The progress of the rebellion and the course of events described on pp.93-103, appears to have been thus:

June 11 Monmouth landed at Lyme Regis
15 Skirmish in the vicinity of Axminster
20 Monmouth proclaimed king at Taunton
21 Monmouth proclaimed king at Bridgwater
22 At Glastonbury
23 At Shepton Mallet
25 At Keynsham, near Bristol
26 Fell back towards Bath
27 Skirmish at Norton St. Philip
28 Fell back to Frome
July 1 At Wells
3 At Bridgwater
5 Night march on the royalist troops under Lord Feversham on Sedgemoor.
6 Battle of Sedgemoor in the early hours of the morning.
Sept. 1 The Assize opened under Lord Chief Justice Jeffreys.

number was increased to several thousands; divers also of the brethren belonging to this church marched along with them. And as this army went forward, so companies of soldiers belonging to King James pursued after, but durst not overtake them. There was likewise another army sent by the king to meet them.

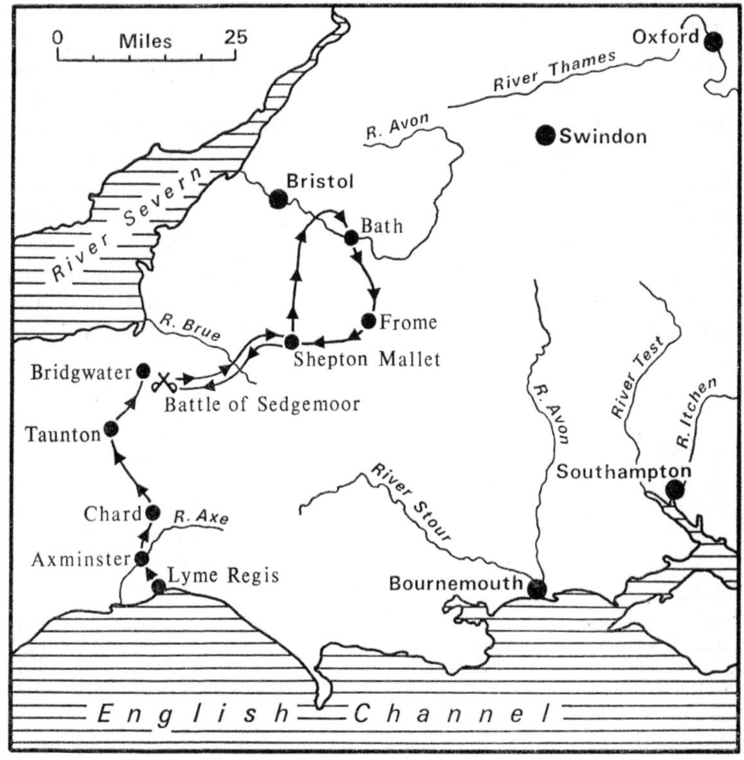

Route of Monmouth's Rising

About four or five days after they marched out of the town of Axminster, whilst they lay in the town of Taunton,[1] some few persons were chosen out of the companies, and sent to view the motions of the enemy that was behind them, amongst which one

[1] See, E. Everett Green, *In Taunton Town; A Story of the Rebellion of James Duke of Monmouth.* 1896.

of them was a member belonging to this society, a faithful brother named Samuel Rampson. Those persons riding forth to descry the enemy, met with a party of them, and engaging with each other had a very smart battle, in which a great person belonging to the enemy was slain. And in this sore skirmish this Samuel Rampson was mortally wounded, who endeavoured to get to an house not far from the place to seek some help and relief in his wounded and afflicted case, but finding none to relieve him, lost his life also.

After some few days more were passed, as the army marched onwards, and meeting with the enemy that came against them, there was a more sharp battle fought, and greater slaughter, in which one Henry Noon, a pious and lively christian, a useful member related to this body, was also slain. Thus these mighty men that had potency with God, and jeoparded their lives in the high places of the field for the cause of Christ, fell in the midst of the battle, and this church began to be diminished. In the meantime their communion was much interrupted in regard both the pastor, the ruling elder, and several of the brethren were with the army.

About the 6th day of the 5th month there was a terrible battle[1] in which many of the enemy were slain, and yet the victory was on their side; for the whole body of this great army belonging to the Duke of Monmouth was broken and routed and the Duke himself fled away, and was in a few days after taken, and being carried to London, was there beheaded. A sore rebuking providence, by that very way in which salvation for the interest of Christ was expected, greater distresses came in. Multitudes were under dreadful amazement of spirit, great trouble of soul and failings of heart for fear what the issue of these things would be. And needs it must be matter of heart aching when the Lord shall, as it were, cast off His people, and put them to shame, and not go forth with their armies, yea make them to turn their backs upon their enemies. Now did the rage of the adversary increase, and like a flood swell to a great height, insomuch that many poor creatures, yea, many of the Lord's own professing people were constrained to hide themselves in woods and corners, where they could find places for shelter from the fury of the adversary, divers being taken captive, some shut up in prison houses, others hanged

[1] The Battle of Sedgemoor, barely a mile north west of the village of Weston Zoyland, 6 July 1685. (See Maurice Page, *The Battle of Sedgemoor, Ed. 2,* 1932).

Sedgemoor and its aftermath

up immediately by the hands of the enemy. Ah! how did the Lord, by this amazing providence, correct the vain confidence, creature dependence, and trusting in an arm of flesh, which was the great sin of the nation in this day; yea, of the Lord's own professing people also, looking too much to men and instruments, and not so firmly relying upon the Lord.

A little before this dreadful battle was fought, some of the brethren belonging to this church were inclined to leave the army,[1] and if by any means to return back to their own habitations; and, by the good providence of God some of them returned home in safety, amongst whom Mr. Towgood, pastor, and Thomas Lane, elder, returned safely. Of those that endeavoured to return back, there were two of the brethren, namely Mr. John Ashwood,[2] son

1 There was a considerable defection from Monmouth's standard following the retreat from Bristol on June 26th.

2 John Ashwood, (1656-1706). Born at Axminster, the son of Bartholomew Ashwood, he was admitted a member of his father's church about 1671-72. He was educated by his father, and in London under Theophilus Gale. Becoming a schoolmaster at Axminster and Chard, he was persecuted for his Nonconformity, and removed to Haviland. He planned to emigrate to America in 1683, but was prevented by illness from doing so. Succeeded Lewis Stucley as pastor of Castle Lane Independent Meeting, Exeter, 1689-98. He was a member of the Exeter Assembly, and scribe for some years from 1693. Removed to London in 1698 preaching in Hoxton and Spitalfields; settling as pastor at Peckham, Surrey, in 1701. Died while on a visit to Axminster and Exeter in 1706. (See Appendix C).

James, Duke of Monmouth

of the former pastor, Mr. Bartholomew Ashwood, who had for some time before addicted himself to the work of the ministry, and Thomas Smith, a very pious christian and useful member of this body. These being on their way returning, were apprehended and imprisoned. Such as tarried with the army were preserved from the power of the sword, though afterwards some of them were exposed to no small trouble. Another of the brethren, named John Spiring, being taken by the rude soldiers after the battle was past, was stripped of his raiment, and barbarously used by their hands, and imprisoned, as divers others of poor christians were.

And now did the calamity increase apace, the Lord permitting a bitter and hasty people to tread down and take the spoil, making great waste in divers places and families, taking and imprisoning many, both ministers and good people. There was also great treachery used by many that were taken by the adversary, in betraying their fellows and basely complying with the adversary. In some places horrible wickednesses were committed, as ravishing of women, blasphemously mocking at religion, and scoffing at the sacred institutions of the Lord Jesus. Meanwhile, the assemblies of the people of God were broken, the ways to

Zion did mourn. This congregation also was much broken and scattered that they could not assemble together for some time. O! doleful day, never to be forgotten; sabbaths even forgotten in the land. Instituted worship did cease in a great measure, the enemy insulting and saying, "Where is your God and what is become of your prayers?" However, it was not many weeks before this church began to revive their communion seasons again, the Lord having by the good hand of His providence, returned back the pastor in safety. Some of the members had the privilege to enjoy some seasons together with him in the worship of God in the evening tide of the sabbath.

About the beginning of the 7th month, the judges of the land came in circuit into the western parts. The great work that lay before them was to call forth, sentence, and condemn those poor prisoners that had lain in bonds for the late rebellion, as they termed it. Those judges exercising great severity, especially one of them named George Jefferies,[1] who was Lord Chief Justice, a man of violence and blood, who, with madness and rage, caused great cruelty to be exercised on the bodies of many poor innocents,

[1] George Jeffreys (1648-1689). Royal retribution for the Monmouth rebellion was administered by this the most notoriously brutal of England's criminal judges. Fresh from browbeating the aged Richard Baxter in London, Jeffreys rode into the western circuit to conduct the Bloody Assize. Beginning at Winchester with the condemnation of Lady Lisle for harbouring John Hickes 'a snivelling Presbyterian', he proceeded via Salisbury, Dorchester, Exeter, Taunton and Wells to Bristol. He stormed at the prisoners, harried their witnesses, and silenced any who dared to speak for them. In the space of one month he conducted a campaign of judicial murder. Three hundred and fifty persons, men, women, lads, and maidens, were hanged. Eight hundred and fifty persons were transported as slaves to the West Indies, while a still larger number were publicly whipped and/or imprisoned in the wake of Jeffrey's progress through Dorset, Devon and Somerset.

> The story is memorable for the fact that notwithstanding all his fury, his blasphemous ravings, and incredible cruelties, Jeffreys met men and women of humble peasant rank who were not afraid of him. Browbeaten, bullied, falsely and maliciously accused of every abomination, they were not intimidated, and could not be made to confess themselves ashamed of their cause . . . When Jeffreys returned to London . . . he left behind him a name that through all posterity will be the synonym for cynical and murderous cruelty. But the proof that his work was wasted was to be found in the fact that when William of Orange came at last to rescue England from the tyranny of James II, it was in this very district that he landed, and the undismayed farmers and peasants of the West Country were the first to flock around his standard, as if Sedgemoor had never been lost and the Bloody Assizes never held. (C. S. Horne, *History of the Free Churches*).

and whose infamy will not be wiped off to the latest posterity, being the principal person in the management of those bloody assizes.

And now was a time of sore distress and perplexity, for multitudes were involved in the ensnaring dangers of the day. And Oh! how many were sentenced by that cruel judge; some to death, others to banishment, many that were hanged up, barbarously and cruelly butchered.[1] O what an amazing time was it, many even at their wits end, filled with tremblings of heart and sorrow of mind. Yea, many eminent pious christians fell in the same common calamity with others. Ah! what an heart affecting sight was it to behold the blood of many even of the precious saints of the Lord to be spilt as water upon the ground and their dead bodies hung up in the open air, and none permitted to bury them. Ah! what hath sin done. Yea, how legible might the sins of a professing people be seen this day in the calamity of it. Many who inordinately scraped after the world, loath to part with their earthly interests to follow the Lord Jesus Christ in His pure instituted ways, now all they have in the world is plucked from them. And O the decays of love, the epidemical evil of this latter age of the world, too, too, common among a professing people; little bowels for their brethren. Now must the bowels of many professors be plucked out by the enemy; and those dreadful breaches and divisions, the cursed effects of pride, must be punished, in their being chopped bone from bone, and limb from limb. This should be for a lamentation. But the design of this narrative is not to give an account of public national affairs, only so far as it respects the state of this church, and may more evidently manifest and set off the wisdom and power of Jehovah,

[1] The only comprehensive first hand account of the sufferings that followed Jeffreys' circuit is that of John Tutchin (c.1661-1707), a whig pamphleteer and himself a participant in the Monmouth Rebellion. Sometimes published anonymously, and sometimes pseudonymously under the name "Thomas Pitts, Gent", it was occasionally called *The New Martyrology,* but usually, *The Western Martyrology; or Bloody Assizes. Containing the Lives, Trials, and Dying Speeches of all those eminent Protestants that suffered in the West of England, and elsewhere, from the year 1678 to this time.* (1687). It is a sad record, much despised by literary and historical purists who nevertheless have derived more from it than they have been willing to acknowledge. Tutchin himself was fined, imprisoned for seven years, and ordered to be whipped once a year through all the market towns in Dorset, although the sentence was later reversed. The *Martyrology* had reached its fifth edition by 1705, and has been reprinted many times since.

in protecting and defending it, and demonstrate His gracious dealings with this people through all the revolutions and changes of times and seasons that passed over them in a howling wilderness.

Now were those brethren belonging to this church, which had been shut up for some time in one prison and another, brought forth before man's judgment seat, and received the sentence of that unjust judge. The aforenamed Mr. John Ashwood, the Lord had made him useful in his prison house for the publishing of His truth and gospel amongst those that were in bonds with him. And now was he sentenced to die as a traitor, and the place of his execution appointed by the judge. But "Who is he that saith, and it cometh to pass, when the LORD commandeth it not?"[1] The blessed God in whose hands are the times of all persons, so over-ruled this sentence, that by endeavours used, a reprieve was granted him and afterwards a pardon procured, and his life prolonged, the Lord having some further work for him to do for His church and interest, he being afterwards called to the pastoral office to a congregation in Exon.

As for Thomas Smith, he was sentenced also to die, and the time being come to be led forth of the prison house in order to his execution, another prisoner standing forth in his name was carried out of the prison in his stead, and the said Thomas Smith continuing in the prison a little time longer, having a fit opportunity, made his escape. But he being a man of a weak constitution of body, though he had a prosperous soul, being unable to undergo much hardship, and somewhat timorous, by reason of the dangers of the day lest he should again be apprehended, wanting such accommodations as his age and weakness required, before he could get amongst his relatives, he grew very weak. Afterwards, being tossed from place to place, he remained but a few weeks before he died, so exchanging this troublesome life for those mansions of rest and peace with his dear Lord Jesus, which is best of all. Thus was another very useful member of this body removed from the church militant here below, to the church triumphant above in glory.

Concerning the said John Spiring, he was likewise sentenced for banishment, and accordingly was carried captive into the Isle of

[1] Lam. 3.37.

Barbadoes, where he was sold as a slave once and again. Yet the Lord made him very useful in the land of his captivity and house of bondage. And after some time was past, a door was open for his redemption by paying a sum of money; which was agreed unto and, the money being collected of christian friends, who readily communicated to the same, was sent for his ransom.[1] Now being redeemed from his bondage state, and returning home to his family and to the house of God, which was no small grief and matter of lamentation to him to be banished from it, whilst he was on the seas, both the ship in which he sailed, with the persons and wares in it were cast away and drowned. Thus this church sustained the loss of another useful member, he being a pious man and of a sweet and heavenly spirit.

There was also another brother belonging to this society named William Comb, who suffered imprisonment at the same time, he being stedfastly purposed by the grace of God to keep himself pure from the corrupt worship of the nation, and notwithstanding all the menaces of a severe neighbouring justice of the peace, he could not sin against his conscience, but stuck close to the pure institutions of the Lord Jesus Christ. Wherefore by reason of the violence and rage of the said justice against him, he was constrained to abscond, and on a day as he was in a retired place alone, some informer or petty officers rushing in upon him apprehending him, and carrying him before the magistrate, who immediately sent him to prison. But no matter of fact could be charged against him of having an hand in the late rebellion, as it was termed, so was he afterwards acquitted by the judge.

These were the only persons belonging to this congregation that suffered bonds and imprisonment at this time. The rest of the brethren that escaped the edge of the sword and the hands of cruel enemies were constrained to lurk in holes and hide themselves in secret corners where the providence of God did open a way for their safety, which was the common lot of many hundreds this day. Did the prophet Jeremiah write a song of lamentations in the day of Jerusalem's calamity, bewailing the sad state of the church of God at the time, and shall none take up a wailing for

[1] There was a large trade in the sale of pardons, both before and after 'conviction'. Jeffreys shared large sums of money thus procured with the King. Edmund Prideaux of Ford Abbey, patron of the Nonconformists, forfeited (in keeping with his status as a landowner) £15,000 for his misdeameanour of providing hospitality for Monmouth. John Spiring's ransom is likely to have cost £10-£15.

the miseries and calamities of this day? None that cry out with the prophet, Alas for the day, it is even the time of Jacob's trouble![1] A day of darkness and gloominess indeed. O the breaches that were made in many families. What hanging of husbands and sons![2] How many places even soaked with blood! What imprisoning of divers persons! Others wandered about in holes, in secret corners and caves of the earth. O the violence and spoiling that was in many places, dreadful oppression and cruelty. What an ungodly generation swarmed up and down full of malignity and all manner of wickedness, having their mouths set against heaven! What horrible oaths and blasphemies were belched out! A generation of scoffers walking after their own ungodly lusts, being filled with all malice and fury like incarnate devils, as if hell were come forth upon the earth. In the meanwhile religion lay a-dying. The poor interest of Christ was in grave-clothes, light departing. The gospel seemed to be going, the righteous taken away and the faithful failing from among the children of men, and can any tender heart forbear to cry out and say, Lord help for the glory of Thy Name?

[1] Jer. 30.7.

[2] "At Axminster one also was executed, his name Mr. Rose, he was a gunner that landed with the Duke of Monmouth, he had a great resolution, and not at all startled with the fear of death. He said, that he defied death, and all them that were the occasion of it. He was very courageous and died so. He spent some time in private prayer..." (*Western Martyrology*, 218,9). The Axminster parish book adds its melancholy confirmation:

		£	s	d
1685—Nov. 3	Laid out about the execution of John Rose	2	18	10
	Paid for building the gallowse	0	16	0

Other entries of interest are:

		£	s	d
1685	Paid Thomas Whitty for taking rebells	0	1	6
	Paid for taking and carrying to prison Caleb Bragg, John Beere, Ric. Samson,...	8	0	0

Whitty was connected through his family with the Axminster Independent Church, and Bragg was a member.

13 

A TABLE..... IN THE PRESENCE OF MINE ENEMIES

(1685)

But lo! How remarkable were the gracious dealings of God towards this poor congregation, even in such a dismal time as this; for in this very same month[1] this people had revived their assembling together again, and notwithstanding all the dangers and dreadful calamities of the day kept up their constant communion together every sabbath in the night season. And though the people of God were now brought into a blacker and more howling wilderness, yet the Lord was graciously pleased to spread a table for this people in this wilderness, and to make choice provisions for them.

1 September 1685.

There was also one Nicholas Lowring, who, though he was not actually joined as a member in fellowship with this congregation, yet usually frequented their solemn assemblies, and had for a long time before in dangerous days been very ready to open his door for the congregation to meet in his house. And now the Lord stirred up his heart in such a day as this to prepare a place for them to assemble together in a secret lonesome place, having wisely contrived it so that it could not be suspected any people could get under the covert that was over it, it being beneath a bank of the earth. And there did this people enjoy many sweet, refreshing and comfortable seasons together, with several others that assembled with them; and though there was no external glory, yet the Lord was the glory in the midst of them, and His gracious presence made it a sanctuary to them. There had they eminent protections from the Lord, and choice anointings poured out upon the pastor, who from time to time discoursed to them from that scripture in *Micah 4.10,* "Be in pain, and labour to bring forth, O daughter of Zion, . . . for now shalt thou go forth out of the city, and thou shalt dwell in the field, and thou shalt go even to Babylon; and there shalt thou be delivered; there the LORD shall redeem thee from the hands of thine enemies". O what seasonable messages did the Lord send this people by their pastor from this portion of scripture; very pertinent to the day and providences which were passing over them. Thus they continued to assemble together every sabbath in the evening or night season in this secret cave of the earth, for the space of three months or upward, without any interruption.

Now in the tenth month, the 6th day of the month, which was sabbath day, the church being assembled in this desert place, according to an appointment, celebrated that great and sacred ordinance of the Lord's Supper; and it was a night much to be remembered for the wonderful protection the Lord gave this people in such a dangerous day, when bands of rude soldiers were in divers places round about them. Mr. Towgood then preached from the Scripture, *Rev. 12.6,* "And the woman fled into the wilderness where she hath a place prepared of God, that they should feed her there a thousand two hundred and threescore days." And the Lord made this a feasting season to them, and, which must not be omitted, notwithstanding the dolour and dismalness of that day, there was this night a member more added to this church. Thus the Lord was still building them up in the most troublesome time. Surely, "The works of the LORD are great, sought out of all them that have pleasure therein." Well may this people say, "He hath made his wonderful works to be remembered."[1]

O what remarks ought to be set upon those special seasons and providences in which the Lord did so eminently hide and feed this people in the wilderness. We read in *Exod. 16.32,* "This is the thing which the LORD commandeth, Fill an omer of it to be kept for your generations; that they may see the bread wherewith I have fed you in the wilderness . . . And Moses said unto Aaron, Take a pot, and put an omer full of manna therein, and lay it up before the LORD, to be kept for your generations." Now that the generations to come might hear and know what the Lord hath done for this people, what a table He furnished for them in the wilderness, and that the churches of Christ in after ages might have a taste of that spiced wine wherewith they were often refreshed in the desert, it was thought requisite that the sacramental speech delivered by the pastor this night before they did eat the supper, be here recorded as a remark on the privileges of this night, and as a cluster of those grapes wherewith they were richly and sweetly fed this evening.

A Sacramental Speech: being the very same words taken from the mouth of the pastor immediately before the celebration of the sacred ordinance of the Lord's Supper!

Beloved, God hath placed us in the wilderness. He hath brought us into a state of obscurity and dispersedness. We are now amongst thorns and briers, but hath not God provided refreshment for us? O let us come and see whether our God hath not been indulgent to His people in their wilderness, desolate condition. What, is there nothing in this wilderness but briers and thorns? Is there nothing but sandy mountains, barren deserts, prospects of blackness, wild beasts, and furious enemies to assault us? O, hath not our God provided for us both a place and provision for our refreshment and nourishment? Cannot He make a wilderness a place of delight? Cannot His gracious presence make a wilderness a heaven? It was the murmuring infidelity of the children of Israel when they said, "Can God furnish a table in the wilderness?"[2] God did furnish a table for them, and God can furnish a table for His people in their wildernesses in gospel times. O beloved, is there not in this ordinance unto which we are now

[1] Ps. 111.2,4.
[2] Ps. 78.19.

approaching such soul satisfying provisions as may mitigate the troubles, afflictions, and sorrows we may meet with in the wilderness? Consider here the provisions Jesus Christ makes in the wilderness, and then see what this wilderness is.

First of all, Jesus Christ, by these provisions He makes for His people, doth turn the wilderness into a Patmos, a valley of visions. Ah! what did John see when he was in the Isle of Patmos in a banished and exile state. What revelations were made to him. What discoveries had he of wonderful things to come. He was wrapped up and ravished in his spirit. This wilderness may be a valley of visions. In this ordinance here we may see the Lord Jesus Christ presenting Himself to us. Here we may see the banner of His love displayed. Here we may behold the glory of His grace beaming forth in His love. Here we may see the law's enmity slain by a dying Jesus, and the devils dragged in chains at His chariot. Here we may see justice satisfied, sin pardoned, the favour of God bestowed upon us. O here are other kind of prospects in the wilderness than the prospect of ruin and desolation, blackness and darkness.

Since then we may see such glorious sights, O let us open our eyes at this time, and let us behold the Lord Jesus Christ in His glory. He will come to visit us in the wilderness. He will be an habitation in the wilderness. He will spread a table gloriously in the wilderness. Open therefore your eyes; come and see what Christ is, what Jesus Christ hath done, what Jesus Christ hath suffered for poor souls. And oh! in this, let your eye affect your heart. When you see these things, ah! do you see them with an affected heart? Let your hearts bleed for your sins that hath brought such dolours on Jesus Christ, and let your hearts love the Lord Jesus Christ, who is willing to come from heaven into the wilderness to see you, to commend to you the love of His Father, and His own love, by laying down His life for you, and shedding His blood for you. Behold Him with desire. Be enamoured at Him. O look at Him as God and your salvation. "Looking unto Jesus." Look off from yourselves. Look off from your sins. Look off from the world to the Lord Jesus Christ, so the word in the original imports; not only a looking on, but a looking off. Poor soul, thou lookest upon thy sins? Thou dost well, if thou dost not so look upon them as to conclude thou art a damned creature.

O look upon thy sins so as to mourn for them, to be humbled for them; but look off from their damning power to Jesus Christ. Look off from thy works, from all thy righteousness, from all thy frames, and look wholly to the Lord Jesus Christ. What are your works, but defilements, and cannot stand before the justice of God, but when weighed in the balance of the sanctuary will be found too light. The wilderness may become a valley of vision to you, in which you may see glorious things.

Secondly, the wilderness may be made a garden of Eden, a place of sweet delight. So Eden signifies. Ah! the wilderness may be made this to you. Look upon the provisions the Lord Jesus Christ makes for you in the wilderness, and you will find the wilderness a place of sweet delights to you. 'Tis true, there's a great deal of affliction the people of God meet withal, but this may be made delightful. O! If the Lord Jesus Christ shall feed your souls with the application of the pardon of sin to you, and the revelations of the love and favour of God unto you, and with the abundant pourings out of the Spirit upon you, and sealing to you all the promises and blessings of the covenant; will not this be sweet unto you? All your wearisome paths, all your troublesome walks will be made easy. Christ will bring His bottles to stay your spirits; here they are in this ordinance. Since then, the Lord Jesus Christ can make the wilderness as a garden of Eden to you, do you apply to your souls the blessings the Lord Jesus Christ hath purchased for you that the wilderness may be pleasant to you, that your troubles may be more light.

Thirdly, the wilderness may be made a land of springs. Ah Beloved! all our springs are in Jesus Christ, and all our streams are in Him. If He will be pleased to open to us springs in the wilderness we may refresh ourselves with the sweet waters thereof. God will make us to drink of the brook in the way. God will give us water out of the Rock, streams flowing from Christ. Then may we have comfort, refreshment and much satisfaction in this wilderness. Ah! sirs, Jesus Christ is living waters to poor souls that will feed on Him.

Fourthly, the wilderness, through the provisions Jesus Christ makes for His people, may become a little heaven. What is it that makes heaven? Is it not the presence of Christ? In this Ordinance you may have the glorious manifestations of God in Christ to you, and this Ordinance may become a little heaven to you, a heaven before heaven. O you may see Christ here by an eye of faith; here you may enjoy Him; here you may satisfy yourselves in Him. You may rest in His bosom, be dandled upon His knee. You may have an earnest of the blessed inheritance. These things will make a little heaven in your souls. What though you be, as to your outward state and condition, in the wilderness, your souls may be in heaven, and heaven in your souls, through the precious manifestations of Jesus Christ to you. Here's a table for you in the wilderness. Here you may have all you want, pardon of sin, peace of conscience, victory over corruptions, the love of God sealed up to you. Whatever you can desire, here you may have it. Therefore now, souls, long for His coming, expect His appearance, make ready for Him. Call forth your graces that they may be all in readiness to praise Him as He comes by. Reach forth the hand of faith as Christ passeth by. Look up to the top of Pisgah.[1] God is pleased yet to continue His ordinances and doth rain down manna. We have not that peace which formerly we had; we are not in those circumstances as formerly we were, but in far worse circumstances. Therefore, let us eat and drink heartily, for we know not how long and tedious a way we may go, and how many brunts we may meet with, and how many thorns and briers we may go through. Therefore, let us feed heartily in this ordinance, whilst in this wilderness.

Thus far as to the privileges of this season.

Now, on the 27th day of this 10th month, it being the last sabbath in that month, this church met with an interruption as to their communion seasons. Bands of rude soldiers were ranging up and down in those parts, so it became dangerous for many persons to travel abroad, so that this people could not possibly assemble together as they had done, but were in a scattered posture, pastor and people, each from other, to the end of this year, which increased the dolour of the day. Sanctuary privileges failed, temple work ceased. The solemn assemblies broken, teachers removed into corners, many sorrowful for the solemn assemblies, so that things appeared with a sad aspect, iniquity abounding more and more, popery, profaneness, blasphemy, enmity and rage against

[1] Deut. 3.27.

religion, persecution and oppression still growing up to a greater height, and the poor people of God that walked humbly and mournfully before Him, were trodden down under the foot of pride. Ah; in what a doleful plight was this poor land. The judgments of God abroad, the Lord marching through the land in indignation, His arrows flying thick; pestilential and infectious fevers, and other diseases that had swept away many in divers places. Fearful apprehensions in many of more sore amazing calamities yet approaching, the lives of many still in jeopardy, the Lord in His providences threatening to cut off two parts and to bring the third part through some purifying fire.

14

WITHOUT WERE FIGHTINGS, WITHIN WERE FEARS.....

(1686)

At the beginning of this year, *1686,* the judges of the land rode in circuit as usually. And now was a time many were in great fear what the event would be, doubting there would be cruel butcheries used, as it was in the last assizes. But whilst the judges were in their circuit, a proclamation was issued forth by the king for the releasing of such as had been in the late insurrection, and had for some months past lain under sore distresses and in great obscurity. Upon which Act of Oblivion[1] such as were in bonds

[1] Act of Oblivion, 1686. A general amnesty for those convicted of participation in the Monmouth Rebellion of 1685.

AE 9

upon that account were set at liberty, and the outcasts returned again to their habitations. Here was much mercy in the midst of deep affliction. A dreadful storm on a sudden turned into a calm, the mischievous designs of rude soldiers in many places broken in pieces. The fears of many a sad and pensive heart abated; some blinks of light did shine in the darkness, and great revivings in a house of bondage, a little pleasant way in a howling wilderness, the lives of many spared that were appointed to the slaughter, and many souls delivered from all the expectation of the people. Blessed be God that a remnant do yet survive to the poor church of God, and that any are spared in a day of great consumption.

Now it is worthy of observation and deserves to be recorded, the wonderful goodness of God to this poor congregation in preserving their pastor in such a desolating day, especially considering the circumstances he was under. Yet through the tender care of the Lord both towards him and towards this church, the blessed God hath prepared a place for him in a christian friend's house where he was safely and comfortably hid all along through this late dreadful storm of blood and persecution. Yea, which was more to be admired, that he had opportunities and capacity to exercise his gifts in preaching almost every sabbath day to some persons of the neighbourhood near the place where he was hid. And about this time did he appear more publicly again as to his ministerial work, and in travelling abroad.

And now the Lord in tender pity and lovingkindness was returning again to this congregation, who had been broken as to their communion and disprivileged as to their enjoying the sacred institutions of the Lord Jesus Christ for several weeks past. For on the 4th day of the second month, it being the sabbath, in the evening tide, several members of this church with divers other persons assembled together in the sacred worship of God in the dwelling house of the afore named Nicholas Lowring, where Mr. Towgood, pastor, preached to them from the former subject, *Micah 4, 10.*[1] He having before in the blackness of this night of affliction, finished his discourses on the former part of the verse, and, as his own words were in the beginning of this his sermon, treated on the afflictions and distresses of Zion, her station in the wilderness, and her oppressions by her enemies, together with her groans under her afflictions, and her travails in order to a deliverance. Now he began to insist, as he then said, upon a more pleasant subject, of Zion's deliverance, from the latter clause of the words,

[1] Autumn 1685; see p.106.

"There shalt thou be delivered; there the LORD shall redeem thee out of the hands of thine enemies." And the Lord made this a peaceful and refreshing season to them, though vile and rude soldiers were not far from them.

The next sabbath in the night season the church assembled together again in the secret cave where they had formerly met. But on the last sabbath day in this month the congregation met publicly in the morning in one of their usual places of assembling in the wood where were a great number of people, the Lord giving them a calm and peaceable season with much of His refreshing presence. And in the third month this congregation enjoyed their gospel privileges with as much publickness and frequency as ever, with a great concourse of people constantly in one place in the wood for some space of time.

Now in this day of sore temptation, and under these sifting, winnowing providences, which had passed over the churches and people of God, much chaff was discovered. Many professors appeared to be as light grain. O the stumblings, O the falls were amongst a professing people. Some had fallen back, and turned out of the good ways of God, and left the pure institutions of Jesus Christ, which before they attended upon. Others had fallen and broken their bones, made woeful work for repentance, fallen very scandalously, and many good souls, through fear of sufferings, had stepped aside and too much fallen into a sinful compliance with a formal generation in the national way of worship. And indeed it was a day of sore staggerings and shakings, enough to make any tender heart to bleed to see the sad shipwreck was made of faith and a good conscience this day.

Also, which was a matter of lamentation and grief of heart to many of this society, there were found even amongst those related to this church that had defiled their garments, and got foul spots upon them in this day of defection and abounding iniquity. Wherefore, the violence of the storm being a little abated, and this people now having a little more breathing time, they thought it requisite to call a solemn assembly, and to make some enquiry into the state of the church.

Now on the 28th day of the 5th month the church was solemnly assembled together. The principal work of the day was to seek the Lord by prayer and supplication for counsel and direction in a case that lay before them concerning the unlawfulness of attending upon the present national ministry of the Church of England. Some of the members of this congregation having gone aside in this matter, which became matter of offence and trouble to some amongst them. Now for the recovery of such, and preventing any further spreading of this evil practice, as they judged it to be, they thought it expedient that after solemn supplications be made to the Lord, this matter be debated that all might know how to steer a right course and keep out of the way of temptation.

Wherefore the church being thus assembled, first of all the pastor directed his speech to them as followeth, which were the very same words he delivered at that time.

My friends, this is a day of very close consultations against the interest and authority of Jesus Christ, against the liberties and privileges of His subjects, against the practice and power of godliness, and ah! it is a day of great shakings and searchings, a day of backslidings and apostacies amongst professors. Now antichrist is undermining the churches of God and bending his force against Zion, seeking to defile her, to overthrow her and lay her in the dust. O my friends, we are a people who have congregated ourselves according to the appointments of Jesus Christ, to bear testimony to His Name, to walk in His sacred appointments, and it is our principal concernment to keep the truths of Jesus Christ inviolable, and to maintain to the utmost of our power His authority, which the world seeks to undermine. It behoves us to be in consultation how we may according to the Word of God behave ourselves in this sinful generation, and how we may establish ourselves in the truth as it is in Jesus. Do Zion's enemies plot its overthrow, and shall not we seek its establishment? Are devices framed for the undermining of the churches of God, and shall not we labour to disappoint the designs of the church's enemies? We are a poor, broken, shattered people, yet blessed be God for any strength that yet remains. Blessed be God for any liberty we enjoy to seek His face, hold forth His truth, and wait upon Him in His ways.

O let us seriously consider what the Lord Jesus Christ now expects of us, what He requires at our hands in such a day, in such a place, and under such a juncture of affairs as now we are. The worse the times are, the better we should be, and the more truth is opposed, the more should we maintain it. It is an honour God puts upon a people when He makes them His church, and causeth them to approach to Himself in sacred things, and it is a trust God commits to all His people to maintain His honour, to defend His truth, and to keep to His pure institutions. We are entrusted with God's word, entrusted with God's honour and entrusted with Christ's laws, and it is our great business to see these be promoted whatever become of our own outward interests.

We are here met together to this purpose to strengthen and establish one another. We may look into God's Word, and see what course we should take in these evil times, and that we may prevent those scandals and apostacies which may be in the midst of us, to the dishonour of God and the grieving of many a poor soul. Now let us in the fear of the Lord beg His assistance, address ourselves to this work that lies before us. It is a great and weighty work, to know what we should do, and how we should behave ourselves in such a day as this. Let us apply ourselves unto God, and beg His direction, counsel, and the presence of His Holy Spirit with us, without which we are able to do nothing.

After the pastor had thus spoken to the congregation, by way of introduction to the solemn work of the day, solemn and fervent supplications were made to the Lord for His presence and counsel in that weighty case that lay before them, which was as followeth: "Whether a people separating from the national ministry, and national way of worship, because of its corruptness and pollutions, and had gathered themselves together, and are become a church of Jesus Christ, may attend upon that national ministry, in such a polluted national way of worship from whence they have made a separation?"[1]

1 'Occasional Conformity', or taking the sacrament in the Anglican Church, was an expedient to which some Nonconformists resorted in order to qualify for certain civil and municipal offices from which they were debarred by the Corporation Act of 1661. The expedient itself was banned by the Occasional Conformity Act of 1771. The question now presented to the Axminster Church is one that had agitated the minds of Nonconformists generally ever since the ejectment of 1662, and there was no uniform answer given to it. Sometime before his death in 1672 Philip Nye had written, *A Case: Whether we may lawfully Hear the Now-Conforming Ministers*. London 1677. In 1683 there had appeared, *The Lawfulness of Hearing the Public Ministers of the Church of England Proved;* by Ph. Nye, John Robinson, &c. On the other hand, Calamy speaks of Francis Holcroft of Cambridge, as being "Much against holding any Kind of Communion with the Parish Churches . . . and was angry with his Dissenting Brethren that were more Catholick-spirited." As early as 1664 there had appeared an anonymous treatise running to 98 pages, entitled *Marturion Christianon,... Or A Christian and Sober Testimony against Sinful Complyance. Wherein the unlawfulness of Hearing the present Ministers of England, is clearly demonstrated. ... By Christophilus Antichristomachus, a Mourner in Sion, waiting for the day of her Salvation, and coming of her King...*" It was therefore well known at Axminster that, "this case being the great controversy of the day and many pious

Now, in the conference of this day, whilst this case was debated liberty was given to each member to offer their opinion and to declare what they had to say either for or against such a practice, that, if possible, all might have satisfaction in this matter. Now this case being the great controversy of the day and many pious persons not being of the same mind or judgment, some judging it lawful, others unlawful, wherefore it was thought meet that the debates of this day should not be inserted in these records. Notwithstanding, that the judgment and practice of this church as to the major part of them might be known and understood, it was after judged expedient that somewhat of the debates of this day be transmitted to posterity that those who hereafter might become members of this church might rightly understand what was the judgment and practice of their ancestors who kept faithful with God in an evil day.

Take then some brief hints of what was delivered by the brethren, principally the eldership of this church:

> I conceive that persons under the case before mentioned to attend upon such a national ministry, particularly this of our English ministry, is not according to the Word. It is not a keeping to the Word, to the rule, to the institution of the Lord Jesus Christ, because that such a national ministry is not the institution of the Lord Jesus Christ, but stands in opposition to Him, to His Word, to His institutions, and appointments. Hearing the gospel is part of instituted worship, for when I come to hear the gospel preached I do expect that something extraordinary beyond the power of nature should be conveyed to me therein, therefore, say I, it is part of Christ's instituted worship, for it is the Lord Jesus Christ only that conveys the blessing of the preaching of the gospel beyond anything that nature can do. Now, hearing being an instituted part of Christ's worship, I must have respect to such an administrator or minister as the Lord Jesus Christ hath instituted and appointed that by them I may expect a blessing. Now the Lord Jesus Christ hath appointed ministers for the preaching of the Word. He gave pastors and preachers; and their qualifications are set down also by Jesus Christ.

---

persons not being of the same mind . . ." An opening address by the pastor, a season of prayer, speeches by brethren (one of whom was Thomas Lane), and contributions and questions by members, led to a general though not unanimous verdict against Occasional Conformity.

But this present national ministry is not a ministry of Christ's appointment, but it is a ministry of man's appointment. The church in which this national ministry is set is not of Christ's appointment. Christ hath appointed congregational churches, such churches in which the members thereof may assemble together in one place for their mutual edification. But this national church is of such a vast compass and circumference, instituted merely for the advancing of human grandeur and pomp, that the end of the institution can in no wise be attained. Such as these are set by such officers as never were of Christ's making, namely diocesan. The prelates claim such power and jurisdiction as the Lord Jesus Christ never gave them; laws of their own making, statutes of their own devising, as Jeroboam had laws which he made after his own heart. Nay, these do stand in opposition to Christ's churches and ministers, seeking to root them out and destroy them. Yea, there is such an opposition betwixt Christ's churches and ministers and this church that they cannot both stand together, but if the one stand, the other must fall. They oppose the power and authority of Jesus Christ in His churches, because they submit themselves to the wills of men, follow the injunctions and impositions of men, bind up their hands, give up their power to the prelate. Christ hath appointed His ministers to teach and rule in His churches, but now these give up their power to such as have not received any authority from the Lord Jesus Christ. In this they are treacherous. They oppose the Lord Jesus Christ, and seek to root out His institutions, so that we may not lawfully attend such a ministry as this.

So far he. Afterward another brother, one of the elders:

The ministers that are now set in the national church which claim the power and authority of Christ's ministers; that they are no ministers of Christ, and principally, to warn you of their betraying their authority in teaching and ruling. According to their own canons they cannot preach without a license, for by a canon made it was decreed that none should preach without licence. God hath instituted a gospel ministry, told us what qualifications it should be, that they should be elected by the people and their work is to preach the gospel and teach the people and govern the flock of Christ. This they have betrayed. They do not preach the gospel of Christ, according to the virtue of their office, for their office is only to read, and they must have a licence[1] before they can preach; and for government they have given up that into the hands of the diocesan. How these men can be said to be the ministers of Christ, though they may sometimes preach by virtue of their licence, and how christians can submit to them as to the ministers of Christ, I cannot understand, seeing they have so cast off the authority of Christ as they have done.

It is true they say, 'We preach the gospel'. So we might say of Jeroboam's priests and others. They had the substance of things, for they had sacrifices. They had circumcision and they had a feast ordained by Jeroboam upon the 8th month, a month which was of his own devising, like as they had at Jerusalem. And herein was one part of Jeroboam's sin in altering the feast from the 7th to the 8th month.[2] I hope that none will say that Jeroboam's priests were the priests of the Lord, since they had gone off from the institution. If the Lord Jesus Christ hath appointed ministers to minister in His holy things, then no persons ought to be attended upon in the ministration of holy things by virtue of office, who never received the office from Him. We cannot hear those as ministers of Christ who are no ministers of Christ. You find in *Lev. 10. 1, 2,* Nadab and Abihu met with a very severe rebuke from the Lord because they offered strange fire which the Lord had not commanded.

You may say, 'What fire was it the Lord commanded? How could Nadab and Abihu come to the knowledge of what fire it was?' See in the foregoing chapter. There it was appointed what fire should be offered. God having appointed this, and in the latter part of the chapter, God having caused fire to come down from heaven extraordinarily, and their not heeding this appointment, they met with a strange rebuke. So we may plainly gather; if the Lord Jesus Christ hath appointed ministers to minister in holy things, and shewn us what their qualifications are, and set them in their places, then we are

1 No person whatsoever, not examined and approved by the bishop of the diocese, or not licensed, as is aforesaid, for a sufficient or convenient Preacher, shall take upon him to expound in his own cure, or elsewhere, any Scripture or matter of doctrine; but shall only study to read plainly and aptly (without glossing or adding) the Homilies already set forth, or hereafter to be published by lawful authority, for the confirmation of the true faith, and for the good instruction and edification of the people. (*The Constitutions and Canons Ecclesiastical.* (1603), 49).

2 1 Kings 12.31-33.

to heed such, and in heeding others we offer up strange fire. Jesus Christ in appointing ministers to minister in holy things excludes all others that cannot shew His warrant, for it belongs to Christ only to be the Legislator of His church.

It was objected: That the bishops of old were the same with these now; had the same ordination, and conformed to the same worship.[1]

Answer: First, let it be considered that then was the Infancy of Reformation. That which those worthy witnesses did was wonderful in their days, but we are set upon their shoulders. It hath pleased God to give unto us a larger and greater inspection into the mysteries of the gospel, and the things of the kingdom of Jesus Christ which was hid from them. It was much they did in their days.[2]

Let it be further considered, that the state of the present ministry, I suppose, differs much from the state of the ministry in the Marian days. The present ministry I conceive to be a more defiled and polluted ministry, not only because they have resisted greater light, but also because they have protested against a reformation. When it pleased God so far to enlighten the nation that there was a covenant set on foot to reform the churches according to the Word of God and the best reformed churches, these men declare this covenant to be utterly unlawful.[3] And what shall we say of persons that are arrived to such a degree as to swear against all reformation. God may say to them as *Ps. 50;* What hast thou to do to take my word into thy mouth seeing thou hatest to be reformed?

[1] i.e. that Cranmer, Ridley, Latimer, Hooper & Coverdale, were technically in the same 'apostolic succession', and committed to basically the same liturgy as Juxon, Sheldon, and Sancroft.

[2] This reply reiterates the view expressed in the opening paragraph of Chapter 2.

[3] The Solemn League and Covenant (1643). A declaration accepted by the General Assembly of the Church of Scotland, the English Parliament, and the Westminster Assembly.

> We ... having before our eyes the glory of God ... and calling to mind the treacherous and bloody plots, conspiracies, attempts, and practices of the enemies of God against all true religion and professors thereof in all places, especially in these three kingdoms, ever since the reformation of religion ... do swear that we shall ... sincerely ... endeavour ... the preservation of the reformed religion in the Church of Scotland, in doctrine, worship, discipline, and government, against our common enemies; the reformation of religion in the kingdoms of England and Ireland, in doctrine, worship, discipline, and government, according to the word of God and the example of the best reformed churches; ... That we shall in like manner, without respect of persons,

That Latimer, Ridley, Cranmer and others of those glorious lights were the ministers of Jesus Christ, nobody will contradict. But that they appeared to be the ministers of Christ by a popish ordination is the matter in debate. What was that which did constitute these men to be the ministers of Christ? Answer:

(1). The election of the people,

(2). God's public owning them and spiriting them for the work of the ministry, and,

(3). The people's acceptation of them, which was the main thing they and many of their successors stood upon.

It was not a popish ordination but the people's acceptation, for ordination is not essentially necessary to the work of the ministry. The essence of a minister lies in the consent of three wills: the will of God, the will of the people, and the will of the minister. The will of God is declared in the consent of the two latter, that is, when a people agree to elect, and the minister agrees to accept of the call of a people. Ordination is for order sake. Now our ministers which did receive their ordination from the bishops of old did publicly declare that which they stood upon was the acceptation of the people. Now these worthy men had this acceptation of the people, but I humbly conceive the present ministry cannot be said so to have. In few places but they are imposed upon the people without their choice or consent.

Thus by what was delivered in answer to this case, the judgment of this church might be understood, especially the eldership and major part of this church. We find it recorded in the holy Scriptures that the children of Israel when they were going up from their captivity, began to reform those disorders that were crept in amongst them whilst they lay amongst the heathen, namely, to put away their strange wives. And they searched into the Book of the Law which was read distinctly amongst them, and the Levites caused the people to understand the sense and the meaning

---

endeavour the extirpation of popery, prelacy (that is, church government by archbishops, bishops . . .) . . . superstition, heresy, schism, profaneness, and whatsoever shall be found contrary to sound doctrine and the power of godliness . . . (Full text in Bettenson, *Documents of the Christian Church*).

Not surprisingly, the English bishops at the Restoration repudiated the Solemn League, and its total renunciation was required of ministers by the Act of Uniformity, 1662.

thereof, and they set upon the performance of what was written in the Book of the Law, which had been omitted from the days of Joshua the son of Nun to the day that the children of Israel should dwell in booths in the feast of the 7th month. Afterwards they assembled with fasting and sackcloth and acknowledged God's great goodness toward them and their own wickedness and sinfulness, and so renewed their covenant with the Lord and entered into a curse and into an oath to walk in God's laws and to do all the commandments of the Lord and His judgments and His statutes.[1] Now suitable to this was the practice of this people at this time, the dawning of a deliverance beginning to break upon them.

On the 19th day of the 6th month, this congregation was solemnly assembled by fasting and prayer as preparatory in order to the sacred ordinance of the Lord's Supper which was appointed to be celebrated on the sabbath day following. And now did they on this day once again pass themselves into a covenant with the Lord and with each other; with their right hands lifted up to heaven, solemnly and publicly declaring their purposes and resolutions to cleave to the Lord and unto each other, and to stand off from all the abominations, will-worship, superstitions, and idolatries of the day. And the blessed God was pleased wonderfully to favour them with His gracious presence, some further addition being made to the church this day.

The sabbath after, being the 22nd day of the month, was a very great assembly of some hundreds of people with much peace and a good day, when this church was signally privileged and admitted once again into the chambers of the King of glory, feasted in His banqueting house, and wonderfully treated with His love. O the changes that have passed over this congregation. A little while ago, what a black and terrible wilderness were they in, fierce men riding over their heads; now they could go up to the house of God in troops with a multitude to keep holy day. O what quick turns can the Lord make in the way of His providence, and how should this be told to generations to come what the Lord hath done for an unworthy people merely for His own Name's sake!

[1] Neh. chs. 8-10.

On the last day of the 8th month,[1] it being the sabbath day, the church being met together, they adventured into their ancient meeting house at *Wickcroft,* from whence they had been driven ever since the year 1681, (as before noted in this narrative).[2] A great concourse of people were now assembled together with great peace and much of the presence of the Lord with them. O how wonderful have the leadings of divine care and providence been all along towards this people. Surely the right hand of the Lord doth valiantly; the right hand of the Lord bringeth great things to pass. Thus this church continued their assembling together afterwards in the open public place from sabbath to sabbath with much peace and freedom and were no more shut out.

1 October 1686.
2 p.77.

15 

THEN HAD THE CHURCHES REST....

(1687-88)

At the beginning of this year, *1687*, a decree was issued forth by the King for free liberty of conscience for persons of all persuasions to worship God according to their own way. A stop was put to any further execution of any penal law against such as dissented from the Church of England on the account of conscience; no disturbance or molestation to be given to any in the matter of religious worship. A strange and astonishing providence the people of God passed under at this time. Now the broken, scattered congregations were gathered again, and such who a while ago were constrained to skulk up and down in the solitary darksome night seasons in secret corners and caves of the earth to worship God, that did gather bread for their souls with the peril of their lives because of the terrible persecution, could now go in flocks and droves and assemble by hundreds in the streets in open public places, and in the view and sight of their enemies to wait upon the Lord in His pure instituted worship, and none that durst make them afraid. O what a surprising providence was this, and worthy of due and serious observation.[1]

When Moses saw a bush burning with fire and yet not consumed, he said, I will now turn aside, and see this strange sight, why the bush is not consumed.[2] Such a curious piece of providence was now on the wheel this day that did call for the most serious contemplations of the most judicious and considerate christians to pause awhile upon the wonderful doings of the great Jehovah; and it might well cause all observing souls to admire at the wisdom and power of God in beholding it. The poor church of God that has been in the fire burning and flaming so long, and yet, behold! it is not consumed, and why? For the goodwill of Him that dwelt in the bush. O wonderful! If it be duly weighed and considered, when the time of this enlargement came; after a black and doleful day of tribulation and persecution, when the Lord had been wroth with His inheritance, and His jealousy burnt like fire, when the adversary had devoured His people and fierce men had made a prey of them. After great spoils, oppressions, and sore calamities and that mostly on the professing party of the nation, so that to the upright did light arise in the darkness, and the Lord turned for them the shadow of death into the morning.

[1] The Second Declaration of Indulgence, 1687. On April 4th 1687 James II repeated his brother's feat of 1672 with a royal Declaration that all laws penalizing Nonconformists and Roman Catholics were to be swept aside. There was to be complete freedom of worship, this time without licences, and also without fear of future conviction under old laws. James was an avowed Roman Catholic and his motive was wholly in the Roman interest; Nonconformists were regarded merely as puppets in a plot to restore the Roman Church in England. The Church of England under Archbishop Sancroft now strove for comprehension with the Nonconformists. "Those who had lately been designated as schismatics and fanatics were now dear fellow Protestants, weak brethren it might be, but still brethren whose scruples were entitled to tender regard." (Macaulay, *History of England*, 1858. II.217). Nonconformist reaction was varied. Some quietly accepted the freedom and used it without regard to the wider implications of the Declaration. Some wrote flattering addresses of thanks to the king. A substantial minority, however, awed by the king's duplicity, and by the danger of their own predicament, stood aloof from these fulsome 'addresses' which in any case only misled the king into thinking his attempts at toleration were more acceptable to the Nonconformists than was really the case. Many stedfastly refused to make any open acknowledgement of the Declaration, as did the Axminster Church (see p.133). On the other hand, many waverers among Nonconformists who had gone back to the parish churches under the repressive legislation now returned to the meeting houses. The king pursued his Romanizing policy in the Universities, in the State, and in the Church of England, finally promulgating his Indulgence a second time, in April 1688, ordering the bishops to have it read in all the churches. Seven bishops refused and were imprisoned in the Tower of London for sedition. This led finally to the Revolution, and cost the king his throne.

[2] Exod. 3.3.

It was also a time when nothing less was expected by the generality of a professing people but more dreadful ruins and desolation, greater havoc to be made of the church of God, a removal of gospel privileges and the pure institutions of Jesus Christ; and when many of the enemies of the Lord's people hoped to have swallowed them up, and to have cut off the name of Israel that it might be no more in remembrance. 'Twas a critical time indeed with poor Zion that it might well be said as in *Gen. 22.14*, "In the mount of the LORD it shall be seen."

Also, to consider the way and method of the infinitely wise Jehovah in bringing about this enlargement; what unlikely instruments doth the Lord sometimes make use of for the carrying on His work in the world. That a potentate so enraged, so incensed, should be so indulgent, that such wonderful liberty and enlargement should be granted by one from whom the quite contrary was expected. O how may this providence in many respects be paralleled with the state of the Jews when in their captivity in Babylon, when Cyrus proclaimed liberty for the poor captives to go up to Jerusalem and build the wall and the temple.[1] Then a heathen potentate was raised up by the Lord to do great things for His people's sake; and now a popish prince was instrumental for easing the burdens of many that did truly fear the Lord. Surely the hearts of kings are in the hands of the Lord, and as the rivers of waters He can turn them whithersoever He will. He can dispose of nations, churches and persons as seemeth good to Him, for the government of kingdoms and nations are in His hands. He can make the earth to help the woman, men of earthly spirits and principles to shew favour to His Zion. And the due consideration of this dispensation of providence might well cause all wise observing christians to cry out and say, "What hath God wrought"!

Now a great and wide door was opened for the publication of the gospel of Christ, and though there were many adversaries yet they were under restraint. Freedom was granted to wait upon the Lord in His appointed worship, a great concourse of people everywhere flocking to the ordinances of God, solemn praises given to the Most High in many congregations of His people for so great a deliverance so strangely brought about. And indeed it was a great deliverance, though not so full a deliverance as the Lord hath promised to His Zion, and that the people of God are waiting for, when all the antichristian power shall be broken in pieces,

[1] 2 Chronicles 36.22,23; Ezra 1.1-3.

and all the enemies of the blessed King Jesus shall be made His footstool, and that time come when the blessed state of the church's peace and purity so fully spoken of in the Holy Scriptures, shall be ushered into the world. For though the people of God had now an opportunity to be as holy as they would, and none to molest them, yet what a door was opened and an advantage likewise given for errors, atheism, popery, idolatry, superstition, profaneness, and all kind of abominations to swarm and abound, and none to control these evils. State politicians may intend the carrying on and promoting their own interests whilst they pretend to favour the interest and people of Christ. But whatever their politic designs are, yet God's thoughts are not as man's thoughts, nor His ways as man's ways. Zion's King reigneth still. He rules in the midst of His enemies, and whether they deal proudly, or act by policy, He is still above them and will overrule them.

Thus the Lord was pleased to lighten the eyes of His people, and to give them a little reviving in their bondage. And this being a public mercy, this church enjoyed the benefit of it and had a new song of praise put into their mouths, and on several sabbath days after the pastor preached to them from *Acts 9.31,* "Then had the churches rest throughout all Judaea and Galilee and Samaria, and were edified; and walking in the fear of the Lord, and in the comfort of the Holy Ghost, were multiplied." And indeed there was still ground for holy fear, and to rejoice with trembling lest under these external privileges, gospel showers and dews, there should be inward witherings and soul decays. Great cause of fear, lest this present calm should breed security, engender heats, strifes, contentions, divisions amongst a professing people; too, too usual the sad effects of the church's tranquillity and, which was cause of lamentation, awhile after was too apparent.

Now this church having a little space given them by the God of heaven to set up the house of the Lord amongst them, began to make a further enquiry into the state of the members, for as some had staggered as to their judgment concerning the purity of worship, and too much warped, through the heat of persecution; so others in this day of looseness and abounding iniquity, had been defiled with the gross pollutions of the day, and got such spots as are not ordinarily the spots of God's children.

Wherefore, on the 26th day of the 8th month, the congregation assembled together in order to the regulating of things appertaining to the church, and amongst other debates and determinations that day, it was then agreed by the church that this Book of Remembrance should be procured, in which the most material matters and things relating to this church should be recorded and kept for a memorial for those that may succeed in after times.[1]

The church also understanding the scandalous behaviour of C—— B—— and Anne his wife, both members of this congregation, appointed another day to assemble together to inspect into that matter, and it was ordered by the church that C—— B—— and A—— B—— his wife, have timely notice given them to be present at their next church meeting which was the 9th day of the 9th month.

Accordingly at the appointed time the church was assembled again, and after solemn prayer and supplication made to the Lord, C—— B—— being then present, he was called forth to answer to what the church had to say unto him. The matter of fact he was charged withal was his drinking to excess on a sabbath day in the evening. The pastor opened the heinousness of his sin and endeavoured to set it home on his conscience, calling upon him to make confession of his sin, and to give glory to God by his repentance. But the said Caleb endeavoured to clear himself as not being guilty of this abominable evil, but he was fully and openly convicted by the mouth of several witnesses, which proved it against him before the church, so that he was constrained to make some acknowledgment of his sin. Yet, after all reasonings and arguments with many things spoken both by the pastor and elder of the church, he rather extenuated than aggravated his sin, whereby his confession and humiliation did not appear to be a right gospel humiliation, but rather a forced acknowledgment. Neither was it satisfying to the church. Wherefore he then passed under the censure of the church which was a suspension from communion with the church in all its special privileges, the pastor admonishing him in these words. "Brother B——, you have by your sin offended God, grieved your brethren, opened the mouths of the wicked, you must therefore make confession of your sin, be humbled for it, repent of it, watch against this sin for time to come, give satisfaction to the church; and until you have given the church satisfaction by your humiliation and repentance you must not think to enjoy the privileges of the church as you have done."

Then further notice was given him that both he and his wife A—— B—— be present at the next church meeting, the day being then appointed by the church. But before that day came, he

[1] 1687. See pp.3, 163; and Appendix F.

was cut off from this church. The great and holy God had sent a summons by the hand of death to make his appearance before His awful tribunal.

On the 23rd day of this 9th month the church was assembled again according to their appointment further to inspect into the state of the church, particularly as to those members that had scandalously fallen and brought reproach and dishonour on the Name of God, His ways and people. After solemn prayer to the Lord they entered upon the principal work and business that lay before them that day, which was to inspect into the carriage, or rather miscarriages and disorderly walking of A—— B——, she being then present. An account was given to the church by the elder of several informations had been given them that this Sister B—— had behaved herself very wantonly and unbecoming a christian with those soldiers that lately lay in the town of Axminster. That she was at unseasonable times in their company, and they were at unseasonable times with her, which was become matter of scandal and public reproach; and that both himself with others of the brethren had more privately discoursed with her, and laboured to set before her, her evil in these unbecoming carriages of hers.

Then the pastor endeavoured to make her sensible of her evil, and desired her seriously to consider that she was in the presence of the great God, in the presence of Jesus Christ who is in the midst of His church, that she must shortly give an account to the Lord Jesus Christ the great Judge; therefore he desired her to speak in the fear of the Lord. All her reply was by way of defence, shifting off her guilt, vindicating her innocency. It was proved she had been seen led by a soldier in an unseasonable time of the night. She was charged also with entertaining bad company in her house, that soldiers with their officers usually haunted her house on sabbath days. Enough was spoken by several of the members to convict her and to satisfy the church she was justly charged, but still she had her shifts and excuses for all that was charged against her. The debate continued for the greatest part of the time that day, but she remained without any sense of her evil upon her spirit, and at last went forth from the congregation as one fretted in her spirit, so leaving them, and remained as a maimed member refusing to be healed, and unfit for further communion with this body in those special privileges they did enjoy.

Information also was brought to the church of the scandalous fall of P—— S——, a member of this society, who in the time of the late trouble was one of those that did abscond with many others, and whilst he hid himself from the hands of cruel men that could only kill the body, he was taken captive in the snare of the devil, that murderer and destroyer of souls. Now this day it was ordered by the church that P—— S—— have warning to be present on the next church meeting day.

On the 2nd day of the 10th month, being the day before appointed, the church was assembled again to carry on what further work lay before them as to those offending members P—— S—— being warned to appear, contemned the authority which the Lord Jesus Christ hath committed to His churches, and appeared not. His sin he stood guilty of was adultery, a sin against the express law of God: Thou shalt not commit adultery.[1] The fact was so evidently known, and spread abroad to the great dishonour of God, the public reproach and scandal of religion, and of this church in particular, that there needed no further evidence. Wherefore he then passed under the censure of the church, the pastor pronouncing it in those words,

> In the Name of the Lord Jesus Christ and by the power of His Spirit I do suspend Brother P—— S—— from the table of the Lord, and until he shall manifest his deep repentance he shall not be admitted to the table of the Lord, nor any special church privileges.

Now the church waited long for his repentance and return, hoping he might acknowledge his great and heinous evil and be deeply humbled, and return into fellowship with the church again, and after a considerable space of time was past and he not likely to be reclaimed, the church thought it expedient to proceed to the last act, and on a day the church being solemnly assembled he passed under the censure of excommunication, being cut off from all fellowship with the church and delivered up to Satan for the destruction of the flesh.

Alas! what are the purest churches in the militant state. We find in the primitive church there was an Ananias and Sapphira that lied to the Holy Spirit.[2] And the Apostle John speaks of some that went out from them because they were not of them, and he said, "If they had been of us, they would no doubt have continued with us: but they went out, that they might be made

[1] Exod. 20.14.
[2] Acts 5.1-11.

manifest that they were not all of us."[1] We read of sinners in Zion and hypocrites that are there. All are not Israel that are of Israel.[2] Churches, yea the best of saints, in this militant state are in a state of imperfection. So that there's great need for church members to be watching over one another; great reason of that counsel the Apostle gives to the Hebrews, to be "Looking diligently lest any man fail of the grace of God; lest any root of bitterness springing up trouble you, and thereby many be defiled; lest there be any fornicator or profane person, as Esau, who for one morsel of meat sold his birthright."[3] We find how the prophet Zechariah saw in a vision a candlestick all of gold. Ah blessed state of the church and greatly to be longed for, when it shall be so pure and glorious that it shall be all holiness to the Lord, when every pot in Jerusalem and in Judah shall be holiness to the Lord, and there shall be no more a Canaanite in the house of the Lord.[4]

After that this people had endeavoured to reclaim those that had gone aside amongst them, and to heal the disorders of offending members, they thought it necessary also to supply what was lacking amongst them. For since the time that Mr. Stephen Towgood was invested into the pastoral office amongst them there had been only Robert Bryant to serve in the office of deacons, and now the expediency of the church called for another to assist with him. Mention is made before in these records[5] concerning Robt. Batt, who in the days of the former pastor had the office of a deacon in this church, but he not concurring with his brethren in the election of their present pastor, left his place and office in the house of God. Wherefore now this church began to look out among them another brother whom they might appoint over this business. And after much seeking to the Lord for direction in this case, on a certain day the church being assembled they chose Roger Hoar and appointed him to serve in the office of a deacon in this church.

Now was it a time of great peace and liberty for the churches and people of God, the hands of oppressors bound up. And as to national concerns a breaking wheel began to pass over the enemies of the people of God, many furious justices of the peace who had been hot and zealous in persecuting the Lord's people had their commissions taken away, and others appointed in their

1 1 John 2.19.
2 Rom. 9.6.
3 Heb. 12.15.
4 Zech. 4.1-3; 14.20-21.
5 pp.24, 72.

places, strange overturnings were at this time. The mighty were put down from their seats, and those exalted that were of low degree in the account of their enemies, and it might well be said by all wise observers, Come behold the works of the Lord, what desolations and overturnings He makes in the earth. Surely God is the Judge. He setteth up one and putteth down another.[1] O how may the saints now sing the song of the Lamb and say, "Great and marvellous are thy works, Lord God Almighty; just and true are thy ways, thou King of saints."[2]

Thus the churches and people of God were greatly gladdened with their peace and liberty; as Jonah was exceedingly glad of his gourd and sat down under the shadow of it, so did they begin to sit down under the shadow of this mercy in this sunny day with too much contentment.[3] Insomuch that in divers places many that it was hoped did truly fear the Lord were too much ensnared and entangled by endeavouring to ingratiate themselves into the favour of this popish prince, professing such faithfulness and loyalty to him and presenting several addresses which savoured too much of a temporizing spirit, for it was too evident unto such as were men of understanding, as had any right discerning of the times, that a popish design was still carrying on amain under all the fair and plausible carriages of authority. But blessed be God many were kept faithful, amongst which this church, of which there was not any member that consented to subscribe with the hand to such addresses.[4] However many potent adversaries did even gnash with their teeth and were grieved to see the poor people of God enjoy any peace or liberty, and that the gospel was like to get ground, for it was a torment to them who were so drenched in profaneness and abominable iniquities, as the witnesses that prophesied tormented them that dwelt on the earth.[5]

1 Ps. 46.8; 75.7.
2 Rev. 15.3.
3 Jonah 4.6ff.
4 See note, p.126. Similar addresses had been sent to Charles II following his Indulgence of 1672. They were usually organized on a county basis.
5 Rev. 11.10.

16

TERRIBLE TO THE KINGS OF THE EARTH....

(1688-93)

But the public affairs of the nation continued not long in a settled state under this government, for lo! in *1688,* about the 8th month, there were great rumours of wars and tidings of the nation's being invaded by foreigners. Great preparations therefore were made for war, and great thoughts of heart in many what the issue of these rolling providences might be. Whereupon an ungodly generation of men began to peck up again, hoping by the revolutions that were at the door to get the day once more, and hector over the people of God as they had formerly done, for they held a confederacy with the invaders.

But God's thoughts are not as man's thoughts, nor His ways as man's ways. On the 5th day of the 9th month, the land was invaded by a vast body of men of a strange language, having for their General the Prince of Orange, who in a few days marched through the land with vast preparations for war.[1] A popish army were sent down from the King to meet him. Many of the king's officers and soldiers that favoured the Protestant interest dropped away from the king and joined in with the invaders, and after some few days' march, before the armies met, the popish army through a spirit of fear and consternation were totally routed, scattered and subdued, insomuch that the Prince of Orange with his army came to the great metropolitan City of London with little effusion of blood.

In the meanwhile the churches and people of God held their assemblies for the public worship of God very peaceably, this church enjoying the same privilege even while multitudes of soldiers lay in the town of Axminster and marched along by the public meeting house. It was marvellous to behold the wonderful acts of the Lord this day. It was certainly a day of wonders. All wise observers might well cry out with admiration, "What hath God wrought?" "Come behold the works of the Lord."

[1] The Revolution (1688), was brought on in general by James II's growing defiance of the official protestantism of the Church of England, and his equal disregard for the constitutional powers of Parliament. Its immediate causes were the popular wave of feeling in the country in support of the vindication of seven bishops against the King in June 1688, and the birth in the same month of a son to James and his Queen, Mary of Modena, which appeared to threaten the country with a succession of Roman Catholic monarchs.

William Prince of Orange (1650-1702) was a Dutch Calvinist, an inflexible soldier politician, who in 1677 had married Mary, the daughter of James, Duke of York and later James II, king of England. English noblemen invited William to take the throne in June 1688, his entitlement resting on his wife's descent, and the landing at Torbay on November 5th of this year was the result. Slowly but solidly the people of the West rose to his standard. The line of march of the main body of his army was through Exeter, Honiton, and Axminster where the Prince himself stayed for several days. With risings in many parts of the country, James II fled to France, and William and Mary arrived in London and were proclaimed joint monarchs, though only after assenting to the Declaration of Rights, on February 13th, 1689. Among conditions included in the Declaration of Rights were these: (i) That any claimant to the English throne who 'shall profess the Popish religion or shall marry a Papist shall be excluded, and be forever uncapable to inherit possess or enjoy the Crown and government of this realm and Ireland...' (ii) That any future monarch must swear a 'Coronation Oath' denying the principle doctrines of the Roman Catholic religion. For generations Nonconformists spoke of the events of 1688 and 1689 as the 'Glorious Revolution', hailing it with gratitude to God, often preaching commemorative sermons on November 5th—the anniversary of the landing at Torbay—in which they vigorously asserted principles of religious liberty.

Now did the Lord in the way of His providence give a check to the popish designs, and a breaking wheel began to go over the popish party, and in a few days divers of the great men of the nation who had been for the promoting of a popish interest were apprehended by the hand of justice and closely secured. The King, Queen, many popish lords and others fled and hid themselves. Thus the people of God might well say as the prophet Habakkuk, chap. 3.12,13: "Thou didst march through the land in indignation . . . Thou wentest forth for the salvation of thy people . . . thou woundest the head out of the house of the wicked."

King William III

Especially it is to be remarked how that monster of men, that cruel judge, George Jefferies by name, who was the capital judge in that bloody and barbarous assizes, in the year 1685, before recorded in this Book of Remembrance, p.99. This man of blood and principal agent for an anti-christian and popish faction, whilst he was contriving to convey himself away by sea in a ship, was apprehended, taken and secured a close prisoner in the Tower of London, where he remained for some months, and a little before his trial in order to his sentence, on the 18th day of the second month, in the year *1689,* he miserably departed this life. O how true are the words of Jehovah, "Bloody and deceitful men shall not live out half their days."[1]

Thus was it a time of great mutations and changes.[2] The former governors were passed away, and it was agreed upon by a Convention that was assembled in a parliamentary way to settle the affairs

[1] Ps. 55.23.

[2] In this year of revolution there appeared from the press of William Marshall in London, the 'second edition corrected' of Bartholomew Ashwood's *The Heavenly Trade.* The corrections were minimal and, except for the title page, the second edition is substantially the same as the first. Whoever was Ashwood's literary executor (? John Ashwood; or John Smith "a brother in fellowship who used to write for him") was unfortunate with his first printer. Samuel Lee, who printed the first edition of *The Heavenly Trade* in 1679 was an unprincipled chraracter. "Such a Pirate, such a Cormorant was never before. Copies, Books, Men, Shops, all was one, he held no propriety, right or wrong, good or bad, till . . . the booksellers not enduring so ill a man among them to disgrace them, spewed him out, and off he marched to Ireland . . ." Not surprisingly, *Groans from Sion,* and *The Best Treasure,* appeared two years later from William Marshall who along with his son and another relative, specialised in divinity "at the Bible in Newgate Street". The Marshalls published for John Owen; John Marshall published the *Western Martyrology;* and William published several pamphlets on the Protestant side during the Popish Plot of 1678. (H. R. Plomer, *A Dictionary of the Printers and Booksellers who were at work in England, Scotland, and Ireland from 1668 to 1725.* pp.186-7; 198).

A shorthand passage in the *Exeter Assembly Minutes* . . . records that on January 29th, 1689, pastors and messengers of neighbouring churches had been asked to advise on differences in the Church of Christ in Tiverton. Certain persons broke the peace of the church, as well as breaking signed agreements, and refused to meet arbitrators. They were severely censured, and informed that the arbitrators would "forbid to hold any communion with them till they repent and give satisfaction". The signatories were, James Wood, Pastor at Bideford; Stephen Towgood, Pastor at Axminster; John Ashwood, Pastor of the Church at Exon; . . . Thomas Lane, Robert Brant [Bryant], messengers from the Church at Axminster . . ." (p.123). No indication is given of the nature of this dispute which occurred in the same year as the death of the first pastor, Theophilus Polwheile. Ejected here in 1662, Polwheile pastored the Tiverton Independent Church, calling Samuel Bartlett, son of Robert Bartlett of Over Compton, as his assistant in 1687. Bartlett also succeeded Polwheile, from 1689 till 1705.

THE Heavenly Trade,

OR THE BEST MERCHANDIZING:

The only way to live well in IMPOVERISHING TIMES.

A Discourse occasioned from the decay of Earthly Trades, and visible wastes of Practical Piety in the day we live in, offering Arguments and Counsels to all, towards a speedy revival of dying Godliness, and timely prevention of the dangerous issues thereof impending on us. Necessary for all Families.

The Second Edition Corrected.

By *Bartholomew Ashwood*, Minister of the Gospel.
Author of *The Best Treasure*.

Labour not for the meat that perisheth, but for that meat which endureth unto everlasting life, Joh. vi. 27.
Seek ye first the Kingdom of God, and his Righteousness, and all these things shall be added unto you, Matth. vi. 33.

Ne nimium operæ consumas in rebus levissimis, fugax ætas, & vitrea res valetudo, non quibuslibet est impendenda: quædam despicienda sunt, & animus ad magna est erigendus. Eras.

Αὐτοὺς γὰρ μετ' εὐσεβείας καὶ δικαιοσύνης ζῶντας ἔν τε τοῖς πᾶσι χρόνοις ἀσφαλῶς διάγοντας καὶ περὶ τοῦ σύμπαντος αἰῶνος ἡδίους τὰς ἐλπίδας ἔχοντας.

London, Printed for *William Marshall* at the *Bible* in *Newgate-street*, MDCLXXXVIII.

of the nations; that King James II[1] having endeavoured to subvert the constitution of government by breaking the original contract betwixt the king and people, by the advice of Jesuits[2] and other wicked persons, and having violated the fundamental laws and withdrawn himself out of the kingdom, has abdicated the government—therefore the throne—and is become vacant. Then was the Prince of Orange and his Princess elected and proclaimed to be King and Queen, and the Convention turned into a parliament.

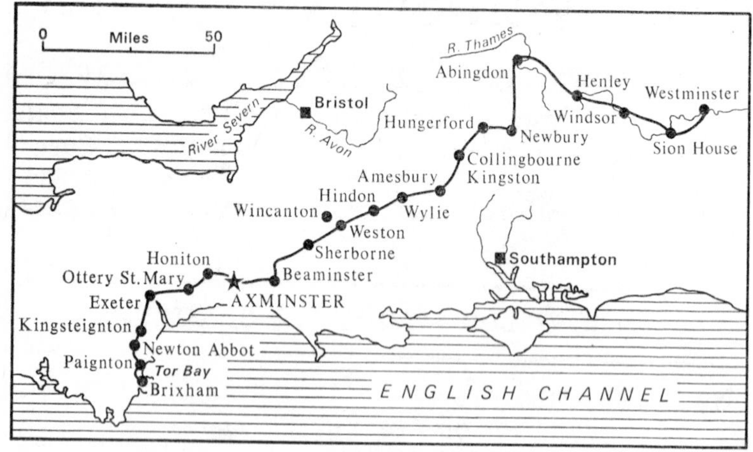

Route of main advance to London by the army of William of Orange

[1] What follows to the end of this sentence is a quotation, almost verbatim, of the resolution of the Convention Parliament in January 1689.

[2] James's closest adviser was his clerk of the Royal Closet, a Jesuit father, Sir Edward Petre. Petre was a member of the Jesuit Mission initiated in England by Edmund Campion in 1580, and well acquainted with the writings of his predecessor Robert Parsons, whose *A Memorial for the Reformation of England . . .'* was written in 1596. Parsons' recommendations which subjugated Parliament to the interests of the Roman Catholic Church, and the policy actually pursued by King James II, are almost identical. In 1690 Edward Gee, rector of St. Benedict, Paul's Wharf, London, published by way of exposure, *The Jesuit's memorial for the intended reformation of England under their first Popish prince. Published from the copy that was presented to the late King James II. With introduction and animadversions.* London, 1690. Petre among others fled to France at the Revolution.

And now the grievances of the nation began to be enquired into, and the Lord was pleased in the way of His providence so to order affairs and changes in the nation to the great content and satisfaction of His poor people who did fear His Name. Thus the Lord changeth times and seasons, removeth kings and setteth up kings. He poureth contempt upon princes and causeth them to wander in a wilderness where there is no way, and snareth the wicked in the work of his own hands. All the glory to Jehovah, Father, Son and Holy Spirit.

Afterwards, the liberty of conscience that was granted to the dissenting party, who separated from the Church of England, by the late king in the year 1687, as is being recorded, was established by Act of King and Parliament.[1] And now had the churches and people of God more rest and peace, freedom from those oppressions and persecutions which they had formerly met with from a malignant generation of men. The hands of adversaries being now bound up by such as were in authority, they dare not molest them without incurring penalty to themselves. And O what a mercy is it when kings are nursing fathers, and queens nursing mothers to the churches of Christ; when rulers are ministers of God for good, to encourage piety, that the people of the Lord

[1] The Toleration Act, 1689, as it is commonly known, was actually entitled "An Act for exempting their Majesties' Protestant subjects dissenting from the Church of England from the penalties of certain laws". This early gesture of William III conferred a welcome but very limited freedom on the Nonconformists. It allowed them their own places of worship, provided they did not meet behind locked doors; authorized prosecution of any who disturbed their services; and exempted them from the penalties of existing laws against conventicles. On the other hand, Nonconformist places had to be certified as such to and by the bishop of the diocese, or the archdeacon, or to justices at the quarter sessions; ministers were required to take the oaths of Supremacy and Allegiance, and to subscribe at least thirty four of the Thirty Nine Articles. Social and political disabilities continued; Nonconformists were still debarred from civil and public office by the Corporation and Test Acts of 1661 and 1673 which remained in force till 1828.

Restricted though it was, this 'freedom' was greeted with relief by the suffering Nonconformists, because it ended twenty eight years of vicious persecution, abolished the ruinous accumulation of unpaid fines, wiped out the miserably prosperous trade of the growing army of informers, and stopped the spectacle of honourable citizens being driven from home and their business ruined simply because they were Nonconformists. Of these developments Benjamin Keach could say, "We do believe that their present Majesties are raised up to be glorious instruments in the hand of God... I am sure we cannot sufficiently adore the Divine goodness for that salvation wrought by His own right hand. Let us strive to be thankful to God, and labour to live in love one with another, and improve the present providence." Preface to *Distressed Zion Relieved*. (Ivimey, *English Baptists*, II.364).

may lead quiet and peaceable lives in all godliness and honesty under their rule and government.[1]

However, there were still wars and rumours of wars, great clashings amongst the nations, and a popish generation of men making great wastes in Ireland. And this new elected king had sent forth a proclamation for a public monthly fast to be observed in the kingdom during the continuance of the war with Ireland, in which solemn work this church was engaged on the prescribed monthly days with all solemnity in their public meeting house. And about the beginning of the 5th month, in the year *1690,* tidings was brought of a great victory which the Lord gave the king with his army over that malignant generation of men, which caused great gladness, and the voices of joy and praises were in the congregations of the Lord's people for what the Lord had done. Public thanksgivings were rendered to the Lord by this church and in other assemblies of the Lord's people for this so signal appearance of the Lord for these nations, and for His people and interest in these lands, in discomfiting the enemy and in giving such a check to those proud insulting adversaries, though, as yet, some of the strongholds and castles were in the enemies' possession.[2]

But no sooner was there a lightsome aspect of a more peaceful day, but lo! another black cloud of judgment hovered over this poor nation. Frequent tidings and great fears there were of the nation's being in danger to be invaded by the French, which was matter of amazement to many and caused great shakings of heart and tremblings of spirit in many persons and of running to and fro in many. Especially in these western parts of the nation where their navy of ships were roving to and fro for several days, braving and domineering on the western coasts, and where on the 26th day of the 5th month early in the morning, some of their men with violence and rage brake into a certain place in the west called Tinmouth, burned some houses, doing some spoil and mischief and so returned back into their ships again. By this the Lord did awaken up many of His people and amongst others this church

[1] Is. 49.23; Rom. 13.4; 1 Tim. 2.2.

[2] James II, now in exile at the court of Louis XIV in France, tried to regain his throne with Irish help. In 1689 he went to Ireland with a French army, entered Dublin as king, and called an Irish Parliament. Roman Catholics welcomed him; the Protestants in Ulster found themselves in grave danger. William III thereupon proceeded in person to Ireland, and with his Dutch army defeated James at the Battle of the Boyne (1690).

and people to pray and cry more earnestly to Him, and in some few days they were turned back by the way they came.[1]

Now, although the churches and people of God did enjoy much peace and tranquillity, O yet, how did the face of times and things look with a sad and lowering aspect this day; scripture prophecies fulfilling apace, the signs of the times frightful and amazing to such as had only an eye of sense and carnal reason, yet such as had the eye of faith clear and open might look up and see their redemption drawing nigh, and their Redeemer preparing to come in those clouds. Now were there earthquakes felt in divers places. Most, if not all the nations in Europe in a flame; wars, rumours of wars, great preparations everywhere for blood and slaughter, many countries dreadfully involved already in war, the Lord of Hosts mustering up His armies this day, shaking of kingdoms and monarchs. Surely the Lord is accomplishing that Scripture prediction. *Zeph. 3.8,* "Therefore wait ye upon me, saith the LORD*;* until the day that I rise up to the prey: for my determination is to gather the nations, that I may assemble the kingdoms, to pour upon them mine indignation, even all my fierce anger: for all the earth shall be devoured with the fire of my jealousy." Likewise, that which was matter of bitter mourning, it was a time of sore decays and declensions amongst the professing people of God as to the power of religion and godliness.

[1] The Revocation in 1685 of the Edict of Nantes by which Henry IV of France had in 1598 granted free exercise of religion to the Huguenots, deprived France of her Protestant alliances and thousands of her best citizens. Many of these were to be found in the towns of Devon at this time, some conforming to the Church of England, others forming Nonconformist Churches with their own pastors. Up to the Revolution of 1688 England had been a wavering ally of France, now, under William III, she became a determined foe in the 'Grand Alliance' with William at its head. The war dragged on indecisively from 1688 to 1697 with battles in the Netherlands and naval encounters in the English Channel. Louis XIV employed the French navy to restore James II to the throne of England, and although in the naval battle of Beachy Head (30th June 1690) the Anglo-Dutch fleet was defeated, the expected invasion did not materialise. The French fleet proceeded westward toward Plymouth where a British convoy of some 200 Mediterranean merchant ships had taken refuge under the protection of the naval squadron of Admiral Henry Killigrew. Louis wanted the French navy to burn the English merchant fleet as a display of French naval power, but his admiral, the Comte de Tourville, disagreed, and compromised by bombarding Teignmouth on 26 July 1690. A small number of houses were fired, and some small ships were destroyed. Shortly afterwards a pamphlet appeared in London: *Great News from Tingmouth, Torbay and Exon; giving an account of the several Actions of the French Invaders and their Majesties forces of Devonshire. The surrendring of several Roman Catholicks, and other Material Occurrences. In a letter from Exon.* London, 1690.

In the year 1691,[1] about the 8th month, it pleased the Lord wonderfully to appear in discomfiting the popish malignant party in Ireland that had been so insolent for some time. All their forts and strongholds were taken, and they were constrained to quit the fields and be gone.[2] Blessed be God for a little reviving for that wasted land and the interest of the Lord Jesus there. Notwithstanding, the proud monarch of France[3] was very potent. A huge host he had prepared for the day of battle and war, and O the tidings, the tidings that should awaken all to look about and be ready for the great and notable day of the Lord that is coming. And O the corruptions, perfidiousness, and treachery that was to be found amongst the great ones of England even sick of the present government, weary of a protestant Prince, hoping, longing, and O that there were not cause to say endeavouring also, to have a popish Prince on the throne again, and the nation once more subjected to an anti-christian potentate.[4] Blessed be God, Zion's King reigneth still, and the nations are angry and mad; but the government both of kingdoms and churches is upon the shoulders of the Lord Jesus Christ.

In the year *1692*, about the beginning of the third month, a mischievous design and plot was discovered and brought to light,

[1] 1691. On 23 and 24 June Towgood attended meetings of the Exeter Assembly at Topsham. John Flavel of Dartmouth was moderator, and John Ashwood, now pastor at Exeter, was present along with some twenty six other ministers. The occasion concerned the union of the Presbyterians and the Independents, for which Flavel made a strong plea. The "*Heads of Agreement assented to by the United Ministers in and about London . . .*" for their Happy Union a few weeks before, were read and "cheerfully and heartily" assented to. Flavel was commissioned to communicate this news to Matthew Mead, John Howe, and Increase Mather in London. He did so from Exeter on 26 June, and died the same evening.

[2] The Treaty of Limerick (1691), by which the Irish surrendered in response to a promise of the same religious and political freedom they had had from the time of Charles II. The promise was not kept.

[3] Louis XIV (1638-1715) King of France 1643-1715; an absolute monarch holding all power in his own person, both in religion and in politics. Though Roman Catholic himself, he constantly set his own authority against that of his church; yet bitterly persecuted Protestants (the Huguenots) arguing that the religion of the king must be the religion of his subjects. His grand aim of imperial aggression led him to wish to dominate all Europe. Princes of western Germany united in the League of Augsburg against Louis XIV, and though they were mainly Protestant the Pope gave them his support. Later referred to in the *Ecclesiastica* as the 'hammer of the nations' and the 'spoiler of the nations'.

[4] The local circumstances leading to these remarks may be reflected by the following entry from the Axminster parish books:

1691. To many hundreds of French prisoners and seamen passing in an extraordinary manner, by the consent of the parish, £14.7.0.

which was to overturn the present government and to bring back a popish prince again. But the Lord defeated their counsels and dashed their hellish designs in pieces, blessed be His glorious Name. His religion in the power and purity of it, is the great eyesore and matter of contempt this day by a profane, treacherous, perfidious generation of men. Nothing pleaseth them while the people of God enjoy their gospel privileges and liberty to wait upon the Lord in His holy ordinances, and whilst the pure institutions of Jesus Christ are faithfully and spiritually administered. Glad would they be could they root out the name of Israel that it might be had no more in remembrance. But in the thing wherein they deal proudly, God is above them, and wherein they deal subtilly and craftily, the Lord defeats and outwits them. "He disappointeth the devices of the crafty, so that their hands cannot perform their enterprise. He taketh the wise in their own craftiness: and the counsel of the froward is carried headlong... But he saveth the poor from the sword, from their mouth, and from the hand of the mighty."[1] Now they began to be detected, and some of the great men were apprehended and closely shut up, a confederacy held with the French, many, especially of the great ones, ready to go down to Egypt, to go over into France, to go down to hell for help, for another change. But, if the Lord say 'It shall not stand', then it shall not stand.

On the 18th day of this third month, the French fleet sailed up by the western coasts with a brisk west wind to meet with the English fleet with expectations of a victory, though the Lord turned it to the contrary. On the next day, which was the 19th day, was a terrible sea fight in which the French fleet were defeated, scattered, and sorely broken.[2] Many of their capital ships being lost, with several others of a lesser size, some sunk, some burnt, other some sanded and split; divers of their transport ships that were prepared for an army to invade this poor land were also burnt. A sore rebuke from the Lord fell upon them. Cruel designs that had been on foot for some time were dashed in a moment. The right hand of the Lord was exalted gloriously for the saving of a poor

1 Job 5.12-15.

2 The Battle of La Hogue, 19th-24th May, 1692. Louis XIV organised an army of 30,000 men at La Hogue, on the tip of Normandy, in an expedition to restore James II to the English throne. James came to witness the embarkation and issued a proclamation to the English nation. But the Anglo-Dutch fleet under Admiral Edward Russell brought crushing defeat and utterly shattered the expedition. Thereafter the allies held command of the Channel.

unworthy people. Now the great spoiler of the nations was in a measure spoiled, and the treacherous dealer was dealt treacherously with. Now the voice of joy and praise was heard in the dwellings of the righteous; the fears of a people fearing the Lord in a great measure removed, and eminent returns of prayer were granted. The hammer of the nations was in a measure broken, and the pride of him that made the nations to tremble, in a measure brought down. The high looks and threatening speeches of such in this nation as held confederacy with them and longed for their success was greatly tamed. Blessed be God, admired be free grace! 'Tis alone for His own Name's sake that He hath wrought salvation for an unworthy people. Surely the Lord reigneth; He sitteth upon the floods. He ruleth in the midst of His enemies, and let all the enemies of this blessed King Jesus be clothed with shame.

However, although the sword did not rage in this land as in other countries, yet it was a distressing time with England. The Lord was bringing it low apace as to men's earthly interests, and it was now a very critical day indeed. The Lord seemed to be doing great things, great work upon the wheel, the nations in a reeling, staggering posture, Europe seemed to be in a flame, great armies appearing in divers parts, the Lord of hosts still mustering up the hosts to battle.[1] Contrary interests seemed to be united, papists and protestants combining, and yet agreeing interests were divided, papists against papists, the Lord setting Egyptian against Egyptian, kingdom against kingdom.

In the year *1693,* about the 5th month, there was a terrible battle fought in Flanders in which several thousands of men were slain, and amongst which were many of the chief commanders and great men cut down.[2] O how are scripture prophecies accomplishing apace according to that in *Psa. 110.5,* "The Lord at thy right hand shall strike through kings in the day of his wrath."

[1] The battles of Namur and Steinkerk (1692), in which the French were victorious yet both sides suffered terrible losses. France was bitterly impoverished and public misery widespread. "The country is a vast hospital", wrote Fenelon to Louis XIV.

[2] The Battle of Neerwinden (or Landen) in the Netherlands, 19-29 July 1693; in which the French were victorious, 130,000 men were engaged, and 25,000 were killed. It was followed four months later by the Battle of Marsaglia with another French victory, and a further 10,000 dead. Yet the results were trifling and indeterminate. In the war of the Grand Alliance it was a year of pyrrhic victories in which "people perished of want to the accompaniment of *Te Deums.*"

As the summer passed on the Lord gave the sword a commission to do further execution. Blood and slaughter was the lot of those countries. Great numbers of men were cut down, the Lord making a way for a more visible reign of the blessed and only Potentate the Lord Jesus Christ, King of kings and Lord of lords, both in Zion and in the world, by filling the places with the dead bodies and wounding the heads over many countries.

1693, The Exeter Assembly met on three occasions during the year. In April it desired S. Towgood and J. Ashwood, with others, to meet brethren from Bideford to help heal a breach in that church. In June Towgood and Ashwood voted with others to receive as members of the Assembly three French Huguenot ministers settled in their own congregations in Exeter. In October Towgood received £5 from the fund, for the support of Samuel Baker of Axminster, a ministerial student under his care. (*The Exeter Assembly: the minutes of the assemblies of the United Brethren of Devon & Cornwall, 1691-1717, as transcribed by the Reverend Isaac Gilling.* Ed. Allan Brockett, 1963, pp.13-16. Cited hereafter as *Exeter Assembly Minutes*).

17

JOYING AND BEHOLDING YOUR ORDER....

(1693-95)

On the 24th day of the 9th month in this year,[1] it pleased the Lord to remove by death Thomas Lane, who had been a member of this congregation almost from the very first rise and constitution of this church, and has served in the office of a ruling elder from a little time after their first embodying, as may be seen page 19, of this Book of Record. He was a faithful and beloved brother indeed, who in his day passed along through many sore and sharp storms of persecution, and bore the shocks of tribulation with invincible courage, cleaving stedfastly to the pure institutions of the Lord Jesus Christ when all his earthly interests, possessions and comforts lay at stake for so doing, and was not moved out of

1 *1693.*

the good ways of the Lord by all his afflictions. It might be truly said of him, as good old Jacob said of his son Joseph, *Gen. 49. 23,24,* "The archers have sorely grieved him and shot at him and hated him; but his bow abode in strength, and the arms of his hands were made strong by the hands of the mighty God of Jacob." He was a man of good judgment in, and of steady affections unto the things and ways of God, eminently furnished with excellent gifts and graces for service in his place, and was very serviceable and useful in his generation. But, lo, he is gone; he is fallen asleep. A great loss this church sustained, but the Lord Jesus Christ, the Head and Husband of His church, can repair it, for the government is upon His shoulders.

There is mention made before in p.80 of the remove of James Hawker by death, who was one of the ruling elders of this congregation. Now there had not been another chosen since his death to take his place and office. Wherefore on the 5th day of the 11th month, the congregation assembled together in their public meeting house at Wickcroft to humble their souls before the Lord and by solemn prayer and supplication to beg His counsel and direction as to a new choice of ruling elders, that those breaches and gaps the Lord had made amongst them might be repaired. And on the 30th day of the same month the church assembled again and after solemn prayer with instructions given from the Word, by the pastor, the brethren proceeded to election. And the Lord signally favoured this people with His gracious presence, and so directed their spirits, that with one voice, excepting two or three, they voted for Robert Bryant. The only objection against him was, whether, he being in the office of a deacon in this church, could be removed from that office and be placed in the office of eldership. This was immediately resolved by the pastor from that Scripture, *1 Tim. 3.13* "They that have used the office of a deacon well purchase to themselves a good degree." Further, he added that himself was placed to serve in the office of a deacon in that congregation to which he was related before he was called by them to the pastoral office. The brethren being all fully satisfied, Robert Bryant was set apart for the office of a ruling elder at that time. But the church being not so unanimous at this time for a second person it was determined to be debated at another assembly.

On the last day of the 12th month the church being assembled again to elect another ruling elder, as also there being a necessity of another deacon to fill up the place of Robert Bryant who had been called to the office of an elder; after solemn prayers to the Lord for His presence and for direction, the brethren were all unanimous as one man in the choice of Matthew Towgood, a beloved physician, to serve in the office of a ruling elder in the congregation. They then proceeded to the choice of another deacon, and the majority of the brethren chose Thomas Miller, who was appointed for the office of a deacon at the same time. Thus the blessed God eminently appeared for the encouragement of this people and continued His sacred institutions with them. All the glory to Jehovah.

Now it had been the practice of this church from the time of its first constitution ordinarily to assemble together one day in a fortnight besides on the Lord's days, unless some more than ordinary providence prevented it. Which day was spent by the members in prayer and teaching the word for their mutual edification, sometimes more solemnly in fasting and prayer, sometimes in thanksgiving for mercies and salvations[1] received, sometimes by way of conference to regulate matters which did more peculiarly relate to the church. And this had been the practice of the members of this church all along in the most gloomy and dismal times of persecution.

Now after the storms of persecution were past and gone, and there was a prospect of more peace, liberty and freedom from those distractions in the worship of God which for several years past they had met withal; it was resolved by this church that the ordinance of the Lord's Supper should be administered constantly every sixth sabbath. Thereby the members living at a distance might have a perfect knowledge of the time and sabbath when that holy ordinance was administered. And one day of the week before that sabbath was constantly observed by the members as a day of preparation for that ordinance in which they assembled together for prayer and attending upon the Word preached. It was also determined that one of those weekday meetings once in six weeks should be spent in regulating matters respecting this church, and sometimes in resolving cases of conscience in which each brother that would or had a capacity had liberty to bring in his sentiment to which case was then principally to be spoken unto and resolved. Also in such days the brethren had liberty to exercise their gifts in prayer for the edification of each other and of the whole body.

In the year *1694,* in the 4th month, the 8th day of the month, the pastors and elders of three or four churches or congregations met at Exeter to confer together about the affairs of the churches,

[1] i.e. deliverances.

at which time there were four cases proposed to be considered and debated at another season which was then appointed by them. And the place agreed upon was to be at Axminster at Wykecroft the usual place where this church assembled. The questions to be debated and resolved were these:

1. What relation the church hath to those children of church members who are baptized by the pastor of the church, and what is the duty of the church toward them?

2. What method is requisite for the church to take to continue a succession in the ministry?

3. What way the church ought to take for a mutual edification of itself in general, and of each particular member?

4. What the church ought to do with respect to those members that withdraw themselves from church communion not being guilty of scandalous sins?

Those questions or cases being communicated to the members of this church by the pastor it was agreed and resolved upon that the brethren give in their answers or judgments unto each of these cases on a day then appointed, which accordingly they did on the 23rd day of the 6th month at Wickcroft. And on the 17th day of the 7th month the pastor and elders of each of the aforesaid congregations or churches met this church at Wykecroft where the day was spent in prayer and conference and each of those cases were debated, and the resolutions of each as drawn up by the pastors of each church was read publicly before all then and there present. What the resolutions and answers to each case as was then given in by this church, was designed to have been recorded in this place, but was omitted through some default and want of due care.[1]

Now was a time in which the churches and people of Christ enjoyed much rest and peace in this land, and a wide door was opened of liberty to attend upon the Lord Jesus Christ in His sacred institutions and none to molest them. But alas, alas! it was matter of great lamentation to consider the sad effects of the peace

[1] The omission is much to be regretted and cannot now be supplied. The dates of conference carefully avoided the meeting dates of the Exeter Assembly, which in any case comprised many more than "three or four churches or congregations", and the Minutes of which do not at this time make reference to the subject-matter of this consultation. It was probably a conference of Independent Churches comprising Axminster, Castle Lane, Exeter (where John Ashwood was then pastor), and possibly Tiverton and/or Taunton. For comment on some of the questions raised see Appendix G.

and liberty of this day amongst a professing party. Oh! what strifes, envyings, emulations, discords, divisions; what lamentable heats, contentions, jarrings, clashings even amongst ministers and persons of more private capacities.[1] The hands of enemies were bound up and now the people of God were biting and devouring one another. Moreover, O what lamentable decays of religion as to the power of it, what lukewarmness, what formality in religion. O how did a selfish, earthly spirit abound. O how eagerly did most professors pursue after earthly interest. O doleful! that there should be such sad effects of so great deliverance and freedom from the hands of cruel persecutors.

It hath been the observation of some that churches have flourished most in a day of adversity, and as one says, 'The blood of the martyrs have been the seed of the church.'[2] It is recorded concerning the children of Israel, the more the Egyptians afflicted them, the more they multiplied and grew (*Exod. 1.12*). O what flocking to ordinances in a day of trouble and persecution; the Word and Gospel more prized than in this day of peace. And this was too much the evil of this church; a careless and an indifferent spirit in attending upon the ordinances of Christ; and especially week-days privileges were less prized and their assemblies less frequently than formerly.[3]

1 On May 30, 1694, an assembly of ministers at Bristol, including some from many parts of England was greatly concerned about "heats, scandals, slanders etc.", and resolved that "upon all occasions relative to the publick good, there be no clashings allowed, either with moderate Churchmen or with men of other communions, but that as far as possible we cultivate all endeavours towards a union upon those common principles notwithstanding any little differences between us on other accounts." The resolutions were referred to the Exeter Assembly, among others, for consideration. (*Exeter Assembly Minutes* . . . pp.19,20).

2 Tertullian (A.D.c.160-c.225). Plures efficimus quoties metimur a vobis, semen est sanguis Christianorum. (*Apology* XVII.1). More accurately rendered; The more ye mow us down, the more we grow, the seed is the blood of Christians.

3 In April 1695 the Exeter Assembly was informed that some members of the Independent Church at Uffculme (where there was also a Baptist Church) had turned Baptist. Also that some young men tutored with a view to the ministry by Stephen Towgood at Axminster, and Matthew Warren at Taunton, had espoused Baptist sentiments. It was held to be "inconvenient" for those who kept academies to "receive or continue" students who held such views. (*Exeter Assembly Minutes* . . . pp.23,24).

18

THE LORD SITTETH KING FOR EVER....

(1695-98)

About the latter end of the year *1695* an horrible mischievous plot was hatched and ready to break forth and to be put in execution; i.e. to assassinate the king, bloodily to murder him and so overturn the government of the nation. This was contrived by some of the great ones, but the Lord in His infinite wisdom and mercy for His own Name's sake carried their counsels headlong, their hellish plot was discovered and he escaped their bloody hands, so that their violent dealings came down upon their own heads, and those wicked ones were snared in the work of their own hands.[1]

[1] Queen Mary died in 1695, leaving the King as the lone object of Jacobite hatred. James II was in Calais in consultation with the Jacobite underworld. The plan was that as William drove home from his weekly hunting in Richmond Park to Kensington Palace, he was to be ambushed

'Tis the gospel in the pure and powerful dispensations that is the great grievance of the great ones of the nation and a great part of the clergy. They have places of trust in their hands, offices, profits, honours and preferments, yet, Haman-like, all this avails them nothing whilst Mordecai sits in the gate.[1] So nothing pleases them whilst the poor people of God have liberty granted them to wait upon the Lord in His pure institutions. 'Tis this hath been the great thing that has made them gnash with their teeth and be so filled with envy because there is an open door for the gospel, and their hands are bound up that they cannot persecute and ride over the backs and trample with the foot of pride on such as fear the Lord. Therefore they hatch plot upon plot, and endeavour by all means if possible to bring on another change, hoping thereby to remove the liberty the people of God do enjoy in waiting upon the Lord in His sacred institutions. There's a malignant generation of men, O how loath are they to have their lusts curbed, and to have a work of reformation carried on in the land.

Howbeit, the Lord was distressing this nation by other means. The coin of the nation being spoiled, there was a great want of current money; besides there was a considerable price on corn and other provisions for the outward man. Likewise the Lord was breaking men in their earthly trades and interest, bringing the nation low, giving it up into the hands of spoilers. The Lord was emptying the nation, making it waste and it was—As with the servant so with the master, as with the buyer so with the seller—men earn wages and put it into a bag with holes, look for much and it came to little. The Lord did blow upon persons' interests, estates and gatherings and it wasted and withered.[2] The nation

[1] Esther 5.9-13.

[2] French privateering in the English Channel had all but ruined English trade, while the cost of the war far exceeded the country's revenue. Business men loaned so much money for the wars that they could not be repaid, and thus originated the National Debt which in turn led to the founding of the Bank of England (1694), as a company of creditors. The average price of wheat under James II was 34s. 8d.; now it was 46s.; and by 1698 it rose to 62s. (See also p.158).

---

and murdered in a narrow lane through which he had to pass at Turnham Green. The men concerned arrived to keep their pledge, but they had not kept their own confidence, with the result that the King himself announced in parliament the details of the assassination plot and the French invasion that was intended to follow its implementation. Parliament responded with the Association Oath, passed on 27 April 1696, which declared: "Whereas there has been a conspiracy . . . we declare that His Majesty is rightful and lawful king . . . and we engage to assist each other in the defence of His Majesty and his government." The plotters were executed.

was much impoverished, poverty coming on like an armed man. O the wants! O the distresses were in many families; and yet, O the stupidity and insensibleness of the most. O the murmuring, the complaining and fretting against the providences of the day, passing along hardly bestead and hungry, fretting themselves, cursing their King and their God in their hearts, looking to the earth and lo! there's trouble and darkness, dimness and anguish.[1] Alas! alas! few that spake aright, few that lamentingly say 'What have I done?' That consider whence is all this that is come to pass, that lay to heart the wastes of God's house, the decays of religion. Most are eagerly pursuing their own things, their earthly interest which as with eagles' wings are flying away apace. Ah! this should be for a lamentation.

Towards the end of this year *1696*, it was determined by this congregation that their church meeting days, being once in six weeks, should be spent by them in resolving cases of conscience, which practice was carried on for some space of time.[2]

In the 7th month of the year *1697*, there was intelligence of a peace concluded betwixt the Princes of those nations that had

1 Is. 8.21,22.

2 In September 1696, the Reverends Stephen Towgood, of Axminster, and John Ashwood, of Exeter, both Congregationalists, were brought to task for assisting at the ordination of a candidate trained by Towgood, Samuel Baker. This had taken place at Bridport but without the formal direction of the Dorset County Assembly, and against the custom of the United Brethren. In May 1697 Towgood brought forward a resolution embodying the strict Independent point of view that there was no authority superior to that of a particular church, that is, that it was not necessary to have all ordinations authorised by the Assembly. This was not accepted and previous resolutions were endorsed. Soon after this Ashwood left the county, but Towgood remained a frequent attender at the Assembly for many years to come. (Allan Brockett, *The Exeter Assembly* ... Introd. p.xi).

By now the 'Happy Union' among the Presbyterians and Independents in London had broken down; the reason there was the same as elsewhere, viz. the tension between the power of synods and the authority of the local church. The Exeter Assembly meeting on Sept. 8 & 9, 1696, at Exeter, received a letter from the Dorset Association meeting at Sherborne a few days before: "We understand that some who are of your association, to wit, Mr. Towgood, Mr. Ashwood etc., have join'd in the Ordination of persons for the ministry who have not addressed themselves for Ordination to the Associated Brethren in the Ministry, when they might have so done..." The account continues: "Mr. Ashwood...came and gave the Assembly an account that being desired he had joined in ordaining Mr. Samuel Baker at Bridport, who had been some time with Mr. Toogood... that he had done nothing herein contrary to the *Heads of Union*, manifesting himself against an imposing spirit, and desiring to be left to his liberty in things of this nature,..."

When the United Brethren met at Exeter in May 1697, the matter was still unresolved. "Mr. Toogood and Mr. Ashwood shewing much

been so long engaged in war.[1] This administered great joy to the inhabitants of this land. And now the hopes of most were raised that there would be a period put to those desolating and expensive wars that had been for some time past in many countries of Europe. It was a mercy the people of God had been long praying for, and it was beyond the faith of many to reach it that it should be brought about so strangely and speedily, considering many circumstances of providence, for though the sword did not rage in this land, yet was the nation peeled and brought low by means thereof. The French monarch had been a great spoiler by means of his pirates or privateers, raving and robbing on the seas, so that sailing was very dangerous and the merchants sustained great losses, so that now the hopes of most were raised upon the account of advancing their earthly trades, of better trafficking to regain those losses and expenses they had for some time past met withal; few that minded the reviving of the heavenly trade, that religion might thrive more, the gospel be promoted and a way made by all those revolutions for the coming of the Lord Jesus Christ to set up His peaceful kingdom in the world. The next Lord's day, after this tidings, being the 19th day of the 7th month, the pastor of this church discoursed to the congregation from *Romans 10* part v.15, "How beautiful are the feet of them that preach the gospel of peace, and bring glad tidings of good things." Oh! how was he directed to speak a word in season; surely 'tis the Gospel that brings the most joyful news.

[1] The Treaty of Ryswick 1697, by which the war begun with France in 1688 was ended. Louis XIV acknowledged William as legitimate King of England, and undertook to help James II and the Jacobite cause no more, a promise flouted in 1701 when, on the death of James II, Louis recognized his son as James III of England.

---

unwillingness to bring ordinations to the Assembly... Mr. Toogood delivered in the following paper desiring the Assemblies assent unto it, viz: 'Agreed, that it is utterly unlawful for any minister of the Gospel or Assembly of Ministers to deny Ordination unto the ministerial office to any person for this reason because he doth not own and will not submit unto any power or jurisdiction in ecclesiastical matters which any may suppose to be lodged in any minister or ministers superior to that in a particular Church.' After much debate upon this paper the majority of the Assembly rejected it, judging it sufficient to declare their own purpose & oblige themselves as to their future practice without condemning most of the Reformed Churches who are of the contrary opinion. The following questions were propos'd but not fully debated: Q. Whether it be not convenient that Candidates for the Ministry be examined before the Assembly before they have an approbation to preach; the better to prevent ignorant and unlearned intruders into the Ministry..." (*Exeter Assembly Minutes*... pp.29,30,38).

In the first month of the year *1698,* J—— S—— a member of this congregation who was judged by all to be one that had the root of the matter in him, the truth of grace in his heart, yet notwithstanding being overcome by his corruptions was led away to drink to excess, and though he was privately admonished by some of the brethren, yet afterwards was guilty of the same evil. Whereupon the church was acquainted with it, who gave him a summons to appear before them, and on the day appointed for their assembling together he was there present, and his sin charged upon him by the pastor. He acknowledged his evil and manifested his repentance, and the Lord so blessed this church act that he was never known to be guilty afterwards, but was received into full communion in the enjoyment of all the privileges of the church, the brethren having an entire love for him, and so remained in fellowship with the church, a solid, humble, judicious christian till he died.

Now there was a design to erect a new meeting house in the town of Axminster, but by reason of some who lived at a distance, who were not so fully reconciled to it, the work was deferred for some time. Howbeit, in the beginning of this year, *1698,* they began to build, and necessary help and supplies being offered the work was carried on with success and speediness, for on the 7th day of the 6th month, that being the sabbath, at the close of the public exercises of religious worship for that day, notice was given to the congregation, that they should leave that place of worship at Wickcroft and assemble the next Lord's Day in the town of Axminster. This place at Wykecroft had been a place of shelter for many years; choice and precious sabbaths the congregation enjoyed there, and though they had been driven out once and again, as hath been recorded in this Book of Remembrance, yet the providence of God opened the door for their return again into this public meeting house. And after some years hot persecution there was a constant assembling together of the congregation for religious worship every Lord's day, and upon all appointed seasons from the last day of the 8th month, 1686, as is before recorded, to this very day that the congregation left it.[1]

On the next Lord's day after, being the 14th day of this 6th month, the congregation assembled in their new meeting house in the town of Axminster. The pastor preached that day from *John 4.21.* "Woman, believe me, the hour cometh when ye shall

[1] pp.124, 192.

neither in this mountain nor yet at Jerusalem worship the Father." His discourse was very pertinent and profitable to the occasion.

Meeting-house at Axminster: 1698-1875

Now the sword of the Lord that was lately made bright and prepared for the day of slaughter, seemed at present to be sheathed up. And the nations in Europe that lately were in a flame of war and ready to dash one against another, at present all seemed to be hushed and still, and the churches and people of God in this land enjoyed much peace and tranquillity, with plenty of gospel privileges. Yet was there too much of a spirit of division amongst a people professing godliness, great formality in their religion with an eager pursuit after earthly interests, though the Lord did surely check and rebuke men with respect to their earthly trading. But alas! alas! the Protestant interest in France, under sore persecution and affliction, and cruel usages they met with from the hands of their bloody tyrannical prince; ah! when shall this limb of anti-christ be cut off?[1] Lord, hasten those blessed days promised; when the oppressor shall be broken in pieces; when the wolf shall dwell with the lamb and the leopard lie down with the kid, when the cow and the bear shall feed and their young ones lie down together, and the lion eat straw like the ox, when they shall not hurt nor destroy in all God's holy mountain; when the earth shall be full of the knowledge of the Lord as the waters cover the sea. When the envy of Ephraim also shall depart, and the adversaries of Judah shall be cut off. Ephraim shall not envy Judah and Judah shall not vex Ephraim.[2]

Now at the end of this year there was further intelligence of great preparations. The French monarch was making for further war and spoiling, and indeed he was the hammer of the nations, the great disturber of the peace of kingdoms, which, through his pride, ambition and perfidiousness, he endeavoured by all means possible to lord it over his neighbour nations, hoping to be the supreme monarch.[3] Besides, things at home in this land did not look with so pleasing an aspect as was to be wished. Many cabals were amongst the great ones of the nation, and too great confederacy with France by many of them. The liberty the churches and people of God did enjoy was a bit that could not be digested by them. Nevertheless, He that is higher than the highest regardeth it, and there be higher than they, and in the thing wherein they deal proudly the Lord is above them. Blessed be God. Zion's King reigneth. He sitteth upon the floods. Yea, He sitteth King for ever.[4]

1 This was the year of the martyrdom at Montpellier (on November 4th) of Claude Brousson (1647-98), intrepid Huguenot evangelist, preacher, and patriot who, even after the Revocation of the Edict of Nantes (1685), had persisted, along with Vivens and others, in his apostolic labours. Hunted and hounded with a price on his head, Brousson fled France again and again, only to return in some other place to minister to companies sometimes numbering four hundred persons. (See, *The Evangelist of the Desert: Life of Claude Brousson, sometime Advocate of the Parliament at Toulouse in the reign of Louis XIV: afterwards a Protestant Minister and Martyr. From original and authentic records*. London, 1853; and Samuel Smiles, *The Huguenots in France after the Revocation of the Edict of Nantes*, London, 1873).

2 Isaiah 11. 6-9, 13.

3 Matters arising from the dissatisfactions of Louis XIV with the first Partition treaty which had been signed between William, Louis, and the States-General October 1-11, 1698.

4 On September 7 & 8 1698 Mr. Towgood was in Exeter at the meeting of the Exeter Assembly. A question raised by Robert Carel of Crediton was: "Whether a capital crime confess'd to a minister, by a penitent under horrour of conscience, ought to be revealed to the magistrate by the minister in order to punishment? Negative." Towgood was appointed to

preach at the following assembly in Exeter in May 1699. He did so, with Henry Backaller as moderator. The following minute says: "Thanks given to Mr. Larkham for praying. Agree that Mr. Toogood having continu'd above two hours in sermon all future preachers have warning given them to keep to their hour: and that the Clark turn the glass when the text is nam'd & take it away as soon as tis run out." (*Exeter Assembly Minutes.* pp.40,42).

19 THE CHURCH REGISTER

HE WRITETH UP THE PEOPLE

Here followeth a Catalogue of the Names of such as were members of this church, actually in fellowship when it was first agreed by them that this Church Register should be kept.[1] *Also the Names of such as have been added to this church since that time; With a remark upon the names of such members as have since been removed by death.*

[1] i.e. on 26 October 1687. Names here recorded are only those who were members between 1687 and 1698. In the MS this members roll intervenes between the pastorates of Ashwood and Towgood—i.e. between chapters 8 and 9 of this edition. On the places represented see Appendix D. The *Ecclesiastica* refers only twice to numbers actually in membership at a given time. At the Church's formation in 1660, there were "but few, about twelve or thirteen" (p.11). At the settlement of Towgood as pastor in 1679 there were "about one hundred persons." (p.72).

Of the Town and Neighbourhood of Axminster

Mr. Stephen Towgood, *Pastor* Deborah Towgood, his wife
Matthew Towgood. Afterwards *Ruling Elder*
Mary Towgood, his wife
Robert Bryant, *Deacon,* afterwards *Ruling Elder*
John Brewer, one of the first members, deceased the 18th day of the 8th month, 1700
Gathered Brewer, his wife, deceased
Dorothy Lowring, one of the first members
John Whitty, sen.[1] John Whitty, jun.
Nicholas Marder
Mary Marder, his wife, deceased the 26th day of 1st month, 1697
Samuel Quick, deceased the 7th day of the 5th month, 1701
Mary Quick, his wife
Anne Whitty, deceased the 1st day of the 11th month, 1698
Anne Sprake, deceased the 2nd day of the 10th month, 1705
Mary Brown, deceased the 16th day of the 11th month, 1701
Emmett Lucas Dorothy Serle
Elizabeth Deamont, wid., deceased the 27th day of the 6th month, 1706
Hannah Pinney, deceased the 11th day of the 12th month, 1704
Jane Newton, deceased the 28th day of the 4th month, 1702
Elizabeth Clark, wid. Samuel Clark
Agnes Sprake
Anne Reed, deceased the 6th day of the 9th month, 1702
Thomas Miller, *Deacon* Joan Miller, his wife
Dorothy Driver Mary Oliver
Mary Slade Anne Norrington, deceased
William Warren Edward Bilck[2] Grace Turner

1 The Whitty family continued its connection with the church down to the twentieth century. John Whitty, son of Thomas Whitty and nephew of John Whitty jun. above, was born at Axminster 1692 and became minister at Beer, Devon; Lyme Regis 1723; at Waytown—1735; and at Lyme Regis again 1735 till his death in 1762. Six volumes of his sermons were published. Thomas Whitty (1713-1792) clothier, and founder of the Axminster carpet trade, was a near relative, possibly a brother; while his son, also Thomas, was the trustee in whose home the manuscript of this work was shown to James Davidson in 1834. In the next generation, Samuel Rampson Whitty bore the name of an earlier member of the church who was killed in the Monmouth Rebellion.

2 Presumably an ancestor of Henry Bilke who in 1875 owned the principal portion of the Weycroft Manor estate. (G. P. R. Pulman, *Book of the Axe,* Ed.4, p. 581).

OF SHUTE, CULLINTON, WITH THOSE ADJACENT AS HONINTON

Thomas Lane, *Ruling Elder*, deceased 24th day of the 9th month, 1693 — Margarett Lane, his wife
Edward Lane — Mary Lane, his wife
Barnard Lane — Rebecca Lane, his wife, deceased July 11th, 1696
Sarah Lane, a second wife
John Bryant
Elizabeth Heydon, deceased the 4th day of the 2nd month, 1706
Charity Slade — Joan Morrice
Josian Wyatt — Dinah Oake
Gregory Lane — Hannah Lane, his wife
Joan Bishopp — Samuel Rampson

OF CHARD,[1] CHARD LAND, COMB, WITH THE PARTS ADJACENT

Roger Hoare, *Deacon*
Elizabeth Hoare, his wife, deceased the 3rd day of the 7th month, 1703
John Sweet, deceased the 20th day of the 1st month, 1705
John Smith, sen., deceased the 19th day of the 6th month, 1706
Hester Grinter, sen. — Hester Grinter, jun.
Joan Smith, deceased the 29th day of the 7th month, 1708
Hannah Legg — Sarah Pile
Benjamin Shute — Mary Shute, his wife
Elizabeth Vile, deceased the 19th day of the 8th month, 1703
Katherine Atkins, deceased the 6th day of the 7th month, 1697
Elioner Atkins
Philip Hobman — Joan Hobman
Thomas Marder, deceased the 16th day of the 7th month, 1696
Thomas Crandon, deceased the 29th day of the 4th month, 1702
Samuel Bennett — Mary Bennett, his wife
Elizabeth Sweet
Lucretia Gammis
James Pitts, deceased
Sarah Marder
Sarah Crandon, deceased the 13th day of the 12th month, 1706-7
James Williams

[1] See also Note 3, p.194.

OF WINSHAM, AND ITS NEIGHBOURHOOD

John Grimsteed, deceased the 20th day of the 9th month, 1705
Timothy Turner, deceased the 27th day of the 7th month, 1696
Priscilla Turner, his wife. Deceased — Susannah Whitty
Susannah Harvey, deceased the 14th day of the 4th month, 1697
William Comb, deceased the 23rd day of the 8th month, 1697
Susannah Wills, of Crewkern — William Paul
Hannah Whitty

OF MEMBURY, STOCKLAND, KILMINGTON, CHARDSTOCK

Edward Sprake — Anne Sprake, his wife
Mary Sellard, deceased the 22nd day of the 1st month, 1703-4
Thomas Anley — Daniel Clark. Deceased
Richard Keath, deceased the 1st day of the 11th month, 1708
Anne Stooker
Mary Burton. Deceased — Sicily Davies, wid.
Elizabeth Manning — Tabitha Rugg
Joan Bagwell, wid., deceased the 20th day of the 1st month, 1699-1700.
Martha C——, suspended from Church Communion, afterwards received into Communion again, and denied Communion again.
Tho. Guppy

OF HAWKCHURCH AND THORNCOMB, WITH ADJACENT PARTS

William Bennett, Esq., of Gabriels, deceased the 20th day of the 8th month, 1703
Dorothy Bennett, his wife, deceased the 16th day of the 7th month, 1699
Stephen Card, of White Church
John Bettiscomb, deceased the 21st day of the 11th month, 1707
Richard Baker, deceased the 8th day of the 3rd month, 1709
Mary Baker, his wife, deceased the 6th day of the 4th month, 1702

Samuel Baker. Afterwards pastor of the church of Christ at Bridport[1]
Sylvanus Dollin, deceased the 23rd day of the 6th month, 1702
Elizabeth Dollin, his wife — Edith Abbott, wid.
Sarah Newberry, deceased the 3rd day of the 5th month, 1706
Joan Burridge
Judith Bennett, deceased 19th day of the 5th month, 1695
Joan Wakely
Thomas Mitchell[2] — Susannah Mitchell, his wife
Hannah Symns

Of the Towns of Taunton and Ilmister

John Dunster. Afterward had a letter of dismission to join with a church in Taunton. Deceased
Hannah Dunster, his wife
Roger Dunster
Elizabeth Dunster, his wife, deceased the 16th day of the 11th month, 1708
Agnes Serjeant, wid.
Susannah Noon, wid. — Elizabeth Baker

Of Wotton, Lyme Regis, with their Neighbourhood

James Cumming
Hannah Cumming, his wife, deceased 12th day of 3rd month, 1697
Anthony Cumming — Susannah Cumming, his wife
William Norly — Joan Norly, his wife
Susannah Love
Margarett Oliver

1 Samuel Baker. Minister at Bridport 1696-1727; immediate successor in office of Richard Downe who had assisted at the ordination of Stephen Towgood at Axminster in 1679. Towgood, along with John Ashwood assisted in Baker's ordination at Bridport (see p.157f). In 1715 Samuel Baker's congregation numbered between five and six hundred persons. He had the reputation of being an excellent evangelical preacher, and published, among other works, *Heaven begun here on Earth, or a Help to young persons under their first convictions and closure with the Lord Jesus Christ, contained in Three Dialogues between a minister and a private Christian*, in 1727.

2 Thomas Mitchell's house at Hawkchurch was licensed for worship in April 1729.

Mary Wakely
Susannah Stanbey
Sarah Sampford
Richard Owsley,[1] deceased the 13th day of the 6th month, 1707
Sarah Oliver
Susannah Morgan
Grace Stooks

Of Remote Places

Josias Chaffey
Stephen Strong. Deceased
Ralph Chambers
Joan Chambers, his wife
John Smith, jun. Afterwards pastor of a congregation.[2]

More of the Town and Neighbourhood of Axminster

Jane Ffreer
Sarah Warren, deceased the 28th day of the 2nd month, 1707
John Sprake
Nathaniel Rice, deceased the 14th day of the 2nd month, 1707
Anne Turner
Rose Turner
Elizabeth Cussens

[1] Probably related to James Ously/Owsley who in 1672 received a licence under the Declaration of Indulgence for his house at Wotton Fitzpaine, in which he preached.

[2] John Smith. A minister of this name attended the Exeter Assembly in 1698 and 1703.

POSTSCRIPT

Of the course of the Axminster Church and its Pastor in the years immediately following the close of this record but little is known. The pastor continued to attend the Exeter Assembly until 1707. He was still at Axminster with 500 hearers in 1715. His son, also Stephen, appeared at the Exeter Assembly as a candidate for the ministry in 1713, and was ordained at Axminster in 1716. Unlike his father, Stephen junior was a Presbyterian, and the ministers who assisted at his ordination were all Presbyterians; viz. Richard Evans of Cullompton, John Ball of Honiton, and James Peirce of Exeter. Of these, the first two were doctrinally orthodox in 1716, but Peirce had recently arrived in Exeter tinctured with William Whiston's unitarianism, to become the dominant figure in the Arian controversy of 1717-19. The non-participation of the Axminster pastor in his son's ordination would appear to have been as much from hesitations of conscience as from divergent views of ordination procedures. Another son of the Axminster pastor was Matthew, who settled at Colyton in 1696 and afterward at Wilton, Shepton Mallet and Poole; that his name should not appear on the Axminster members' roll is strange. It is less strange that the Axminster pastor's name does not appear on the list of Presbyterian and Congregational Brethren in 1718; he had probably withdrawn from the Exeter Assembly altogether. Finally he removed from Axminster to Newport, I.O.W. in 1721, and died in 1722.

The Ruling Elder, Matthew Towgood M.D., became the father, in 1700, of Michaiah Towgood, the best known of all the Towgood family. Michaiah was ordained in 1727, and authored a classic treatise on dissent, *The Dissenter's Apology; or their principles and conduct justified*. . . . 1739, which was many times enlarged and reissued. In 1750 Michaiah and his cousin Stephen were joined as co-pastors of a church in Exeter, each having forsaken the faith of his father and adopting high Arian principles.

Stephen Towgood's immediate successor at Axminster was James Stucley. A letter written by James Small, who was pastor 1785-1834, to James Davidson, the Devon antiquary, dated August 21, 1826, to give him "a few things extracted from the Church Records", says in conclusion, and doubtless with the trinitarian controversy which engulfed the Exeter Assembly, and the transition to Unitarianism of more and more ministers and churches in the district as the eighteenth century progressed, in mind: "And here the Record ends. I believe this Church has continued *sound* in the Faith from the beginning." (Davidson's MS *Collections for Axminster*, East Devon Record Office, Exeter). What did Small mean by "sound"? He underlined the word, so he had definite ideas as to its meaning. Fourteen years before he wrote this letter James Small received into the Western Academy which was under his presidency and in his home at Axminster, a student named Richard Knill, later to make his mark in the field of missionary endeavour. In 1814 Knill took his turn to "read a discourse for the criticism of his compeers and tutor . . . He selected as his text, 'Ye who sometime were far off are made nigh by the blood of Christ'; and proceeded to illustrate the words from his own experience, and to urge the claims of Christ to the gratitude of redeemed men with such force and pathos, that several of the students, forgetting their judicial character, were melted to tears. The conclusion was followed by a long pause, after which the president, observing the general impressions, and drying his own tears, rose and left the room, saying, 'Brethren, criticism is disarmed today.' " (C. M. Birrell. *The Life of the Rev. Richard Knill, of St. Petersburg.* p.40.)

After many years, Richard Knill found himself deputising for the London Missionary Society in Essex, in 1844, and became interested in the ten year old grandson of the Independent minister in whose home he stayed at Stambourne. But let the grandson tell his own story:

> There stood in my grandfather's garden two arbours made of yew trees... We went into the right hand arbour, and there, in the sweetest way, he told me of the love of Jesus, and of the blessedness of trusting in Him and loving Him in our childhood. With many a story he preached Christ to me, and told me how good God had been to him, and then he prayed that I might know the Lord and serve Him. He knelt down in that arbour, and prayed for me with his arms about my neck. He heard my childish talk with patient love, and repaid it with gracious instruction. On three successive days he taught me, and prayed with me; and before he had to leave, my grandfather had come back from the place where he had gone to preach, and all the family were gathered to morning prayer. Then, in the presence of them all, Mr. Knill took me on his knee, and said, 'This child will one day preach the gospel, and he will preach it to great multitudes. I am persuaded he will preach in the chapel of Rowland Hill, where (I think he said) I am now the minister.' He spoke very solemnly, and called upon all present to witness what he said.

The prophecy was in due course fulfilled, both at Surrey Chapel in London, and at the Independent Chapel at Wotton-under-Edge; the grandfather was James Spurgeon, and his grandson, Charles Haddon Spurgeon. (C. H. Spurgeon, *Autobiography,* 1897. I.33-38; *The Early Years.* 1962. 27-31. C. M. Birrell, *Life of Richard Knill.* p.220-23.)

What is the connection? It is the connection of authentic, orthodox, biblical, historic Christianity; a spiritual succession which is apostolic in its doctrine, heart moving in its experience, fervent for the souls of men, and utterly unchanging in its relevance to every generation. In short, it is the religion that compelled the Axminster chronicler on more than one occasion to stand back in wonder and cry,

Admired be free grace!

APPENDIXES

A Bartholomew Ashwood and John Owen

B Ashwood and his *Heavenly Trade*

C An Account of John Ashwood

D The Axminster Circle

E The Towgood Family

F The Story of the *Axminster Ecclesiastica*

G The Axminster Churchmanship

APPENDIX A

Bartholomew Ashwood and John Owen

The connection was incidental, though real. Probably the two never met, but they were kindred spirits in their esteem of the Person of the Lord Jesus Christ. Two years after publishing his *Christologia: or, A Declaration of the Glorious mystery of the Person of Christ* (1679), Owen read Ashwood's *The Best Treasure* (1681) and wrote for it the commendatory preface which follows. Three years after this Owen published his dying work, *Meditations on the Glory of Christ* (1684). Ashwood's *Treasure* and Owen's *Meditations* are parallel works on the same theme of the incomparable glory and inexhaustible wonder of Christ's Person. Comparison of the two works is instructive. W. H. Goold in tracing the background and associations of the *Meditations* quotes Owen as saying he drew them up "for the exercise of his own mind", but, although he lists the preface to Ashwood in his List of Owen's Prefaces to the Works of other Authors, overlooks the fact that Owen's mind had been recently prompted on the theme by his reading of Ashwood. (Owen's *Works*, ed. Goold, I.274; XVI.550. See also Owen's *Works*, ed. T. Russell I.395—appendix to Memoir by Wm. Orme).

TO THE READER

The wisdom and grace of God in Christ Jesus, are frequently in the Scripture expressed by the name of Riches and Treasures. These it is the duty of believers in all ages, diligently to search after, to enquire into and possess for themselves. And it may be more diligence or with more success, as to the doctrinal revelation of them, hath not been used in this enquiry in any age than in that wherein we live. But still they continue unsearchable, though not absolutely as unto their truth, reality and substance, or such a possession of them as may enrich us unto a meetness for the inheritance of the saints in light; but as unto their unmeasureable dimensions, their breadth, and length, and depth, and height in degrees of fulness.

Wherefore, after the utmost and most diligent search made into these things by the best and wisest of the sons of men, there is still and ever will be, new work for the church whilst it is in this world, to enquire farther after and into these treasures. Nothing but the sight of Christ Himself in glory, can give us a full comprehension of them. Whilst we are here below, no man can exercise his spiritual wisdom and faith about a more noble, a more useful, and beneficial object. They do best for themselves who are conversant herein, and will be found to be the most spiritual and thriving christians. And therefore those who are not only wise for themselves herein, but do moreover communicate unto others the knowledge that they have obtained of these unsearchable treasures, and their insight into them, that they also may be made partakers of them, do deserve well in an eminent manner of all that do believe.

Among these, the reverend author of the ensuing discourse (if I mistake not) doth deserve our praise and our thanks to God for him and his labours. For as he hath given evidence that he was himself in a good measure, admitted into the enjoyment of these unsearchable riches; so he hath with great skill and spiritual wisdom, unfolded and laid them open to the view of others. And this he hath done so briefly, plainly, and practically, that the most learned will find nothing in his discourse to be despised, and the generality of believers whose edification he designed, will meet with that which will be to their use and advantage.

The times also wherein we live, do render this and discourses of the like nature exceeding seasonable. For the uncertainty of the continuance of all other riches, should stir us up to look with diligence after an indefeasible interest in the certain and unsearchable riches of Christ. For as these alone are sufficient for us in every condition, so we know not but that e're long, they alone will be left unto us; blessed are all they who are possessed of them. Besides, the opposition that hath been made of late by some unto these and the like mysteries of the Gospel, doth give a value unto a sober testimony given unto them. Of this nature is the ensuing discourse, which, that it may be useful to the reader, unto all the ends whereunto it was designed by its worthy author, shall be the prayer of his servant in the work of the Gospel.

John Owen.

APPENDIX B

Ashwood and his *Heavenly Trade*

The following extract from Ashwood's own preface to his work *The Heavenly Trade* (1679) begins, "Epistle to the Readers, especially those who are the peculiar objects of my care, love and labours." It supplements the *Ecclesiastica* with its further disclosure of the author's gracious character, earnest pastoral zeal, and general ministerial competence.

. . . I have chosen to prosecute this metaphor of Trading throughout this discourse . . . the better to insinuate into the mind of ordinary Christians the knowledge of heavenly things, of men's duties, neglects, and backslidings. If thou art one who never made a profession of God farther than blindness, formality, or superstition might lead thee; and a stranger to this great, pleasant, and gainful trade of godliness, here thou mayest find arguments to persuade thee to this rational and necessary undertaking in order to life and salvation, grace and glory, with counsel and instructions how thou mayest attain to this high and heavenly calling.

If thou be one who drivest furiously after the world, pursuing thy earthly interest with greediness, neglecting the things that concern thy peace, and subjecting the concerns of heaven and thy immortal soul to the poor and perishing trifles of this world; here thou wilt find reasons to convince thee of that folly, and helps to loosen thy heart from that ensnaring, soul-ruining bondage.

If thou meetest with rebukes upon thy earthly interests, and crosses on thy affairs and undertakings in the world, this book will help thee to find out the cause of thy disappointments and those consuming moths on thy estate, and instruct thee to get honey out of these rods, good from these evils, and how to comport with divine ends, and thy own advantages by such dispensations.

Hast thou made a profession of godliness, and formerly driven this heavenly trade to advantage, but art now fallen back and decayed in thy spiritual substance, and become poor in thy inward man and toward God? Here mayest thou find the discoveries of a backsliding soul, with the causes of it; thou wilt also meet with awakening considerations to affect and afflict thy heart with the sense of thy evil case. Here also mayest thou know whether thy decays are curable, and what course thou mayest take to get out of thy languishing estate.

Art thou one that dost profess this *Heavenly Trade*? This piece will tell thee what thy work is, and wherein this employment lies; what are the important duties of piety to be driven on every day, with directions and rules about it.

If thou art one who keepest up this trade for heaven and thrivest therein, here hast thou marks of a prosperous trade in godliness, and several doubts cleared up about thy soul-thrivings, with those important duties opened which this peculiar mercy calls for. Gather out of this garden what physic or food thou needest, and apply and improve it, praying for the assistance of that Spirit that hath been frequently and solemnly begged both for the forming and blessing of this discourse unto all that read it.

You who have been hearers of this subject, though in somewhat different expressions suited to your capacity and advantage in the delivery of it, have reason above others to receive and improve this message twice sent unto you.

But you especially my dear friends, the care of whose souls is upon me, for whose sake chiefly these truths were at first delivered, and are now made public, have the most obliging reasons to get them copied out upon your hearts, and in your lives. To you firstly, more especially, yea, most affectionately was and is this word of salvation sent and presented again to your view, that you might have these things abiding with you, and that they might live in your eye which have sounded in your ear, and be speaking to you when I shall be removed out of your sight, and be beyond all capacity to serve your precious and immortal souls, that when I can plead no more for God or with you, I may in this be speaking to you and others in the behalf of Christ, and glorious though despised holiness. This has been the prevailing argument with me to discover my weakness to the world, and expose myself to the censure or scorn of some.

I have the greatest reason to expect from you the entertainment of these truths, who have chosen and received me in the Lord, to declare the Gospel of His Son to you. You also have known my labours, infirmities, and afflictions with you and for your sake; that for twenty years space I have served you in the Gospel, in reproach, wants, weaknesses, dangers, and sufferings, neither count I my life dear unto myself, so that I may finish my course with joy, and the ministry which I have received of the Lord Jesus, to testify the Gospel of the grace of God. Yea, being so affectionately desirous of you, I have been willing to have imparted to you not the Gospel of God only, but also my own soul. Because you were dear unto me, you know and have acknowledged the suitableness of this subject unto your own cases, and how evidently the condition of most of you is opened here and suited, by the convictions, counsels, reprehensions, and consolations of this discourse. There are some among you that I am jealous of with a godly jealousy, lest I should have laboured in vain for you, and your minds be corrupted from the simplicity of the Gospel through the temptations of this present world. I have often cried aloud in your ears against the sin, and have warned you of the danger of an earthly spirit and conversation, and do tell you now even weeping, that such are enemies to the cross of Christ, who mind earthly things. Until you are crucified to the world, you have no saving benefit of the cross of Christ, or can ever behold the face of God in heaven, until you are redeemed from the earth. All your profession, parts, duties, and enjoyments, will be but so many witnesses against you, if after all you are lovers of this present world. Coveting to be rich will also make your souls poor, and deprive you of the refreshments of His presence and consolations of His blessed Spirit, and will be a manifest evidence that you have little of those pleasures that are from above. 'Twas said of pious Mr. Bain,[1] that he sought not great matters in the world, being taken up with comforts and griefs to which the world was a stranger. The more a soul converses in heaven and lives upon the first-fruits of the other world, the less will he be taken with things below. When Abraham came to live by faith, and in a view of that city whose maker and builder is God, the plains of Sodom and spoils of Canaan were to him but mean things. "I never cared much for the world," saith one, "since I came to know better things."

[1] Paul Bayne, lecturer at St. Andrews in Cambridge, [d.1617]. "In which station he so demeaned himself for some years, that impiety only had cause to complain. But all that favoured the wayes of God... rejoiced, and gloried in him and his Ministry, as in a Spiritual and Heavenly Treasure. Sometime after Master Baines was silenced, yet preached sometimes where he might have liberty... He was indeed all his Life after pressed with want, not having (as he often complained to his friends) a place to rest his Head in. Yet he did never so much as consult with himself about his denying his sincerity, and complying with the Bishops; of whom, and their courses, he was wont to say, 'They are a generation of the Earth, earthly, and favour not the Ways of God.'" (Samuel Clarke, *Lives of Thirty-Two English Divines*... Ed.3. London, 1677, p.23).

You have tasted that the Lord is gracious, you have fed on the fat things of His house, and have found a day in His courts better than a thousand elsewhere, and must be self-condemned if you prefer not God above ten thousand worlds, and count the enjoyment of Himself riches enough; yea, if you esteem not the reproach of Christ greater riches than the treasures of Egypt. 'Twas a brave speech of that noble Galeatius when he had left his honour, interest and relations for Christ and the Gospel sake—"I have", saith he, "riches, honour, and joy enough while in this cottage I may live in the Church of God, enjoy His word and people, and have time to converse with God by holy meditation, and with my friends about God's great goodness to me in my conversion. Cursed for ever be that religion which weds men to the world, and divorces them from God."

There are others of you, I fear, fallen back in your spiritual state. Former days were better than now; and the shadow gone back some degrees upon the dial of your hearts, who it may be have left your first love, have lost your spiritual taste, more dead to the things of God, cold and formal in duty. Possibly you have hid your face from God, and He hath compassed Himself with a cloud before you. You have neglected your walks with God, and He hath withheld converse with you. For the recovery of such from whence they have fallen to their first love and labours, is part of this discourse framed. Hear what the Spirit saith therein. Attend and obey those counsels. Return to your first love, and do your first works, lest the Lord take the candlestick out of his place, and leave you in that wilderness into which you wander.

Some of you who are fearers of God yet walk in darkness, and see no light, have your frequent exercises and continual complaints, that He who should have comforted your souls is far removed from you. My advice to you is, to walk in the light when you sit in darkness, and wait for the light, when the evening shadows are upon you. 'Tis but a little while and He that shall come will come, and will not tarry; the Son of righteousness is upon His journey towards you, and 'twill not be long ere it be risen upon you.

Are there any of you who have better days? Does your bow abide in strength? Are your affections warm towards your Beloved, and your hearts sometimes burn within you while He is talking to you in His word? Do you long for His appearance, and delight in His presence, and press hard after Him in His appointments, do you love the word of His mouth more than your necessary food? Can you be content to let your own things sit, that you may seek the things that are Christ's, and sit at His feet? When others are in the market-place, and abroad in the crowd of their earthly affairs, are you alone with Christ in a corner? If so, your mercy is singular, and your obligations strong to be entirely the Lord's; to be no more your own, but wholly devoted to His fear, to live a life of praise and well-pleasingness unto God, to think well of Christ, and to bear His pleasure; to be patient in tribulation, continuing instant in prayer, to long for the well-head of your mercies, and to be beginning a life of glory while you are here in a life of grace. I shall close up this discourse with a few words of general advice to you all.

First, lay the foundation sure on which you build all your temporary labours and your eternal hopes. You cannot be too certain in that on which depends your all. Consider how often hath Satan battered down; yea, your own hearts have disputed away those evidences, on which you could sometimes have adventured your souls, and yet the strongest assaults are to come, and the greatest forces of hell reserved for the last battle. Bottom not your hopes on anything short of a crucified Christ, not on your frames, but on His favour; not upon your duties, but His righteousness; nor upon any kindnesses received from Him short of a saving union with Him. Rest not till your convictions be clear, deep, and distressing, such as discover sin to be the greatest evil in its nature and fruits, and its residence and indwelling in you, a burden intolerable; such convictions as will not admit of after-favour or reconciliation to the least known or most beloved sin; that can make your heart to bleed afresh upon every new touch of it, and never at rest till the whole kind of it be destroyed out of your souls. Labour to see such a beauty in Christ as may render all created glory as dross and dung in your eye. Stop not till you come to the excellency of the knowledge of Jesus Christ as your Lord; till you can discern such a worth in the person as well as the purchase of Christ, as will make you content to throw all overboard, to take in Him, and be sick of love till you enjoy Him. Be sure your close with Christ be right with His whole person, will, and designs, to be one with Him upon all His own terms. And that this union be not in judgement and consent only, but in heart and will from your whole souls, finding an inward likeness and love to Him in your renewed nature.

Secondly, go on towards perfection, press after nearer and more complete conformity to the nature and will of Christ every day. Think how short your highest measures do come of perfect holiness in the sight of God. Set the Pattern before you every day, that you may be the more ashamed at your present attainments in grace, and more provoked to higher aims and achievements. Compare yourselves with them that are above you, with the Rule of Righteousness, and with all your obligations, time, means and mercies to keep you humble in your own eyes. Look upon your wants as well as enjoyments, that you may be as poor in spirit as in condition; that which is wanting in you cannot be numbered. "Who am I, and what is my people, that we should be able to offer so willingly after this sort?" (1 Chron. 29.14). Keep low thoughts in yourselves under the greatest services you do for God, and the highest honour you receive from God. Alas, said the Lord Duplessis[1] to one who commended him for the improvement of his talent, "What is there of mine in that work? Say not that it was I, but God in me". "I know more", saith another, "by myself to abase me, than any man could know to extol me. So much humility a man hath, so much grace he hath, and worth, and no more." (Dr. Harris).[2]

Thirdly, keep up a life of faith upon Christ in the promises. As the first quickening of a Christian is by faith, so his whole life is maintained by believing. No longer than you believe can you live. (Gal. 2.20). Your life is hid with Christ in God. Draw fresh influence thence by faith upon your hopes, comforts and graces under every want, fears, and deaths within you. Make not your graces or duties the grounds of believing, but encouragements to faith. Study more the nature, freeness, fulness, and unchangeableness of redemption grace, and get acquaintance with the promise and persuasions of the truth of them in Christ. "To live only by faith", saith Dr. Harris, "and a bare promise without a pawn, and to give all to free grace and to Christ alone, are mighty works";[3] and some of those things he found most difficult.

Fourthly, walk in love as Christ hath loved you. This is the life of heaven, and the beginning of that excellent glory which shall never be removed. There is nothing does make thee more like to God, more near and dear to Him, and more fit for His use than this grace of love. Let your affections be extended as large as the objects of them; unto God, His word, ways, and people. Love God to obey Him; His ways to walk in them; His people to delight in them; to sympathize with them; to mourn over them in their sufferings; to help them in their necessities; to rejoice with

1 Philippe de Duplessis Mornay (1549-1623). French Huguenot apologist, lawyer, and diplomatist. Founder of the Protestant academy at Saumur.

2 Robert Harris, D.D. (1578-1658). (S. Clarke, *Lives* ... Ed.3. London, 1677. p.335).

3 S. Clarke, *Lives* ... Ed.3. London, 1677. p.335.

them in their consolations, counting their mercies your own, which is no easy part of your duty. "It is far harder", saith one, "to adopt another's comforts than his sorrows, and to hold one's self exalted in another's exaltation."

Fifthly, in the enjoyment of the world, get above it; and while you live in it, be daily dying to it. So much as you get above the world, so near are you to God and glory, and no nearer. Covet not another's goods; the world is none of your portion if God be your part. Oh how much beneath the extraction, dignity, and duty of saints is the love to, and life upon this low and dirty world. Leave not childrens bread to feed on such carrion dogs-meat, with which Satan feeds his labourers.

Sixthly, Make much of the time and means of grace while you have them. Your glass runs; your sun hastens, and the wind blows when and where it listeth. O make use of time while you have it. God who made nothing in vain, hath work for every hour of your short day. Work as hard as you can, you will find something to do when you come to die. "Loss of time", saith Dr. Harris on his deathbed, "sits very near upon me. Work, work apace; assure yourselves nothing will more trouble you when you come to die, than that you have done no more for that God which hath done so much for you."[1] Wait upon, and walk in the light while you have it. If Grace thinks it not much to spread a table for you, don't you think it much to spare time to sit down at it. You that find so many things to do when God calls for your company, will shortly find that God hath other things to do than to mind you when you need His cordials. How glad would you be of enjoying time to hear the voice of peace when you are entering upon eternity, who are not at leisure now to hear divine precepts while in the possession of time. Neglect not hearing, praying seasons, which are your seed-time for glory. "O that every day", saith one, "were a sabbath or a fast-day, for then I should be well". Buy not your ease or earthly interest at so dear a rate as the loss of salvation, time, and helps. Evidence your love to God by your valuation of His presence in His ordinances. How can you long for the enjoyment of God in heaven, who care not for His company on earth, or His glorious appearance in His sanctuary? Stick at nothing that may yield Him delight, or give Him glory, how expensive soever it be on your dearest comforts and interests. When one told Du Moulin in his sickness that he wronged himself by speaking so much, " 'Tis true", said he, "but I will aye glorify-

[1] S. Clarke, *Lives*... Ed.3. London, 1677. p.326.

ing of God".[1] A soul that supremely loves God, will count nothing too much to do, part with, or suffer, that may bring Him glory.

Seventhly, Rest not in your enjoyments of means, without improvement of them. What's a full table if thy soul abide empty, and frequent feeding if thy inner man languish. 'Tis a time of dying and secret waste in most Christians. O covet earnestly the best gifts, that you may flourish in the courts of God, and grow as the cedars of Lebanon; that you may be thoroughly furnished to every good work, and your profiting appear to all men. Be deeply sensible of your little fruit under great dressing, and be humbled. Take heed of spiritual pride, and puffings up in your apprehended excellencies or privileges; 'tis the humble soul is the most thriving soul. Keep your hearts pure, and your lives unspotted. As sound bodies, so sincere souls are most growing. Pare off luxuriant branches as they sprout out, and lay the axe to the root of them every day. Keep up faith in the promises of soul-prosperity to them that serve Him in sincerity (Ps. 92.12,13), and stay on Christ by faith for help. When you see nothing but discouragements in yourselves, and when you are afraid to apply the promises, even then bless God for them: "These promises," said a doubting soul, "are none of mine, yet I am glad that God hath made them, and for their sakes that shall partake of them." (Mr. White).[2]

Eighthly, Neglect not secret transactions between God and your souls, to which I fear some of you may be too great strangers. No wonder that intimacy between God and souls does fall, when they are seldom together in retirements. Oh take heed of passing by thy closet or secret corners one day (Matt. 6.6); or posting out of them before God and your souls have some converse together. And be not only constant in it, but careful to please God in the spiritual performance of it. Let not custom or formality deprive thee of the sweetness of that bread eaten in secret.

Ninthly, Make conscience of every duty you owe towards others, in your relations, places, and callings. Keep up family duty, or write heathen upon thy doors, that the world may know thee. If you neglect God's service, He will not be your sanctuary. Prayerless houses have broken walls and doors, and no defence against

[1] Peter Du Moulin (1568-1658), French Protestant divine. The reply was, in fact, "But I will die glorifying God." (Erasmus Middleton, *Biographia Evangelica.* 1784. III.374).

[2] John White (1575-1648), a puritan divine known as the 'Patriarch of Dorchester'. A principal founder of the Massachusetts colony, though he never left England; member of the Westminster Assembly.

the last evil. If you will not give God your breathings, how can you think He will give you His blessing? 'Tis sad that any, especially such as God hath taken into His house, should shut Him out of their doors; or give Him such pitiful service as some do, scarce ever reading the scriptures in their families from one Lord's day to another; only send Him a little hasty fruit, some short and shuffled prayers once a day. No wonder that salvation comes not to their houses, or converting grace into their families, but a flying roll is over their habitations, and the black marks of ruin on their children and servants. Think it not strange that God makes thy pleasant roses pricking briars and thorns to thee, who hast made them spears and swords to Him. Oh keep with God in every duty of His service, your relation, calling, and employments.

Lastly, in every condition walk with God, and wait for God. If He lead you in ways of mercy, follow Him in ways of duty. If you have comforts, take heed of doting on, or abusing of them. When He sends you afflictions, receive them. Be not fainting nor forward under them, but sanctify God in them, and by their hand return to Him. Do not overlove your mercies, or overfear your troubles. Prepare for changes, but live upon Immutability and be settled under all your unsettlements. Count nothing strange but sin, and nothing hard to bear but the absence or anger of a gracious God. Lose not your fears in time of peace, neither cast away your confidence in the day of trouble. Let your lamps be always burning, that you may see the way of your duty in the night of your danger; and how to get comfort in your adversity. And let your loins be girt, that you may be ready both to do your work, and to meet your wages; and be always looking and waiting for the coming of your Lord, who will welcome you in the acceptance of your duties, unclothe you of your sins and sufferings, and crown your sincerity and faithfulness with a "Come ye blessed of my Father, inherit the kingdom prepared for you." This is the longed-for fruit of all his labours with you, and the subject-matter of his daily prayers for you, who is in Him that was, and is, and is to come.

Your affectionate Labourer,
Fellow Servant,
and
Brother,
Barthol. Ashwood

APPENDIX C

An Account of John Ashwood

Extracted from *A Sermon preached on the death of the Reverend John Ashwood with an account of his life and character ... by Thomas Reynolds, to which are added two sermons preached by the deceased a little before he died.* London. 1707.

He was descended of eminently pious ancestors, being the fourth generation of those, who in an uninterrupted line of succession had feared God, and the third, if not the fourth that served Him in the work of the ministry. He was born at Axminster in Devonshire A.D.1657.

The Lord began to work upon his heart when he was about fourteen or fifteen years old; and that upon a very accidental occasion that struck him with a sudden impression and most terrifying fear of death ... and it grew at last to that height as to force him to his bed. The next sabbath after he was thus siezed, which was also the next day to it, his father preached in the chamber where he lay, with these words, "But one thing is needful, and Mary hath chosen that good part, which shall not be taken away from her," Lk. 10.42. A seasonable and suitable word, the real evidence of the piety, prudence and affection of a godly minister and tender parent; which had the desired effect from the blessing of God attending it, for it made a very deep and lasting impression upon him.

Thus did our brother continue under much affliction and exercise of spirit till He who healeth the broken in heart, and bindeth up their wounds, and knows how to speak a word in season to him that is weary, did in a special manner lead unto and powerfully apply by His Spirit to his soul that exceeding precious promise, the remembrance of which was ever after most dear unto him: "Remember these, O Jacob and Israel; for thou art my servant: I have formed thee; thou art my servant: O Israel, thou shalt not be forgotten of me. I have blotted out as a thick cloud thy transgressions, and, as a cloud, thy sins: return unto me, for I have redeemed thee". Most gracious words, which cannot but be entertained with melting joy and unspeakable wonder where they are spoken and effectually applied to the heart by the Spirit of God. Thus the same hand that bound him gave him a release, and that mouth which condemned, proclaimed liberty to the captive, and brought this poor prisoner out of the prison house.

After this remarkable change by the special work of God, he was admitted a member of his father's church and soon after that sent up to London where (having first had the advantage of education which his pious father thought proper) he was received into the family, and pursued his studies under the learned Mr. Gale.[1]

He taught school at Axminster about the time, or but a little before he began to preach, after which he pursued the same employment at Chard, where he did not long continue, being driven out of the town by persecution. After this he went on for some time undisturbed in his work, till new troubles arose, and frequent attempts were made to sieze him, though they were as often frustrated. But at length, upon the change of the magistracy in the town, he thought it not safe to continue any longer in Chard, but removed to Haviland, where he entertained some thoughts of going with divers others of his friends for Carolina. Whereupon several days of prayer were set apart to seek the Lord in reference to this affair. Divers of his friends afterwards laid aside their design; however he and three more still prepared for their intended voyage which was to commence in January 1683. But the Lord remarkably prevented it by afflicting him with the small pox.

After this, meeting with fresh troubles, he removed from Haviland to Westy, and from thence to Buckland. He records the signal favour of God to him at this place in these words:— "During my abode here, I had most glorious influences of the grace and mercy of God towards me". After this he had a call to a people at Exeter, where being ordained he did with great solicitude and pains discharge all those parts of a vigilant and faithful minister for about the space of ten years till he was induced to come and exercise his ministry at London. He had first an evening lecture near Spittalfields, besides which he preached

[1] Theophilus Gale (1628-78). Ejected from Winchester Cathedral, and also from his fellowship at Magdalen College, Oxford, 1662. He became tutor in the family of Philip. Lord Wharton, later commencing a small nonconformist academy at Newington Green, also assisting and succeeding John Rowe in his church in Holborn. (W. Wilson, *Dissenting Churches... in London*... 1810. III. 161-68).

one part of the day at Hoxton. After about two years he received a call to a people at Peckham near London, in Surrey.

Under much weakness he went to Axminster where he preached the sermons that follow. From thence with difficulty he travelled to Exeter to pay a visit to his former flock, and among them (it pleased God) he finished his public work, preaching his last sermon to those unto whom he first officiated as an ordained minister, from Ephesians 1.22. He published two works; *An Address to the Orphans of Religious Parents;* and, *A Minister's Legacy to Fatherless Children.*

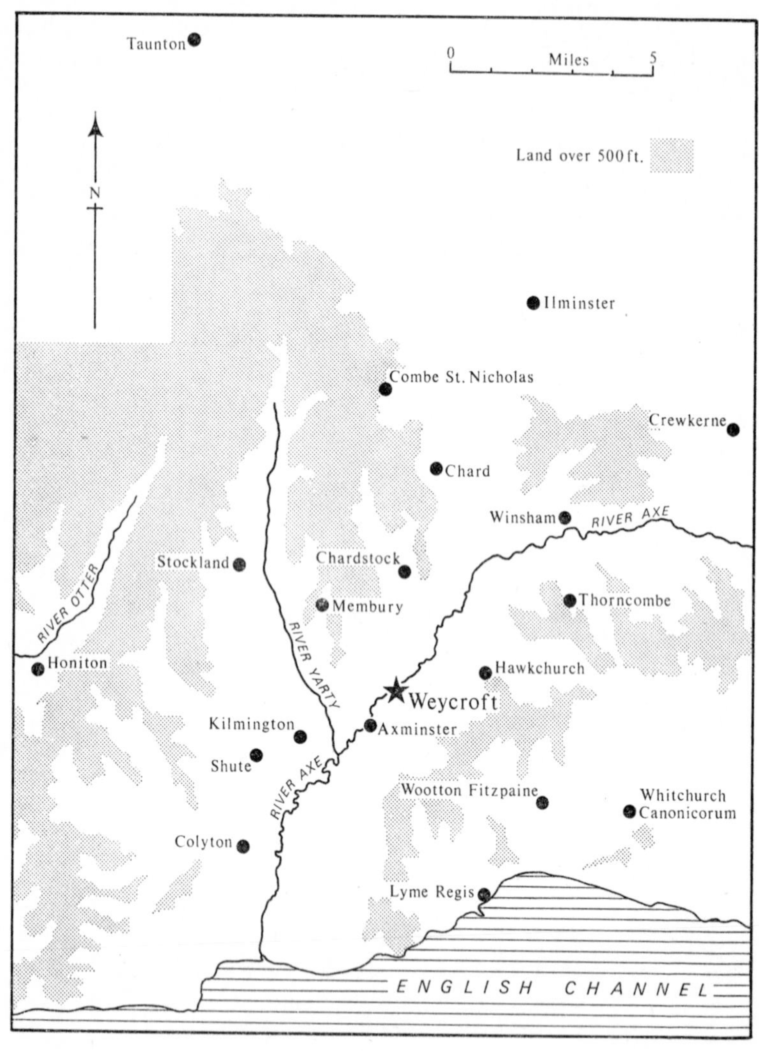

The Axminster Circle

APPENDIX D

The Axminster Circle

One cannot but be impressed by the wide area from which the one hundred and fifty two persons named in the Axminster member's roll were drawn. Of the nineteen places named (Chard Land being regarded as part of Chard), Taunton at twenty miles was the most distant. The counties of Devon, Dorset, and Somerset were all represented, and one may only wonder what were the unnamed 'Remote Places'. Axminster was not alone in its widespread catchment area. It was said in London that the Independent Churches were "gathered out of many parishes". In other country districts it was the same. At least a dozen Northamptonshire villages were represented in Thomas Browning's Independent Church at Rothwell. Francis Holcroft and Joseph Oddy ministered to a Cambridge Church that comprised members from a wide area of Cambridgeshire and Hertfordshire. The same was true of Bunyan's Church at Bedford, which could appoint a service in any one of nine or ten places up to twelve miles away, and count on local members being present. In the Axminster circle there was a certain spontaneity in the mutual attraction of likeminded souls:

> Now the Lord was pleased to engage the hearts of some serious pious christians of the neighbouring villages to attend frequently on the ministry of this holy man. These got into an intimate acquaintance with him, and also with those few souls in the town of Axminster whose hearts the Lord had wrought upon by His word and Spirit, who likewise resolved to join in and walk with them in the same order and fellowship of the gospel. (p.8).

Further, the *Savoy Declaration* of 1658 which may or may not have been known in Axminster (it was printed four times in 1659), had said "Saints living in one city or Town, or within such distances as that they may conveniently assemble for divine Worship, ought rather to joyn in one Church for their mutual strengthening and edification, then to set up many distinct Societies."[1]

Circumstances of persecution often dictated the necessity of meeting in different places. But that there was a further reason is

[1] *Savoy Declaration of the Institution of Churches, and the order appointed in them by Jesus Christ.* XXIV.

evident from the following notes, the object of which is to indicate in the briefest outline and so far as may be possible at this distance of time, the general state of religion in the various places named in the Axminster roll. In all but two of these places there had been ejectments in 1660/62. In all but the one place on which no information has been discovered (Stockland), there was immediate and persistent conventicling. In all these places there were both householders and ministers forthcoming in 1672 to declare themselves and take advantage of the Declaration of Indulgence. And in almost every place named there was someone (and in some places many) who suffered imprisonment or death rather than recant principle. Moreover, while the available information in some cases is little more than names, facts, and dates, what is disclosed when a fuller picture is forthcoming, is the existence of a godly, learned, discriminating, and compassionate ministry, with a constituency of a consistent calibre, episcopal sneerings about the 'vulgar sort' notwithstanding.

Why, then, did not all such godly folk in a given locality attend some local assembly as a matter of course? From the origins of the Puritan movement within the English Reformation there had been two views of the local and visible church; the parochial system favoured by Anglicans and Presbyterians, and the voluntary or 'gathered church' principle, favoured by Independents or Congregationalists, and Baptists. Because Puritanism was no more than a segment of the total church structure of the nation, neither party had at any stage been able fully to develop all its principles. Compromises had of necessity been made all along. Now, under the oppression of the Restoration regime in Church and State there was a general tendency to comprehension between Presbyterians and Independents, in common cause against the persecuting policy of the crown and the bishops. Sheer force of circumstance compelled many Presbyterians to constitute what amounted to gathered churches in practice, while renouncing the idea in theory. On the other hand, many Independent Churches were themselves governed by elders, while sternly refusing all aspects of synodical government. There was a drawing together as in the Exeter Assembly and the 'Happy Union'; yet the Assembly was always divided on issues arising from the churchmanship principle, while the 'Happy Union' soon became sadly unhappy from the same cause.

In the Axminster circle it should be noted that the dominant churchmanship, with but few exceptions, was Presbyterian, though doubtless with varying degrees of rigidity and charity. On the other hand the Axminster Church was strongly and, it seems, uncompromisingly Independent. Thus although there was a common heritage and union in the Reformed Faith, there was a distinct divergence in matters of church constitution and practice which the Independents of Axminster considered vital. It were too much to insist that there was no other Independent or pro-Independent Presbyterian Church within the Axminster 'Circle' during the period represented by the *Ecclesiastica,* but the likelihood seems small until at least toward the end of that period. And it was that change which eventually brought about the entirely happy division of the Axminster Independent Church.

Axminster Puritanism was represented in Axminster before the arrival of Bartholomew Ashwood in the form of his immediate predecessor, one Richard Cresson, appointed in 1647. He too was an Oxford graduate, and one of some seventy Devon Presbyterian ministers who signed the Devon '*Testimony*' of 1648. (These '*Testimonies*' were documents of support for the outcome of the Westminster Assembly of Divines, drawn up and signed in various parts of the country. They declared allegiance to the Westminster Standards and the *Solemn League and Covenant,* and denounced rising fanatical sects). Cresson was not sequestrated; he resigned for personal reasons in 1655 and went to a small living in Dorset. He was admitted by the Triers as vicar of Kingston by Taunton in 1659, and conformed in 1662 when he became vicar of nearby Musbury on the ejection of Richard Farrant, till his death in 1671. He was at heart a Presbyterian and must have left behind some following when he left Axminster. Thus, when Ashwood's house was licensed under the Declaration of Indulgence, 1672, for worship after the Independent way, another licence was issued for "the house of Tristram Cop of Axminster in Devon, Presbyterian."[1] This latter licence, however, was sought for "a house or room in Wycroft In Axminster in ye County of Devon in ye occupation of Trusham Cop. Ye people of ye Congregationall persuasion."[2] Tristram/Trusham Cop is otherwise unidentified, and no minister was licensed specifically for his house. The question arises whether he was the tenant/occupier of Weycroft Manor when it was hired for Ashwood's church? It is possible that there may have been confusion in the licence applications; Ashwood's having been made by John Hickes,

1 *SPD. Chas. II. EB38A.266.*
2 *SPD. Chas. II. 320.56.*

and Jas. Innes, Jun, and Cop's by Stephen Ford, ejected from Chipping Norton, Oxon, and himself then licensed as the Congregational teacher at Miles Lane, London. Ford also made application for licences for John Hodder, and for John Wakely's house at nearby Thorncombe, both Presbyterian. We are left with these alternatives: either Cop's house and Ashwood's house were in fact the same place of meeting of the Axminster Independent Church; or, alongside Ashwood's assembly at Weycroft there was also a Presbyterian congregation vaguely descended from Cresson's earlier ministry, but concerning which there is otherwise no information.

Axminster was also acquainted with the Baptists at an early stage, some seventeen persons from Axminster being members of the church at Dalwood in 1653. (See p.213).

It must be noted with thankfulness that Ashwood's successor as vicar of Axminster was an ally and not an enemy. Joseph Crabb (1619-1699) was born at Sandwich, Kent, educated at Wadham College, Oxford, graduating B.A. in 1641. He was ordained by presbyters as curate of Beaminster in 1647, and was chaplain to a regiment under the Commonwealth; during which time he had preached against Anglicanism and prayed publicly that Charles II might not come to the throne. Appointed vicar of Netherbury in 1656, he was ejected at the Restoration in 1660. He had a part in the forming of a dissenting congregation in Beaminster, although he afterwards conformed and spent the rest of his life as vicar of Axminster.

> Tho' he was in the established church, yet in his principles, and manner of preaching and praying, he so resembled the nonconforming ministers, that he was still looked upon as one of them. He visited some of his ejected brethren when persecuted and imprisoned; sheltered and did good offices to others, and shewed on all occasions that his heart was with them. About 1683 he was accused to Dr. Lamplugh, Bishop of Exeter, for . . . not coming up to the height of Conformity; but the bishop after he had heard his defence, dismissed him with kindness, to the disappointment of his accusers. He joined with Mr. Wm. Ball the ejected vicar of Winsham, and others, in publishing a volume of Abp. Ussher's sermons . . . [1]

[1] Samuel Palmer, *Nonconformist's Memorial.* II.176.

Crabb had previously appeared in literature as co-signatory with Hugh Gundry, later ejected from Mapperton, of an Epistle Dedicatory to a posthumous work of his own predecessor at Netherbury, Jerome Turner (1614-1655): *A Breastplate for the keeping of the heart:... Sermons by Mr. Jerome Turner, late pastor of Netherbury,* London, 1660.[1]

Between Ashwood's ejectment and Crabb's institution on November 21, 1662, a shadowy figure named Thomas Ayshford appears in some lists of Axminster incumbents. Nothing further is known of him, unless he is the "Thomas Ayshford minr. of Topisha" (?Topsham), who subscribed the articles of the Exeter Assembly on 22 May 1656.

The observant visitor to present-day Axminster may notice in the main street not far from the parish church an old house bearing on its door the name 'Ashwood House'. It was at one time the residence of some of Ashwood's successors in office.

Old Axminster

1 C. H. Mayo, *Bibliotheca Dorsetiensis* 1855. p.178.

Meeting Places of the Axminster Church

1660-1672	No settled place. Houses, woods, solitary places, obscure places, desert places—are all mentioned as venues in this period.
1672-1681	The house at Weycroft, licenced under Declaration of Indulgence 1672. No other venue mentioned in this period.
1681-1686	No settled place. Woods, houses, nightwatches, from place to place, desert place, secret cave of the earth; and for some months unable to meet at all.
1686-1698	The house at Weycroft.
1698-	The 'new meeting-house' in Chard Street, Axminster.

Chard & Chardland The one was the borough, the other the parish, long since united. In the time of our narrative there was a longstanding feud between the inhabitants of each, and separate identity was vigorously maintained.

Baptists were the earliest Nonconformists, a church being founded by Captain Wallington, an officer in Cromwell's army, at a date prior to 1653. Associations of Baptist Churches met here in 1655 and 1657; and in 1689 the minister, Mr. Wilkins attended the Particular Baptist Assembly in London.[1]

There was no ejectment at Chard in 1660/1662. In 1669 the Episcopal Returns speak of conventicles at the house of Mrs. Bond and Mr. John Chapman, "The numbers uncertaine, but always very great, sometimes 200, 300, 400, 500, 600 and oftentimes 700". The six "Teachers or Preachers" were all ejected ministers who, in 1672, were licensed as Presbyterians. First among them was Robert Atkins, born at Chard, an Oxford graduate, one-time chaplain to Oliver Cromwell, ejected from St. John's, at Exeter. Then there was Henry Berry, ejected from Dulverton; Benjamin Mills from Chardstock; Robert Pinney from Charlcombe; Richard Smith another native of Chard, from Whitestaunton; and Henry Parsons from Burstock.[2]

[1] See, *Association Records of the Particular Baptists of England, Wales, and Ireland to 1660.* Ed. B. R. White. Pt. 2 The West Country and Ireland. (1973).

[2] *Cod Tenison.* 639.145.

Under the Declaration of Indulgence, 1672, licences for five ejected ministers in Chard, all Presbyterian, were issued: Benjamin Mills from Chardstock; Robert Pinney from Charlcombe; Henry Backaller from Combe St. Nicholas; William Samson from Bradpole; and John Cudmore from Exeter College, Oxford.[1] As to meeting places, licences (Presbyterian) were granted for "A large Roome in the midst of the Street at Chard belonging to Wm. Atkins, Nathaniel Pitts and others", and for the houses of Robert Pinney, and Robert Batt,[2] the latter being a deacon of the Axminster Independent Church. On two occasions James Innes Junr. applied for a licence for "Mr. Henry Backaller, Presbyterian, the new Hall in the midst of the towne of Chard in Somersett", and each application is marked "not approved".[3] The Declaration itself had suggested no limitation on what buildings might be used but after perhaps a dozen public or semi-public buildings such as town halls, guild halls and the livery company halls in London, had been so licensed, it became clear that a change of policy behind the scenes now forbade this. Thus the New Hall in Chard—presumably the 'New Work' also known at the time as the Guild Hall, and demolished in 1834—was refused a licence. Similar refusals were generally made throughout the country, in fact three licences already issued for such public buildings were withdrawn. Says Professor Lyon Turner, "The magnates both in Church and State were determined to keep the 'places allowed' for Nonconformist worship, as much in 'holes and corners', in 'out-of-the-way places', and in private houses; as perforce their meeting-places had been before, when unrecognized by the Crown."[4]

With the Axminster Church still embracing members at Chard, and its pastor still certainly preaching there between 1672 and 1684, there were no less than five other ejected ministers preaching in the town from 1672. It becomes a question as to when a distinct church was formed in Chard. Three opinions have been expressed. (i) "A separate church was formed in Chard in 1672, and its first pastor was Rev. Henry Backaller (1672-87). He was succeeded by Rev. Aaron Pitts who held office for 50 years."[5]

1 *SPD.EB38A*. 68,69,79,133,174.
2 *SPD.EB38A*. 79,208.
3 *SPD.320*. 67,156.
4 G. Lyon Turner, *Original Records of Early Nonconformity*. III.650.
5 Congregational Union, Somerset. *The Annual report . . . 1896, with historical sketch of the churches*. (1896).

(ii). "From a record of the proceedings of the ministers in Devon in Dr. Williams's Library we learn that 'Mr. Aaron Pitts was ordained, with Mr. Samuel Atkins, of Exeter, 18 May 1687, by the laying on of the hands of the Presbytery'... After he was ordained, Mr. Pitts most likely took Mr. Towgood's place, alongside with Mr. Backaller, till 1693..."[1] (iii). "The ecclesiastical history of Wyke-Croft ends with the building of the meeting house (in Axminster) in 1698. About the same time another meeting house was built at Chard, and the church was divided."[2]

The only written evidence is that of the *Ecclesiastica.* In 1687, the very year of the suggested division, the Axminster Church resolved to compile its Book of Remembrance, and included in its membership roll the names of the members living at Chard and Chardland.[3] Its churchmanship had been strongly Independent from the beginning, and this appeared again in the calling and ordination of Stephen Towgood in 1679, and in his own persistently Independent position in the Exeter ordination controversy of 1696. (See note p.157). While on practical grounds the division of the Church would seem to have been desirable, on grounds of churchmanship it seems hardly to have been possible, there being no Independent minister at Chard. A second church of distinctly Presbyterian flavour may well have come into being in the "large Roome in the midst of the Street at Chard", as early as 1672, but there is no real evidence of a separate Independent Church until well toward the end of the seventeenth century. By that date, as Wyatt says, the Axminster Church was divided; and the Chard Independents may have coalesced with the Chard Presbyterians in the new chapel built 1700-2, the deed of which, dated 1703 shows Aaron Pitts among others as trustee. Having stressed the importance of not over-playing the distinctions between Presbyterians and Independents at this period, here is a case where such distinctions must certainly not be under-played.

[1] Henry Mayo Gunn, *History of Free Churches in Chard and the Neighbourhood to 1867.* (1867). p.33.

[2] Francis Bullen Wyatt. *Congregational Historical Society Transactions.* IV.110. (1909).

[3] See Chapter 19. H. M. Gunn (1817-1886) was son of a former minister at Chard. His identification of the Chard names in the *Ecclesiastica* members roll, based as it is on local knowledge, is worth comparison. "Roger Hoare and his wife. Katherine Atkins probably related to Robert Atkins. James Pitts probably father of Aaron Pitts. Benjamine Shute and his wife. John Smith and his son who became a minister. Hannah Legg. Sarah Pike (Pile). Stephen Strong. Hannah Symes (Symms). Nathaniel Rice. Mitchell. Sarah Warren." (*Free Churches in Chard.* p.29).

The 'New Work', Chard

Chardstock Coaxdon Hall, in Chardstock parish, already referred to as the home of the Cogans (p.81), had previously been in possession of the D'Ewes family. Sir Symonds D'Ewes (1602-50) was born there and spent his boyhood there. Later he lived in Suffolk, was knighted in 1641; a strong Parliamentarian and ardent Puritan, he was expelled from Parliament under Pride's Purge in 1648. He wrote, among other things, *The Greek Post-scripts to the Epistles to Timothy and Titus,* 1641; and, *The Primitive Practice for Preserving Truth,* 1645; and a *Diary* in which he gives in much detail his childhood at Coaxdon.

Benjamin Mills was vicar of Chardstock from 1654. Calamy notes that "He had a full congregation while he was in the public church, and it was observed that the parish in general was, at that time, more civilized than it was known to be either before or since."[1] He was ejected in 1662; a Presbyterian, he later ministered in Chard, dying in 1689.

James Strong, the ejected vicar of Ilminster was born at Chardstock.

In the Episcopal Returns of 1669 demanded by Archbishop Sheldon, Seth Ward, Bishop of Salisbury, reported that he could find no conventicle in Chardstock;[2] the Nonconformists were well catered for at nearby Weycroft and Chard!

1 Palmer, *Nonconformist's Memorial.* II.124.
2 *Cod. Tenison.* 639.247b.

On Coaxdon Common is the remains of what appears to have been a beacon, and an earthwork which is considered to have been the scene of the 'sore skirmish' (p.96) in which Samuel Rampson was mortally wounded in the Monmouth Rebellion of 1685.[1]

Coaxdon Hall

Colyton It is Colyton's distinction to have been the place in which Thomas Manton, afterwards chaplain to Cromwell and one of the leading London Presbyterian ministers, began his public ministry, which he sustained from 1640 till his settlement at Stoke Newington in 1643. Born at Lydiard St. Lawrence in 1620, Manton graduated at Oxford and was ordained deacon by Bishop Joseph Hall at Exeter at the early age of 20. After his first sermon at Sowton, near Exeter, he began his well attended and highly esteemed weekly lecture at Colyton. "There", says his biographer, "he had an occasion of reforming the disorderly practice of those who, after the example of a leading gentleman, fell to their private devotion in the congregation after the public worship was begun".[2] The gentleman concerned was Walter Yonge Esq. of the Great House, Colyton, a Justice of the Peace and Sheriff of Devon, Member of Parliament for Honiton from 1640

[1] G. P. R. Pulman, *Book of the Axe,* 1875, 643.
[2] William Harris, *Some Memoirs of the Life and Character of the Reverend and Learned Thomas Manton, D.D.* (Manton's *Works,* 1870, I.vii-viii).

Colyton Parish Church

and reputedly an ardent Puritan. Yonge was the author of a fascinating *Diary* 1604-28, published in 1848, and of an unpublished MS diary of proceedings of the Long Parliament 1642-5.[1]

John Wilkins succeeded Manton in 1647 continuing the Presbyterian tradition, and was joined as curate by John Gill (who was also vicar of Shute) in 1657, till both were ejected for Nonconformity in 1662. Wilkins then preached to a Presbyterian congregation in his own house till his death in 1667, and was buried in the parish church where a tablet describes him as minister from 19 September 1647, till 24 August, 1667, and adds:

Such pillars laid aside,
How can the church abide?
He left his pulpit hee
In Patmos God to see.

The congregation was then ministered to by various ejected ministers from time to time: John Gill from Shute, Bartholomew Ashwood from Axminster, Thomas Godwin of Uplyme, Richard Farrant of Musbury, Francis Soreton of Honiton, and Ames Short

1 G. P. R. Pulman, *The Book of the Axe,* 1875, pp.812,3.

of Lyme Regis. John Kerridge (d.1705), an ejected schoolmaster from Lyme Regis appears to have served in some regular way at an early stage. In the Episcopal Returns of 1669, Bishop Anthony Sparrow of Exeter reports: "Colyton: one conventicle; once in a fortnight or three weeks, sometimes in one house, sometimes in another and in fields and orchards. Teacher, Ames Short."[1] In the record of licences issued under the Declaration of Indulgence, 1672, the following entries tell their own story:—

The howse of Bernard Dwight at Callison in Devon, Presbyterian Meeting place. 8 May 72.

The howse of Widow Drake in Culliton, Devon. Presbyterian.[2]

Nonconformity in Colyton being predominantly Presbyterian, the Baptists gravitated to Dalwood and the Independents to Axminster.

Combe St. Nicholas Henry Backaller (1615-1713) ejected from the vicarage here in 1660, was born at Axminster, matriculated at Oxford, and appointed to Combe St. Nicholas in 1647. When he gave up his living he had sixteen children and nothing to keep them on. Later he became chaplain to Edmund Prideaux at Ford Abbey, and also preached at Chard and Winsham.

In 1669 the Episcopal Returns reported a conventicle here attended by 200 persons, and ministered to by John Baker and — Colford. The 'persuasion' was evidently Presbyterian as Baker, the ejected rector of Curry Mallet was such, and also ministered to similar conventicles at Bridgwater, Fivehead, Ilchester, and West Monkton.[3] Hence the Independents of Combe affiliated with those of Axminster.

Crewkerne Jacob Tomkins curate of Crewkerne since 1647 appears to have been ejected in 1660, but according to Calamy he afterwards conformed and became vicar of Misterton, of which Crewkerne was a curacy. His Presbyterian sympathies had already been indicated by his signature to the *Attestation* of

[1] *Cod. Tenison,* 639.185.
[2] *SPD.EB38A.77;* 178.
[3] *Cod. Tenison,* 639.144,146.

the Somerset ministers in 1648. "Some of his hearers, however, were less flexible, and having adopted the principles of Nonconformity, steadily adhered to them. For two years, from 1665 to 1667, they had the ministerial services of Mr. James Stevenson, who had been ejected from the living of Martock . . . He then removed to Crewkerne and preached in his own house . . . he met with many enemies some of whom threatened to burn down his house."[1]

In the Episcopal Returns of 1669 a conventicle was reported "At the house of Henry Ellyot called Tayle Mill. Numbers uncertaine. Teachers or Preachers Mr. Pinney, Mr. French, Mr. Westley." These were Robert Pinney ejected from Charlcomb, Jeremiah French ejected from South Perrott, and John Westley—grandfather of the founders of Wesleyan Methodism—ejected from Winterbourne Whitchurch; all of whom were Presbyterians.[2]

Under the Declaration of Indulgence of 1672 three houses in Crewkerne were licensed for Presbyterian worship; those of John Serry, William Clares, and William Bennett. By the same device Thomas Marshall received licence to preach at William Bennett's house, and William Cooper, ejected from St. Olave's, Southwark, received a general licence to preach in Crewkerne, Martock, and Coat.[3]

The first settled minister after the Act of Toleration was Robert Knight, (1690-1738) also a Presbyterian.[4]

Although Quakers were active in the town, the strength of Nonconformity in Crewkerne lay with the Presbyterians. One wonders what story lay behind the one lone Independent "Susannah Wills of Crewkerne" who joined herself to the Axminster Church.

Hawkchurch John Hodder was ejected here in 1662, and thereafter lived and laboured at Thorncombe. John Gill, ejected from Shute and Colyton settled at Hawkchurch and preached here till his death in 1688. Under the Declaration of Indulgence, 1672, Gill was licensed as a Presbyterian teacher, and his house as a Presbyterian meeting place. A further licence was

1 Jerom Murch, *History of the Presbyterian and General Baptist Churches in the West of England*. 1835. pp.239-48.
2 *Cod. Tenison*. 639.144.
3 *SPD.EB38A*. 198,256,285.
4 Murch, *op. cit.*

issued for "The howse of Thomas More Esqr in Hawk Church Dorsett Presbyterian Meeting place"[1] thus establishing another 'conventicle in a mansion', for More was the occupant of Wylde Court, one of the three manors of Hawkchurch.

Gill, among other worthies whose names appear in the *Ecclesiastica* and its notes, signed the *Address* of the Dorset ministers to Charles II, as under:

To the Kings most Excellent Majesty
The humble acknowledgement of severall Nonconforming Ministers of the County of Dorset.
Most Gracious Soveraigne

Wee your Majesties Loyall and peaceable subjects having to our abundant joy and satisfaction, seen your Majesties Royall Declaration of March the 15th, 1672, doe from our Soule bless God who hath put such a thinge as this into the Kings hearte to extend soe greate favour to us; ...which Encourageth us humbly to make this thankfull Address devoting our selves . . . to the preaching of the Gospell of peace and Salvation And continue to pray for your Royall person family Councill and Government, as Dutie obligeth us Your loyall Subjects and Ministers of the Gospell.

Wm Ben	*Ame Short*	*George Thorne*
John Gill	*Richard Downe*	*Josiah Banger*
John Brice	*Robert Bartlet*	*James Owsley*
John Kerridge	*Henry Backaller*	*Benjamin Mills*
John Hodder	....	(and 25 others)[2]

Honiton Francis Sourton/Soreton (1622-1689), was ejected from the rectory of Honiton in which he had been settled since 1648. "He was", says Calamy, "A man of great learning, a close student, and surprisingly humble. He was an excellent preacher; and his labours were successful to the good of many. His sermons were kept as a treasure in several hands in that town, and were sometimes repeated to the satisfaction of many. He had always such a reverent and awesome sense of God upon his soul, that it gave a majesty to his presence. When the rabble of the town were guilty of any rudeness, he would go and reprove them, and they would retire at the sight of him. Besides a monthly

[1] *SPD. Chas. II.* EB38A. 77,78.
[2] *SPD. Chas. II.* 321.77.

preparation sermon, he set up a weekly lecture in the town, and had the assistance of several ministers in it; which he continued till the act of uniformity ejected him. He then retired to the house of Sir William Courtenay of Powderham, whose aunt he married." In 1665 he was back at Honiton; the following year he was imprisoned at Exeter under the Five Mile Act, but was released and returned to Powderham where he made the translation (published in 1672) of Jean Daille's *Exposition of Colossians,* which, revised by James Sherman, was reissued in Nichol's Puritan Commentaries series in 1863, including the translator's dedication to Sir William Courtenay.[1]

Under the Declaration of Indulgence of 1672, Sourton returned to his flock at Honiton. His licence, which for some reason is undated and unsigned, lies still in the State Paper Office, and is, for its own interest and as a sample of such royal permissions, cited in full:

> *Charles by the Grace of God King of England, Scotland, France, and Ireland, Defender of the Faith &c.*
>
> *To all Mayors, Bailiffs, Constables, and other Our Officers and Ministers, Civil and Military whom it may concern, Greeting. In pursuance of our Declaration of ye 15 March, 167½. We doe hereby permit and license Francis Sourton of ye Presbyterian pswacon to be a Teacher of the Congregation allowed by Us in the Schole house at the Towne of Honiton in Our County of Devon for the Use of such as do not conform to the Church of England, who are of the Perswasion commonly called Presyterien. With further License and permission to him the said Francis Sourton to teach in ony other place licensed and allowed by Us, according to our said Declaration. Given at our Court at Whitehall, the .... day of .... in the 24th year of Our Reign, 1672.*
>
> *By His Majesties Command.*[2]

Sourton finally retired to Powderham where he ministered till his death in 1689, when a monument to his memory was erected in the parish church.

Before Sourton was ejected from Honiton in 1662, a native of the town, Samuel Hieron, grandson of a celebrated minister of the same name at Modbury, was ejected from Feniton. He returned to

1 Palmer, *Nonconformist's Memorial* II.41.
2 *SPD. Chas. II.* 320.270.

Honiton, "Oft disturbed", says Calamy, "and a great sufferer for Nonconformity. Once his house was violently broken open by the order of several justices, his goods were rifled, his plate and his very bed were taken from him; and they would have rifled his study had not his mother interposed, and produced her own plate to satisfy their demands. His goods were exposed for sale in the public market place, and he employed a friend to buy them. He was imprisoned upon the Five mile Act in Exeter gaol, with Mr. Soreton, but released . . . He was a very charitable man... His house was a common receptacle of poor ejected ministers and private Christians, who were forced from their homes by the rigour of the times." He was licensed to preach at the school house, as a Presbyterian teacher, in 1672, and continued there as assistant to Francis Sourton until 1685 when he was forced to leave the district, dying in London shortly afterwards. Like John Hodder of Thorncombe, Hieron was a man of some substance, and made bequests to numerous ejected ministers, including Mills of Chard, Backaller of Wootton Fitzpaine, and John Glanvil ejected from Taunton.[1]

Yet another ejected minister who appeared from time to time in Honiton was Richard Saunders, former rector of Loxbeare. The Episcopal Returns of 1665 mention him as keeping conventicles "sometimes lurking in Tiverton, sometymes in Loxbeare, & other places for like ends".[2] He was licensed as a Presbyterian teacher in 1672, and divided his time between Honiton and Tiverton until his death in 1694.[3] Preaching his funeral sermon, Robert Carel of Crediton, said of him:

> I who have known him about thirty years, never saw him angry; nor have I heard of any one that did. When he hath been highly provoked, he hath not been 'overcome of evil', but hath 'overcome evil with good'... His contentment with his daily bread was singular; and so was his love, his peaceableness and moderation. His humility was admirable. He had the art of giving a soft answer, so as not to exasperate. Few, if any, less degraded others, or less exalted himself in his discourses. He was . . . a Jonathan, amiable and pleasant. He was cheerful but not vain, serious but not sullen... He was a good polemical divine, and in a religious sense, a man of war from his youth, fighting the Lord's battles ... He had a body of divinity in his head, and the spirit and soul of that divinity in his heart. Tho' he was a great school divine, he

[1] Palmer, *Nonconformist's Memorial.* II.38,39.
[2] *Cod. Tenison.* 639.307b,402.
[3] *SPD. Chas. II.* EB38A.12.

rather chose to shoot at the people's hearts, in plain, practical, though very rational divinity, than shoot over their heads in high seraphic notions. His style was clear and strong, flowing from a full soul. He was an Ezra, a ready and eminently instructed scribe in the law of God: clear and solid in resolving cases of conscience: in all things 'a workman that needed not to be ashamed.' And the Lord crowned his labours with success."[1]

Ralph Spragg (or Sprake), a godly minister who had already been imprisoned in Dorset for conventicling, was in 1672 granted a licence to preach as a Presbyterian in the vicinity of Honiton.

Baptists had an assembly in Honiton, its origins going back to the Kilmington-Dalwood-Loughwood church of the Commonwealth. In 1655 Henry Jessey, a Baptist of note, later ejected from the lectureship of St. George's, Southwark, was invited "by the saints of Bristol, (i.e. churches comprising persons baptized on profession of faith) to assist them in regulating their congregations." He visited Baptist congregations in Bristol, Chard, Taunton, Honiton, Exeter, Lyme Regis, and Weymouth, among others.[2] The influence of Thomas Collier (*fl* 1645-65), Particular Baptist apostle of the west was felt in the Honiton area. As early as 1649 he had written "General Epistles" to the Baptist Churches, and these, or possibly his *Certain Queries, or Points now in Controversy Examined* (1645), called forth from the Honiton Presbyterian, Richard Saunders, *A Balm to Heal Religious Wounds, in answer to Collier*.[3] By the Declaration of Indulgence 1672 the Honiton Baptists engaged James Innes Jun, impartial licence-agent for Presbyterians, Independents, and Baptists alike, to apply for licences for two houses for their worship:

> The howse of Samuel Serle of Honiton licensed for an Anabaptist meeting place. 1 May 72.
>
> Peter Coles howse in Honiton, Devon. Anabapt. Place. 2 May 72.[4]

The only trace of Independents in Honiton at this period is the presence of their names on the Axminster Church Roll.

1 Palmer, *Nonconformist's Memorial*. II.45-48.

2 *The Life and Death of Mr. Henry Jessey*. 1671. p.84. See also, *Association Records of the Particular Baptists . . . to 1660*. Ed. B. R. White. Pt. 2 The West Country (1973).

3 B. Brook, *Lives of the Puritans, III.27-30*. W. L. Lumpkin, *Baptist Confessions of Faith*. 200-04.

4 *SPD. Chas. II*. 320.295.

Ilminster James Strong was ejected from the vicarage, and William Alsop from the curacy of Ilminster. Tradition has it that an ejected minister conducted services in the town. This may, or may not have been Alsop who, by 1669, was ministering to large numbers at conventicles at West Monkton, Winsham, and Ashills. There was also a Quaker conventicle of some 220 adherents at this date.[1]

In the record of licences issued under the Declaration of Indulgence, 1672, these entries appear:—

The house of Thomas Marshall in the parish of Ilminster, Somersett, Presbyterian meeting place. 8 May.

Licence to Thomas Marshall to be a Presbyterian teacher in his house in the parish and town of Ilminster, Somerset. 8 May.

The howse of Joseph Holmes at Broadlanes end in the Parish and Town of Ilminster, Somerset. Presbyterian meeting place. 8 May.[2]

Those who held to Independent principles in Ilminster at this period apparently chose between the Axminster and the Taunton Churches.

Kilmington Ecclesiastically, Kilmington was a curacy of Axminster, and so fell under the parochial care of Cresson, Ashwood, and Crabb in succession. It had a Baptist congregation founded in the Commonwealth, but which removed to Loughwood under persecution following the Restoration. From this church, the Baptist congregations at Colyton, Honiton and Lyme Regis, among others, were pioneered.[3] John Salaway, ejected vicar of Whitchurch Canonicorum, is said by Calamy to have been "afterwards minister of Kilmington, in Devonshire".[4] He was buried at Shute. As his Puritan successor at Whitchurch (John Brice) was Presbyterian, it may be presumed that Salaway continued this tradition at Kilmington. Independents were thus left to resort to Axminster, their nearest assembly.

1 *Cod. Tenison.* 639.143-5.
2 *SPD.EB38A.86.*
3 See also, *Association Records of the Particular Baptists ... to 1660.* Ed. B. R. White. Pt. 2 The West Country (1973).
4 Palmer, *Nonconformist's Memorial.* II.164.

Lyme Regis Ejected here in 1662 was Ames Short (1617-97), ordained by presbyters in London and appointed to Lyme in 1650, when, although a Presbyterian, he drew up a covenant for a 'gathered' church. After ejection he "discharged his duty to his people in private . . . and was many ways a sufferer for Nonconformity" being constantly hounded, and imprisoned several times. In the Episcopal Returns of 1669, Anthony Sparrow Bishop of Exeter, complained of Short's "excursions into several parts" of his diocese—which would include Colyton; while Seth Ward, now Bishop of Salisbury reported, "Lime Regis. Several conventicles, 200 or 300 people. Teacher, Mr. Amy Short."[1] In 1672 he was licensed to preach at his own house at Lyme Regis.[2]

John Kerridge, Master of Lyme Regis School, was also ejected in 1662. He afterwards ministered at Colyton, and elsewhere, receiving licence as a Presbyterian preacher in 1672.[3]

"Mr. Short", says Calamy, "outlived his troubles; and after liberty was granted to Dissenters, he had a public meeting in Lyme, in which, Aug. 25, 1687, eight candidates for the ministry were ordained. He continued to bring forth fruit in old age."[4]

Nevertheless, a few persons from Lyme Regis were members at Axminster.

Membury Like Kilmington, Membury was a part of Axminster parish, and was served in turn by Cresson, Ashwood, and Crabb, as successive vicars. In 1672 it had a Presbyterian congregation meeting in the house of "Mr. John Webber commonly called Thorp", for which James Innes Jun, sought a licence which was granted on May 8, 1672.[5] Presbyterians in the village being thus catered for, the Independents turned to Axminster.

Shute John Salaway, later ejected from Whitchurch Canonicorum, was curate here 1640-45, and was buried here in 1672. Shute parish was dependent on Colyton, so Salaway would have some contact with his contemporary Thomas Manton. John Gill, appointed in 1656 was ejected in 1662. "After his ejectment he

1 *Cod. Tenison.* 639.247b.
2 *SPD.EB38A*. 18.
3 *SPD.EB38A*. 78.
4 Palmer, *Nonconformist's Memorial.* II.136,8.
5 *SPD. Chas. II.* EB38A.77.

continued a humble, pious preacher among the Dissenters till his death which was about the year 1688".[1] Shute's Independents gathered at Axminster and its Baptists at Dalwood; so we may presume its Presbyterians worshipped at nearby Kilmington with John Salaway. Thomas Lane, the venerable elder at Axminster, along with other members of his family, appears to have resided at Shute.

Old Shute House

Stockland I can find little concerning Nonconformity in Stockland. There was no ejectment; the episcopal returns are silent; no licences were issued under the Declaration of Indulgence. But there were Baptists who gathered with the Dalwood Church, and Independents who gathered at Axminster.

Taunton There was a puritan church in Taunton known as Paul's Meeting, whose Covenant was drawn up and signed in 1654, though whether it was Presbyterian or Independent is in dispute.[2] In 1662 both the vicar of St. Mary Magdalene's and his assistant were ejected for nonconformity. The vicar was George Newton (1601-81), and the curate was the saintly Joseph Alleine (1634-68). Also ejected were the curate of St. James's, John Glanvil, and the chaplain of nearby Hill Bishops, Nathaniel Charlton. Both Newton and Alleine had studied at Oxford;

1 Palmer. *Nonconformist's Memorial,* II.69.
2 C. E. Surman. *Congregational Historical Society Transactions.* XX. 139.43.

Newton signed the Somerset *Attestation* in 1648, while Alleine was ordained by a Somerset Presbyterian Classis in 1655. All these ministers continued their work, in public when possible and in private when necessary. On the spirit of this Taunton circle the following concerning the oustanding character of Alleine must suffice.

Following the Five Mile Act and the Oxford Oath:

> Some of the ministers were more determined than ever to preach openly. Joseph Alleine of Taunton, was a man of this undaunted spirit. Like Paul and Silas, he sang praises to God in prison, and when out of prison prepared to return to bonds if it should be the will of God. On the passing of the Five Mile Act he removed to Wellington, a short distance beyond the prescribed limits, and there appointed for his friends a service of thanksgiving. 'Methinks', he said in his address, 'there are several periods of time, since the time of our calamities, wherein God hath appeared to us when we thought all had been gone. One period was when your ministers were shut out of public by the Act of Conformity. Another, when we were cast out of our private meetings by the Act made against seditious conventicles, so called by the iniquity of the times. Another by this Act that doth now cast ministers out of their habitations. And, methinks, every period should end with praise . . . What! though God hath separated your preachers from you, yet as He said, if the soldier dies fighting, and the preacher preaching, and the swan singing, then the saints should part praising. O! Christians, this is the spirit that should be in you, that whatever God doth with you for the time to come, you should resolve to end in His praise for the mercies past. If it were the last day we should have together, surely, methinks, we should end in praise.'[1]

Alleine's godly life, amazingly laborious preaching and pastoral ministry, together with his numerous publications, have made both before and since his death, a considerable impression. His *A Call to Archippus* (1664) urged ejected ministers to continue in their ministerial calling at a time when some, as the *Ecclesiastica* notes, 'had been silent to the people, like men in their graves' (p.19). His *An Alarm to the Unconverted* (1671) is "a book for which multitudes will have cause for ever to be thankful",[2] it sold a

1 1660-1672: *Black Bartholomew and the Twelve Years' Conflict.* By the Author of *Historical Papers.* 1862. pp.29-30.

2 Calamy. (Palmer, *Nonconformist's Memorial,* III.211).

hundred thousand copies before the end of the eighteenth century, and is still in print. At his death in 1668, George Newton preached, and Alleine was buried in the chancel of the church whence he had been ejected, his tomb being marked:

Here Mr. Joseph Alleine lies,
To God and you a Sacrifice. ('you' being Taunton).[1]

The 1669 Episcopal Returns sent in by William Piers, Bishop of Bath and Wells, reported, "Taunton Magdalen. At the houses of Mr. John Ford, — Bird, Mr. — Gill. 230" hearers. The preachers were six ejected ministers and three others. There was George Newton himself; Timothy Batt from Riston, John Galpin of Ashpriors, George Bindon of Wilton, Emmanuel Harford from Upton Noble, and Nathaniel Charlton of Hill Bishops. John Anderton, Jasper Batt, and Thomas Mercer made up the full complement. In Taunton St. James's parish a further conventicle of 120 hearers was reported, having the ministrations of John Glanvill himself, Lawrence Musgrove ejected at Angelsley, and John Musgrove whose place of ejection is uncertain.[2]

Under the Declaration of Indulgence 1672, applications for licences for seven houses to be used for meeting places were allowed, though a petition signed by ten inhabitants for the use of the Town Hall and the Church House for George Newton was refused.[3] (See note relating to public buildings under Chard). All licences were 'Presbyterian'.

Taunton had an assembly of Baptists at least as early as 1646 when, on April 20th Thomas Collier addressed a letter "To the Saints in the order and fellowship of the gospel at Taunton." Thomas Mercer was pastor in 1655. Henry Jessey had visited them the previous year; and in 1682 the pastor was Thomas Winnell who attended the assembly of Particular Baptists in London in 1689 and signed its *Confession of Faith*.[4]

There must have been substantial reasons why even a few Taunton inhabitants joined the Axminster Church, though some were later dismissed to a church in their own town.

1 On both Newton and Alleine, see Palmer, *Nonconformist's Memorial.* III. 205-12. On Alleine, see, Chas. Stanford, *Joseph Alleine: His Companions and Times, 1861;* Elizabeth Braund, *By Schisms Rent Asunder,* 1969, pp.43-68.

2 *Cod. Tenison.* 639.143,143b.

3 *SPD. Chas. II.* 320.292.

4 See, *Association Records of the Particular Baptists . . . to 1660.* Ed. B. R. White. Pt. 2 The West Country (1973).

Thorncombe There was no ejectment at Thorncombe, the vicar William Bragge, holding the living from 1648 to his death in 1680, and proving no friend to the ejected ministers who found refuge in his parish. In the west country fugitive ejected ministers tended to gravitate together in groups. Thus Ottery St. Mary had a colony of four by 1665, Honiton had three, Chard had five, Dartmouth three, while Exeter had eight in addition to the seven who were ejected within its own bounds; and in the little village of Thorncombe no less than four were gathered together. In the Episcopal Returns of 1665 Seth Ward, with the careful assistance of William Bragge, reported—

> Mr. John Hodder, sometymes minister of Hawchurch in Dorsett, now liveing in Thorncombe on his own demeasne.
>
> Mr. Branker sometymes minister of Sturminster Newton, Dorset teaching schoole in Thorncombe.
>
> Mr. Wakely sometimes minister of Laurence Lydiat in Somersett, now living in Thorncombe on his own demeasnes.
>
> Mr. Trottle sometymes minister in Dorset (Spetsbury) now liveing in Thorncombe.[1]

John Wakely, son of Nicholas Wakely of Thorncombe, had returned to his native place because he had property there on which to live. Hodder likewise had a roof for his head at Thorncombe. Thomas Branker (or Brounker) was married to Wakely's sister and found hospitality with his brother in law; while John Trottle had a daughter and son in law living at Thorncombe. Thus they found refuge.

Four years later the Episcopal Returns of 1669 reported;

> Thorncombe. 3 Conventicles. Att ye houses of Edmund Prideaux Esqr. Presbyterians. About 100 oftentime more. Vulgar sort. Heads and Teachers, Mr. Wakely and Mr. Hodder.[2]

Ford Abbey, Prideaux's residence, was in Thorncombe parish.

In 1672, under the Declaration of Indulgence, Hodder received licence as Presbyterian teacher in his own house, and similarly Wakely in his.[3] Both had signed the *Address* of the Devon ministers along with Bartholomew Ashwood and others. (p.39f). Of Hodder Calamy tells us, "He was a man of excellent abilities and

1 *Cod. Tenison*. 639.402b.
2 *Cod. Tenison*. 639.185b.
3 *SPD. Chas. II*. EB38A. 78,173.

a celebrated preacher. He was so much of a gentleman, and of such singular ingenuity, that his very enemies admired him, and were fond of his conversation. He was also a great Loyalist, as appears from a long epistle of his prefixed to a sermon of Mr. Ames Short at Lyme Regis on the proclamation of K. Charles II."[1] At his death in 1679 he made bequests to several ejected ministers, including William Samson at Chard, John Gill at Hawkchurch, John Kerridge and Henry Backaller at Wootton Fitzpaine, and Benjamin Mills at Chard. Of Wakely, we learn that in 1669 he was preaching not only at Thorncombe, but at conventicles in his old parish of Lydiard St. Lawrence. In 1673 he was presented by the churchwardens of Thorncombe for absence from church, for which he was excommunicated in March 1674. He died in 1678.

Thorncombe's Presbyterian Nonconformity explains why those of Independent sympathies, including, significantly, Joan Wakely, repaired to Axminster.

Whitchurch Canonicorum John Salaway, vicar from 1645 was ejected in 1660 when the sequestered vicar was restored. In 1672, under the Declaration of Indulgence, licence was issued to "John Brice to be a Presbyterian teacher in the house of Eleanor Floyer in White Church, Dorset." Eleanor Floyer's house, Berne, was also licensed, as was "the house of Hen: Pitfeild of Whitchurch in Dorsetshire, Presbyterian".[2] Brice had been assistant to George Thorn at Weymouth; then rector of West Chickerell whence he was ejected 1662. Imprisoned twice in Dorchester for conventicling 1663-65, he became chaplain to Anthony Floyer of Whitchurch (d.1672), and subsequently to his widow (d.1674).[3] Stephen Card a lone Independent from Whitchurch is found among the members at Axminster.

Winsham The origins of Nonconformity in Winsham are connected with the ministry of William Ball (1632-1670) who was vicar from 1653, and ejected for Nonconformity in 1662. He was an Oxford graduate and had been ordained by elders in a Presbyterian Classis in London in 1647.

[1] Palmer, *Nonconformist's Memorial.* II.130.
[2] *SPD. Chas. II.* 38A.177,273.
[3] A. G. Matthews, *Calamy Revised.* p.72.

In the Episcopal Returns of 1669 conventicles were reported in Winsham "at the houses of Henry Henly Esqr. and John Bennett." Henly was of the influential family of that name of Leigh House, who, like his neighbour Edmund Prideaux Esq. of Ford Abbey but a mile away, was host to a conventicle in a mansion. Perhaps for this reason the episcopal sleuths did their work more thoroughly, for they were able to report that no less than nine ejected ministers were engaged from time to time in ministry here. The nine were headed by William Ball; then came Ames Short ejected from Lyme Regis, Richard Farrant from Musbury, Henry Stubbs from Dursley, John Turner from North Cricket, John Langdale from Cricket St. Thomas, Henry Backaller from Combe St. Nicholas, John Galpin from Ashpriors, and William Alsop ejected from Ilminster.[1]

Winsham Parish Church

Under the Declaration of Indulgence, 1672, the houses of William Wheadon and Robert Baker were licensed as Presbyterian meeting houses. Also issued under the same device was a "Licence to Josiah Banger to be a Presbyterian teacher in the howse of

[1] *Cod. Tenison.* 639.144.

William Wheadon at Whotley in the parish of Winsham, Somerset, 22 May." Banger was the ejected vicar of Broadhembury.[1]

As all the above named ministers were Presbyterian, and the houses concerned were licensed for Presbyterian worship, Pulman's statment that "Mr. Ball founded an Independent Congregation at Winsham"[2] is incorrect if by it is meant Congregational Independent as understood at this time. The Winsham Nonconformist assembly was Presbyterian from its inception in 1662, becoming Independent perhaps about 1687. This throws a little light on why some eight souls from Winsham were members of the Independent Church of Axminster, and why in a particularly dangerous situation in 1683 one Joseph Harvey of Winsham offered the Axminster Church hospitality. (See pp.85, 86).

Wootton Fitzpaine John Kerridge (b.1609) was rector here from 1650, and was ejected for Nonconformity in 1662. He had graduated at Oxford and was previously vicar of Abbotsbury. He was father of John Kerridge (d.1705) ejected from the mastership of Lyme School, and who later ministered at Colyton. He may also be presumed to be father of Sarah Kerridge whose house at Wootton Fitzpaine was licensed as a Presbyterian meeting place, 8 May 1672.[3]

Henry Backaller, assistant to Benjamin Woodbridge at Newbury and ejected along with him in 1662 (not to be confused with his name-sake at Combe St. Nicholas), was licensed under the Declaration of Indulgence "to be a presbyterian teacher in the howse of Sarah Keridg in Wotton Fitzpaine, Dorset, 8 May 1672".[4] He was still ministering there in 1685 when Samuel Hieron, ejected from Feniton and a man of some wealth, left legacies to him and to other ejected ministers.

James Ousley, son of the ejected minister of Littleham and Exmouth, entered the ministry and was licensed to preach in his own house as a Presbyterian meeting place, 8 May 1672.[5]

The Nonconforming interest being Presbyterian, Axminster proved to be the resort of the Independents, even of one Richard Owsley.

1 *SPD. Chas. II.* EB38A.133, 172.
2 *Book of the Axe,* 1875. p.380.
3 *SPD. Chas. II.* 320.227.
4 *SPD. Chas. II.* 320.227.
5 *SPD. Chas. II.* EB38A.77.

This exhausts the list of places named in the Axminster roll. It may not escape our notice however that in two other places within five miles, but not named, there were similar situations to those outlined above. At Bettiscombe, Isaac Clifford was ejected in 1661; and at Uplyme, Thomas Godwin shared the same suffering.

The Baptists of Dalwood were also a feature of the overall scene in the Axminster circle. The church was formed at Kilmington as early as 1650, when a record states that five elders and five deacons were appointed. John Pendarves was desired to be their pastor and there were 219 members living at Honiton, Ottery, Colyton, Kilmington, Axminster, Dalwood, and Stockland. In its records for 1653 are given "the names of the members of the Church of Christ at Dalwood, usually assembling at Loughwood, Dorsetshire" (as it then was). This membership roll is strangely parallel to that of the *Ecclesiastica,* including as it does, 15 names from Colyton, 22 from Shute and Dalwood, 14 from Honiton, 32 from other hamlets near, and 17 from Axminster. In 1654 the meeting house at Loughwood was finished and opened, and by 1669 George Allome was chosen pastor. This church was helped considerably in its earlier years by the Baptists at Plymouth under Abraham Cheare who, while a fellow-prisoner of Bartholomew Ashwood in Exeter gaol, had written to William Punchard in London, under date "17th of the seventh month, 1662, . . . they at Dalwood have a very large and increasing meeting, where the Lord is present as a covert to them." Other preachers at Dalwood were James Murch, Thomas Payne, and James Hitt. Both Murch and Hitt came from Plymouth. Hitt and Payne attended the general assembly of Particular Baptists in London in 1689, Hitt being one of the signatories of the *Confession of Faith* issued by that assembly. By 1692 Payne was the stated minister at Dalwood. It is evident that there were the closest links between the Baptists of Dalwood and those of Honiton, and also with the Luppit Baptists who, in 1665, built a meeting house at Newhouse in the parish of Upottery. Both the Loughwood and the Newhouse chapels still exist, the former being in occasional, the latter in regular use.[1]

[1] See, W. T. Whitley, *Baptist Historical Society Transactions,* IV. 129-44. Ivimey, *History of the English Baptists,* I.505; II.105-07, 139-41, 153. H. M. Gunn, *History of Free Churches in Chard and the Neighbourhood.* 1867. p.23. R. W. Oliver, *The Strict Baptist Chapels of England,* 1968. V.119-20. *Association Records of the Particular Baptists . . . to 1660.* Ed. B. R. White. Pt. 2 The West Country (1973).

This survey has turned out to be largely the story of what happened to the ejected ministers of 1662 in this particular area, and of the assemblies, congregations and churches, all officially denounced as 'seditious conventicles', to which they ministered. The Axminster circle was in fact a microcosm of the English nation; it was a nation's tragedy, yet a tragedy not without its triumphs. For Black Bartholomew's Day 1662 as it was long afterwards known among the Dissenters marked a watershed in English religious history. The Axminster circle, by no means replete with great names and oft-repeated heroisms, has its place nevertheless within the overall picture, concerning which John Richard Green was moved to say:

> Nearly two thousand rectors and vicars, or about a fifth of the English clergy were driven from their parishes as Nonconformists[1] . . . the change wrought by St. Bartholomew's day was a distinctly religious change, and it was a change which in its suddenness and completeness stood utterly alone. The rectors and vicars who were driven out were the most learned and the most active of their order . . . They stood at the head of the London clergy . . . They occupied the higher posts at the two Universities . . . men whose zeal and labour had diffused throughout the country a greater appearance of piety and religion than it had ever displayed before. But the expulsion of these men was far more to the Church of England than the loss of their individual services . . . It was the close of an effort which had been going on ever since Elizabeth's accession to bring the English Communion into closer relations with the Reformed Communions of the Continent.[2]

Yet another assessment in the perspective of history may be pondered:

> All hope of unity was blasted by this second most disastrous, most tyrannical, and most schismatical Act of Uniformity; the authors of which, it is plain, were seeking not unity but division. But this strait waistcoat for men's

1 The figure of 2,000 includes the ejectments of 1660 as well as those of 1662 throughout England and Wales. It is approximate, and perhaps as many as 200 in excess. That there were more ejectments in Devon than in any other County, 40 in 1660 and 73 in 1662, reflects both the quality and the numerical strength of Puritanism in the West country.

2 J. R. Green, *History of the English People*. Ed. 1921. p.622-3.

consciences could scarcely have been devised, except by persons of seared consciences and hard hearts, ready to gulp down any oath without scruple about more or less. How grievous was the wound to the Church at the time! How grievous it is still at this day, in its enduring effects! Two thousand ministers, comprising the chief part of the most faithful and zealous in the land, were silenced in one day. Moreover after we had cast out so much faith and zeal and holiness, we had, in this manner, almost cast out the doctrine of Christ crucified from the pale of our Church. The church that does so exclude them, maims herself, by forfeiting the services of numbers who would have served her faithfully; and while the Act of Uniformity thus cast out many of the best fish from the net, all the bad, all the careless, all the unprincipled may abide in it unmolested. The age which enacted this rigid uniformity was addicted to the uniformalizing of all things. It could not bear the free growth of nature—yet even trees, if they have any life, disregard the Act of Uniformity, and branch forth according to their kinds, and none submit quietly except the dead.[1]

Nor were these the only consequences of the Great Ejection.

If it be presumptuous to fix upon particular occurrences as proofs of God's displeasure, yet none will deny that a long, unbroken course of disasters indicates but too surely, whether to a nation or a church, that His favour is withdrawn. Within five years of the ejection of the two thousand Nonconformists, London was twice laid waste, first by pestilence and then by fire . . . But other calamities ensued, more lasting and far more terrible. Religion in the Church of England was almost extinguished and in many of her parishes the lamp of God went out.[2]

And what sort of men as a body were they to whom the men of the Axminster circle belonged? Writing in 1774, Samuel Palmer could say:

They had the best education England could afford; most of them were excellent scholars, judicious divines, pious, faithful, and laborious ministers; of great zeal for God and religion;

[1] Julius Charles Hare (Archdeacon of Lewes). Preface to a Visitation Sermon on the *Unity of the Church.* 1845.

[2] J. B. Marsden, *History of the Later Puritans.* 1852. pp.469-70.

undaunted and courageous in their master's work; keeping close to their people in the worst of times; diligent in their studies; solid, affectionate, powerful, lively, awakening preachers; aiming at the advancement of real, vital religion in the hearts and lives of men, which, it cannot be denied, flourished greatly wherever they could influence. Particularly they were men of great devotion and eminent abilities in prayer, uttered, as God enabled them, from the abundance of their hearts and affections; men of divine eloquence in pleading at the throne of grace; raising and melting the affections of their hearers, and being happily instrumental in transfusing into their souls the same spirit and heavenly gift. And this was the ground of all their other qualifications; they were excellent men, because excellent, instant, and fervent in prayer.[1]

[1] Samuel Palmer. *The Nonconformist's Memorial.* Preface, I.v.

APPENDIX E

The Towgood Family

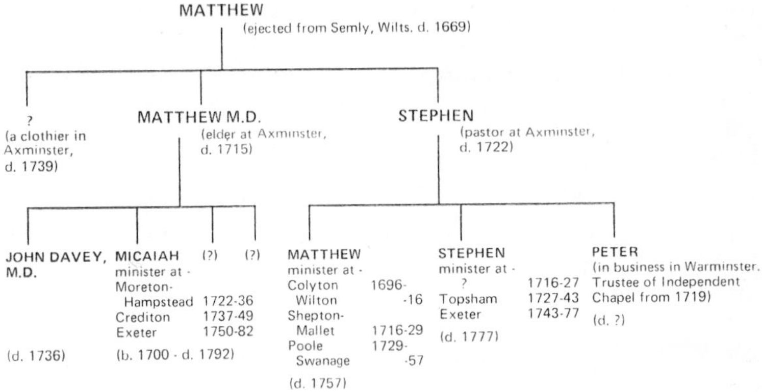

For two reasons, some elucidation of the Towgood family in the period of the *Ecclesiastica* and the years immediately following is desirable. The first is the repetition of the christian names Matthew and Stephen; and the second is the fact that each of these names is found in both the doctrinally orthodox, and in the doctrinally unorthodox circles of the time. These factors have led to unending confusion in all the relevant literature.

The above diagram, limited to the male line, indicates the three generations involved. Scores of sources have been considered in its compilation, and four which are considered of sufficient authority, and which are mutually complementary, are the basis for the above.

(i). The *Ecclesiastica* itself identifies Stephen as the pastor, and Matthew the physician as the Elder, at Axminster.

(ii). Calamy/Palmer, with the concurrence of A. G. Matthews in *Calamy Revised,* provides the basic statement concerning Matthew Towgood ejected from Semly, as follows: "Before he entered on the ministry he was master of a school at Shaftsbury, and educated two of his own sons, who were both of them of considerable learning, the one a minister, the other a physician . . . He was some time minister of Hilperton, but was not . . . ejected from thence, having removed to Semly some time before the Uniformity act took place. After his ejectment he taught school, and preached privately in his own house at Semly about seven years . . . Two of his grandsons were dissenting ministers at Exeter. The one is Mr. Michaiah Towgood, son of the physician, well known in the world by his excellent writings in favour of religious liberty . . . The other, Mr. Stephen Towgood, colleague with him, whose father was a minister."[1]

(iii). Henry Mayo Gunn, (1867): "Stephen Towgood (of Axminster) was the eldest son of the ejected clergyman of Semly . . . He (Stephen of Axminster) left three sons and three daughters . . . the eldest Matthew . . . the second Stephen . . . The third son went to Warminster in business and his family were trustees of the Independent Church in that town from 1719-1800. . . . Dr. Towgood (Matthew, of Axminster) had four sons and two daughters. He died in 1715 . . . his second son was Micaiah Towgood of Exeter."[2]

(iv). In the copy of the *Axminster Ecclesiastica* (1874) in Dr. Williams's Library, there is on p.vii a roughly scribbled pedigree of the Towgood family in an unidentified hand. The writing is as old as the book itself, which, in the opinion of the deputy librarian, Mr. John Creasey, could have come from a member of the Towgood family, three generations of which were trustees of Dr. Williams's Charity.

On the complementary concurrence of these four sources I have to reject the testimony of James Manning, who names the father of Michaiah Towgood of Exeter as "Michaiah Towgood M.D.", crediting him (the father) as "the author of several publications on practical divinity, and particularly an '*Essay for the Reformation of*

[1] Palmer, *Nonconformist's Memorial,* III.374-5; A. G. Matthews, *Calamy Revised,* 489.

[2] H. M. Gunn, *History of Free Churches in Chard and the Neighbourhood.* 1867. pp.20,21.

Manners' ".[1] This attribution of authorship is not verifiable from the British Museum General Catalogue, nor from the Catalogues of Dr. Williams's and the Congregational Libraries; nor from the standard bibliographies of Allibone, Darling, Lowndes, or Watt; nor is the matter resolved from the several titles published between 1732 and 1745 by Matthew Towgood of Shepton Mallet and Poole (d.1757). A. Gordon copied Manning's error in *D.N.B.*[2] as had others before him.[3]

The above has some bearing on the authorship of the *Ecclesiastica,* and also on the orthodoxy of two of its leading figures—Stephen Towgood the pastor, and Matthew Towgood M.D., the elder. Further reference to the Towgood family is to be found on pp.72, 169.

1 James Manning. *Sketch of the Life and Writings of Revd. Micaiah Towgood*. Exeter, 1792. p.5.

2 *Dictionary of National Biography*. LVII.94 (1899; s.v. Towgood, Michaiah).

3 e.g. Lysons, Daniel & Samuel. *Magna Britannia*. VI. pt.2. (1822).

APPENDIX F

The Story of the *Axminster Ecclesiastica*

The origin of the *Axminster Ecclesiastica* lay in a decision of the Axminster Independent Church on 26 October 1687. Six months after James II had issued his Declaration of Indulgence and a small measure of toleration began to appear, the Church took opportunity to put various matters in order. "It was agreed by the church that this Book of Remembrance should be procured, in which the most material matters . . . should be recorded and kept for those that may succeed in after times." (p.128f). This was twenty seven years after the formation of the church, eight years after the death of the first pastor, and only eleven years before the record itself terminates.

The record is anonymous and would seem to be the work of a compiler, or compilers. The earliest published attribution is that of H. M. Gunn (1867), who regards it as "records kept by him (Ashwood) and his worthy and able successor."[1] Next comes the judgment of the un-named editor of the first published edition of the *Ecclesiastica* in 1874, who says of Matthew Towgood M.D. (d.1715), that he "rendered double service in his brother's church, as deacon, and probably as annalist."[2] The said Matthew M.D., however, was never a deacon, and was appointed elder only in 1693, seven years after the decision of 1687 and five years before the record ends. There is in the copy of the 1874 edition in Dr. Williams's Library, London, a MS genealogy of the Towgood family in a hand probably as old as the book itself, and against the name of "Matthew, M.D.", a note says, "sembles the author of this book",[3] but robs itself of independent authority by a further note referring to the editor's attribution quoted above. This is also the qualified attribution of the Dr. Williams's Library Catalogue.

Edward Miall held the opinion, in 1874, that Stephen Towgood, the pastor, was the author;[4] and a slight variation of this is the

1 *Free Churches in Chard and the Neighbourhood.* p.7.
2 *Axminster Ecclesiastica* (1874), p.vi.
3 p.vii.
4 *The Nonconformist.* vol.35, p.943. (Sept. 30, 1874).

attribution of the *Catalogue of the Congregational Library* (II.495, 1910), which credits the *Ecclesiastica* to "Towgood, Stephen, M.D.", thus confusing the pastor with the "beloved physician", his brother. Stephen Towgood settled at Axminster in 1679; Matthew, his younger brother at an unknown subsequent date before 1687. Though it may be natural enough to regard either the pastor or his educated brother as annalist, the argument is no more than presumptive either way; nor is it a simple choice between the two. The pastor would hardly have written the account of his call and settlement at Axminster in the terms presented in Ch.9; nor would other highly favourable passages flow naturally from his own pen, though Matthew could have recorded these on information supplied.

The officers of longest standing in the church in 1687 were Thomas Lane appointed ruling elder in 1662 and still in office at his death in 1693, and Robert Bryant appointed deacon in 1663, raised to the eldership in 1693 and presumably still in office when the record ends in 1698. Both were members from a very early date, although the only foundation member to survive the whole period, according to the members roll, was John Brewer, who died in 1700. We may not overlook the fact that Bartholomew Ashwood, with at least two substantial published works to his credit was a literary man. We might expect him to leave records, either in his own hand, or in that of the "brother who used to write for him." (p.43). This latter was John Smith senior, of Chard, the amanuensis who penned Ashwood's *Epistle to the Church* during his illness at Chard in 1672 (p.43-49), and who recorded his dying sayings, also at Chard, in 1678 (p.61f). Smith was thus a member in possession of Ashwood's fullest confidence some time prior to 1672, and was still a member at his own death in 1706. If either, or both Towgoods compiled the *Ecclesiastica* they were heavily dependent on Lane, Smith, and Bryant, to say the least, for these three between them represented at first hand the total period of the record. On the other hand the literary style of the work is generally consistent; it does not present an appearance of unevenness. The matter of authorship has to be left unresolved, but with the feeling that there is as strong a case for the joint compilership of Lane, Smith and Bryant, as for any other. Whoever has the credit, has also responsibility for the studied anonymity with which the failure to report the results of the conference of 1694 is recorded; though Lane died the previous year, both Towgoods and Bryant must have been present on that occasion (p.151f).

So far as can now be traced the manuscript *Ecclesiastica* disappeared for about a century. James Small, pastor at Axminster 1785-1834, wrote on August 21 1826, to James Davidson, the Devon antiquary who had obviously made some enquiry, "I have sent you a few things extracted from the Church Records," and follows with the barest outline of the church's origin and early history taken from the MS *Ecclesiastica.*[1] In 1834, Davidson, who was then gathering material for a history of Axminster, was allowed to see the MS itself. From it he copied five foolscap sheets headed: "Notes and extracts from a MS. volume in the possession of the Trustees of the Independent Meeting-house at Axminster ~~lent me~~ shown to me by Mr. Whitty, at his house in 1834."[2] The longest extracts are those concerning the Monmouth Rebellion and the Revolution, and comparison shows that all his extracts and the published *Ecclesiastica* of 1874 are from the same source.[3]

The man who brought the existence of the MS *Ecclesiastica* to general notice in the locality was G. P. R. Pulman (1819-80) in his *The Book of the Axe,* a fisherman's description of the general topography and history of the places on the banks of the river Axe. Published in serial parts, there were four editions—1841, 1844, 1853, and 1875, the fourth and last being rewritten and containing "nearly four times as much matter as the third edition." Suffice it to say at this point that the edition of 1853 refers to "a contemporary manuscript preserved in the Axminster Independent Chapel", and that in his coverage of the parish of Axminster, Pulman prints some eleven pages of extracts from the *Ecclesiastica,* interest centering in the national events which it records.[4]

In an Editorial Introductory Note, the un-named editor of the 1874 edition of the *Ecclesiastica,* says of the manuscript volume:

> Twelve years ago, indeed, the file was nibbled to its very through and through by a partizan class of casuists, who disputed whether the Ejected Clergy of 1662 as a body were entitled to the rank ascribed to them—whether they were not rather intruders rightfully dispossessed than heroes entitled

1 James Davidson, *MSS Collections for Axminster.* (East Devon Record Office, Exeter) pp.875-6.

2 James Davidson, *MSS Collections for Axminster.* (East Devon Record Office, Exeter) pp.868-73.

3 In his *Bibliotheca Devoniensis,* 1852, Davidson mistakenly says of John Ashwood, "Mr. Ashwood was vicar of Axminster." (p.135).

4 G. P. R. Pulman, *The Book of the Axe.* Ed.3, 1853. pp.336-50; 362,3.

> to be crowned; but by this time the verdict of the age has been pretty well restored to its former *not* partizan conclusion—namely, that the distinctive nobility of the day were the victims of politico-ecclesiastical stratagem, and the true ignobles in the main were they who contrived to circumvent them.[1]

It is easy enough to see that twelve years before 1874 has some reference to the bicentenary of the ejectment of 1662, which was then celebrated in various parts of the country. Matters were initiated by the Central United Bartholomew Committee in London, representing all the English Free Churches. Its principal literary monument to the occasion was a fat volume of *Documents relating to the settlement of the Church of England by the Act of Uniformity of 1662,* edited by George Gould, to which was prefixed a substantial introductory essay on *English Puritanism* by Peter Bayne. (London, 1862). There was also a series of eleven tracts on subjects such as The Book of Sports, The Savoy Conference, The Act of Uniformity, The Farewell Sunday, etc., etc. by writers including Thomas M'Crie, Peter Bayne, Robert Halley, and Peter Lorimer. The Committee had explicitly stated in advance that they "are unanimous in their resolution that in their collection of historical facts bearing upon the Ejection of the Two Thousand, and in their presentation of them, in whatever form, to public notice, the most rigid impartiality shall be observed. Implicit deference to truth they recognize as the most important moral of the event to be commemorated . . ." By the time the last of a series of public lectures was held in London however, a general furore had broken out both in the religious and general press from anti-Nonconformist quarters, and the lecturer, Robert Halley, began with a lengthly reference to "the unhappy personalities, the insinuations, and recriminations which have unfortunately grown out of our bicentenary celebrations." Somewhere, somehow, in this furore some "partizan class of casuists" made use, or misuse, of the manuscript *Ecclesiastica.* Who these people were, and what were their arguments, it must be confessed, has proved elusive, even though a mass of pamphlet and other ephemeral literature of the period and subject has been examined.

If Pulman brought the existence of the Axminster manuscript treasure to light in a general way, it was Henry Mayo Gunn (1817-86) who introduced it to the Christian public of the west

1 *Axminster Ecclesiastica* (1874) p.iii.

country.[1] Son of John Gunn pastor at Chard 1816-36, himself pastor at Warminster, Gunn used the occasion of the stonelaying of a new chapel at Chard in 1867—in which he himself had a leading part—to publish a slim volume of some fifty pages, the first twenty of which comprise a resume with lengthy extracts from the *Ecclesiastica,* interest focussing on the constitutional and spiritual history of the Axminster church. "The annals of the Free Churches of England", he writes, "have been brought before the public of late years in works of a general historical character, and in narratives of a more local interest. As one of the latter kind, there are few memorials more worthy of being preserved and published than "*The Book of Remembrance*" recently brought to light, describing with much ability and care the forty years of trial, from 1660 to 1700, endured by members of the Independent church at Chard, Axminster, Winsham, and the neighbourhood" (p.4). After referring to the ejected ministers of the area, their sufferings and their testimony, he proceeds: "Among those men of martyr spirit was the rector of Axminster... Bartholomew Ashwood, first minister of the Independent Church in both Chard and Axminster. This is proved by records kept by him and his worthy and able successor, rivalling in interest the most touching stories of persecution in ancient or modern times, and portraying, with much fidelity to the life, the inner working of piety in good people, tried as gold in a fiery furnace." Quoting the *Ecclesiastica's* design that those who read "them may keep the same fresh and green in their memories", Gunn ends his introduction by saying, "This design will be promoted by a brief outline of what is worthy of being printed in full, while in a state of good preservation, in case of so rare and valuable a record being lost, as has often been the fate of others." (p.7). Concluding his extracts he says: "Here the old folio ends... We turn from it with regret, as from a friend who is silent for evermore. Yet in doing so we tender most hearty thanks to those who still guard this old treasure with the greatest reverence and care." (p.19).

The first published edition of the *Ecclesiastica* appeared in 1874. Its title page is reproduced facsimile in this, the second, edition. It is a small 8vo volume of 132 pages, published at Axminster and printed by J. Townsend of Exeter. We are also informed that "Copies of this book may be had of Messrs. Deane and Tapscott,

[1] H. M. Gunn. *The Free Churches in Chard and the Neighbourhood.* 1867.

Ecclesiastica,

OR

A BOOK

OF

REMEMBRANCE

Wherein the Rise, Constitution, Rule, Order, and Discipline of the Church of Christ, ordinarily Assembling at Wykecroft, in the Parish of Axminster; is faithfully Recorded.

Together with the most Remarkable Occurrences and signall Providences which have attended the same from the first Foundation thereof.

BY THE ORDER & APPOYNTMENT OF THE CHURCH.

NUMB. 33. 2. And Moses wrote their goings out according to their Journeyings by the commandement of the LORD.

PSA. 102. 18. This shall be written for the Generation to come; & the People which shall be Created shall praise the LORD.

Axminster; or of any Booksellers through the London publishers, J. Snow and Co., Ivy Lane, Paternoster Row." There is a four page editorial introductory note and a two page postscript by the editor who, with an annoying modesty, fails to identify himself. Mr. Allan Brockett of Exeter University Library says, "I believe the editor of the 1874 edition to have been James Davidson, editor of the *Bibliotheca Devoniensis,* or else his son." James Davidson's interest began, as we have seen, as far back as 1826, and he may well have brought the MS to the notice of G. P. R. Pulman and H. M. Gunn, but his own death in 1864 excludes him from any possibility of writing an introductory note dated 'Axminster, May 15, 1874'. James Bridge Davidson (1824-85), his eldest son, inherited his father's antiquarian interests and doubtless also his father's papers. According to the *Dictionary of National Biography,* J. B. Davidson was the author of many papers, but published no work separately, which nonetheless does not preclude his anonymous editorship of the *Ecclesiastica.*

The editor of 1874 quotes Coleridge's *Notes on English Divines* (on Sheldon), Wordsworth's *Ecclesiastical Sonnets* ('The eternal roll of praise'), Calamy, and Samuel Chandler (1693-1766); refers to his friendship with and indebtedness to H. M. Gunn; and cites Revelation 3.3,5 as his peroration. He was himself thoroughly committed to Nonconformist principles, and sympathetic (though not blindly so) with those whose narrative he edited, saying of them:

> Take them on the whole, it would be difficult to find . . . a people more self-consciously and intelligently *real* in their relation to the Chief Corner Stone nor more apostolically devoted to the interests of His kingdom.[1]

Of the work itself, he says:

> The Narrative comprised in this Book was written by an able and honest chronicler, himself a contemporary constituent of the church, by whose authority it became finally adopted and confirmed, with evidently a public unlimited design. But although two hundred years have since passed away, this design has not had the opportunity of being realized until now. The office bearers of the church in question have, no doubt, proved careful conservators of the relic, and now and

[1] *Axminster Ecclesiastica* (1874) p.130.

then have admitted their friends and neighbours to the privilege of a private or social inspection; but the manuscript in its unbroken continuity and entireness, has remained all this while a hidden treasure—a string of pearls, withheld from the general reach, and kept out of sight, very likely, from many to whom it has proprietorily belonged. So apt is the Church, as well as the world, to put into the shade some of its best heroes as soon as they are departed. Yet how important that it should have been otherwise!"[1]

Yet in 1862 it *was* displayed before the eyes of "a partizan class of casuists"—successors in spirit of the persecutors of the *Ecclesitica's* personnel!

In his postscript the editor of 1874 says:

> Thus our worthy old church has been allowed to tell its own story in its own way, with scarce a word or syllable of correction. The modern reader is asked to take the document from the Press as it was found in the manuscript, and to form his own fair estimate of those whose mind and manners it represents. Clearly they were not like the rest of the world, nor of the church either, in some very noticeable particulars; but nevertheless the comparison need not be to their reproach.[2]

Publication of the *Ecclesiastica* was not overlooked by the religious press of the day. It appeared in July or early August, and had an enthusiastic welcome from *The Nonconformist,* edited then by Edward Miall. In his issue of September 30 he carried a review running to two and a half columns headed, 'An old Church Record':

> There are certain respects in which this *Axminster Ecclesiastica* is one of the most interesting records relating to the origin and early history of the Free Churches of England that has ever been printed. It is the most complete that we have ever met with; it extends over a long period, and it is very illustrative of the history of the times." After lengthy quotations, the unnamed reviewer concludes, "The history of this time has never been more eloquently described than it is in the simple language of these pages . . . "[3]

1 *Axminster Ecclesiastica* (1874) p.iii.
2 ibid. p.129.
3 *The Nonconformist.* vol. 35. p.943.

Two months later, the old established *Evangelical Magazine*, then under the editorship of James Spence, carried the following notice:

> *Ecclesiastica* Or a Book of Remembrance . . . A very interesting record of the origin and history of a congregational church at a thrilling time of our country's history. The manuscript of the chronicler has been preserved nearly two centuries, and has never been published until now. The 'remarkable occurrences and signal providences' connected with the story are full of touching interest. The circulation of this book of remembrance will do good.[1]

After its publication the manuscript drops out of view altogether and must by now be presumed lost or destroyed. No writer who quotes the *Ecclesiastica* after this date mentions the manuscript. The present day successors to the old Independent Church of Axminster, its true custodians, expressly disclaim all knowledge of it. Two years' search elsewhere has filled me with admiration for the kindness of librarians and archivists but has produced no trace of the Axminster treasure.

1873-75 saw the serialisation of the fourth and final edition of G. P. R. Pulman's *The Book of the Axe*. In its final form it is a work standing in a succession which includes John Prince's *Worthies of Devon* (1701), Sir William Pole's *The Description of Devonshire* (1791), and Daniel and Samuel Lyson's *Magna Britannia* (1806-22); all of them general antiquarian and topographical histories of the locality. Its usefulness on several points in the general background of the special interest of the *Ecclesiastica* is duly acknowledged, yet it must be said that the author was no friend of the tradition it represents. His general assessment runs thus:

> The full title of this manuscript is "*Ecclesiastica,* or a Book of Remembrance." Similar records were very commonly kept by the dissenting congregations. They served to show the progress of 'the cause', and to chronicle the persecutions of its early professors. The Axminster manuscript, along with a great deal of interesting local matter, presents a vivid picture of the state of the country generally at the period at which it was written. As a literary composition it is exceedingly

[1] *Evangelical Magazine*, 1874. p.664.

creditable to the author, whose phraseology and style are amusingly characteristic.[1]

Pulman fills some thirteen of his pages with extracts from the *Ecclesiastica;* the longest, which gives the account of the Monmouth Rebellion he introduces thus. "Due allowance must of course be made for the prejudices of the writer and for the cant of his sect, and especially must it be borne in mind that he was smarting under a sense of unrighteous persecution." Elsewhere he refers to the author as "the canting old puritan", to "Cromwell's sour puritanism", and finally, with sublime detachment from truth on either side commits the anachronism of setting the *Ecclesiastica* over against the treatment of Roman Catholics in Elizabethan England.[2]

The *Ecclesiastica's* debut on the stage of general Nonconformist history came in 1879 when Henry Martyn Dexter alluded to it, with brief extracts, in his lectures on *The Congregationalism of the last Three Hundred Years as seen in its Literature.*[3] Two years later John Stoughton who, in his first edition of *The Church of the Restoration* (1870) appears to have been unaware of the *Ecclesiastica,* issued a second edition (1881) with references to the Axminster church and the Monmouth Rebellion drawn from it.[4] In 1885 Edward Windeatt read a paper on *Early Nonconformity in the Neighbourhood of Seaton* before the Devonshire Association for the Advancement of Science, Literature, and Art, at Seaton, and in its published form, ten of its fifteen pages comprise extracts from the *Ecclesiastica,* with comment.[5] Densham and Ogle, writing on Congregationalism in Dorset, in 1899, found it a useful source of information concerning Samuel Baker of Bridport and Robert Bartlett of Over Compton, among others.[6]

In 1901 Windeatt again appeared in print with a series of articles on *Devonshire and the Indulgence of 1672* in the Transactions of the Congregational Historical Society, including the doings of the

1 *The Book of the Axe.* Ed.4. (1875) p.271.

2 *The Book of the Axe.* Ed.4. (1875) pp.652, 686-8.

3 London, 1879, pp.669-71. He also lists the title (No. 7018) in his appendix, *Collections toward a Bibliography of Congregationalism.*

4 *History of Religion in England.* IV.91.

5 *Transactions of the Devonshire Association for the Advancement of Science, Literature, and Art.* 1885. XVII.298-312.

6 Densham, W. and Ogle, J. *The Story of the Congregational Churches of Dorset.* 1899.

Axminster Church in 1672 as recorded in the *Ecclesiastica.*[1] Seven years later, Francis Bullen Wyatt (1864-1939) then pastor at Axminster, issued a brief history of the Axminster Church. It ran to fifteen small pages, ten of which are extracts from the *Ecclesiastica.*[2] In 1908 Frank Bate's valuable work on *The Declaration of Indulgence 1672* included the *Ecclesiastica* in its bibliography.[3] The following year F. B. Wyatt contributed an article on *The Congregational Church at Axminster,* dealing with the Weycroft site, and giving a sketchy outline of the later history of the church.[4] Alexander Gordon's *Freedom After Ejection,* published in 1917, cites the *Ecclesiastica* among authorities for statements in the brief biographies of ejected ministers.[5] A. G. Matthews likewise, in his twin reference works, *Calamy Revised* (1934), and *Walker Revised* (1948), is pleased to acknowledge the authority of the *Ecclesiastica* for certain statements made. In 1957 G. F. Nuttall published his *Visible Saints: The Congregational Way, 1640-1660,* a study of Independent or Congregational Church principles drawn from the original writings of the churches of the period. Although the *Ecclesiastica* falls chronologically somewhat later than his stated period, the author lays it under liberal contribution in his establishment of the Congregational distinctives. And finally, A. G. Matthews editing the *Savoy Declaration,* in 1959, cites in a footnote to the Declaration of Order (para VIII) the *Ecclesiastica's* use of the covenanting element in church institution.[6]

Thus we have sketched the story of the *Ecclesiastica,* for the most part in external terms insofar as these are known. As to the internal story—the story of what 'the generations to come' have in fact learned from the dealings of God with their forefathers here recorded—we may hope to chronicle but little. Such things are "written on fleshy tables of the heart" and "the day will declare it."

[1] *Transactions of the Congregational Historical Society* (1901). I.85-86.

[2] *A Brief History of the Church of Christ of the Congregational Order in Axminster. 1660-1907 A.D.* By the Rev. F. B. Wyatt, Pastor. Axminster: Edwin Snell, Printer. 1907.

[3] p.lxxxvi.

[4] *Transactions of the Congregational Historical Society* (1909) IV. 107-112.

[5] Alexander Gordon, *Freedom After Ejection: A Review (1690-92) of Presbyterian and Congregational Nonconformity in England and Wales.* 1917.

[6] *The Savoy Declaration of Faith and Order 1658.* Edited by A. G. Matthews. 1959.

APPENDIX G

The Axminster Churchmanship

The professed content of the *Ecclesiastica* according to its title page is "The Rise, Constitution, Rule, Order, and Discipline of the Church . . . at Wykecroft." Polity or churchmanship is thus a prominent feature of the record, although nothing is set down in a formal way. There are no lists of rules or procedures; all appears incidentally as part of the unfolding story. This suggests that the church's life was not regimented in legalistic fashion, but that out of a genuine christianity in church form there arose a submission to commonly accepted disciplines. There was a reciprocal balance in other words, between life and order, order and life, neither dominating the other but both derived from "their only Lord and lawgiver" and viewed as gifts of His grace.

Church order, however, is meant to be orderly, and the object of this essay is to draw together the leading elements of the Axminster practice in something approaching an orderly manner. But this cannot be done in isolation, because although seventeenth century Independency (Congregational or Baptist) was by no means stereotyped in its churchmanship, the Axminster order falls well within a wider pattern clearly distinguishable from that of their fellow-nonconformists the Presbyterians. Further, there are several lacunae in the *Ecclesiastica,* and some of these may be at least suggestively filled by reference to contemporary sources. I shall therefore lay alongside the *Ecclesiastica:*

(1). The standard later-seventeenth century Independent document of church order, *The Savoy Declaration of the Institution of Churches, and the Order appointed in them by Jesus Christ,* a brief appendix of thirty articles, being part of *A Declaration of the Faith and Order Owned and practised in the Congregational Churches in England; Agreed upon and consented unto By their Elders and Messengers in Their Meeting at the Savoy, October 12, 1658.*

(2). A document derived from a single contemporary Independent Church in which its church order is codified, viz: *Certaine Scripture Rules, which Jesus Christ hath given to his Churches to walke by: which are approved of, and consented to, by all the Members of the Church of Christ walking in Gospell-fellowship in Chippin-Norton.* It contains 24 articles, together with 50 "More Particular Practicall Rules For walking in Church-fellowship." These were drawn up by the pastor, Stephen Ford (d.1696) who was ejected from Chipping Norton in 1660, continued his ministry among his people there and later in London, and appended to his *An Epistle To the Church of Christ in Chippin-Norton . . . certaine Scripture Rules . . . Published for their use and benefit, and for the satisfaction of such persons as desire to know the Principles and practises of the Church aforesaid.* Oxford, 1657.

(3). To a much lesser extent, the writings of some contemporary Independent divines, in the area of church order.

Regulative Principle

We begin with the question of the professed authority for what was done in church practice. *The Ecclesiastica* mentions no statement of faith. However, the trust deed of the "new meeting house in the town of Axminster" built in 1698 may be taken as a safe guide. It describes the property as "a place of religious worship . . . by . . . Protestant Dissenters . . . called Independents . . . who should adhere to and hold and profess the same religious sentiments and doctrines as those which are taught and professed in what is commonly called the Assembly's Catechism",[1] that is, the *Westminster Shorter Catechism* of 1648. The church's basic doctrinal stance is thus clearly defined as that orthodox, reformed or calvinistic Christianity with its fundamental appeal to Holy Scripture, which was then common to Presbyterians, Independents and Particular Baptists.

In general terms there had been an eagerness on the part of Independents and Baptists to proclaim their affinity with the leading Westminster doctrines, however much they differed in matters of church constitution and government. Thus the Presbyterian *Westminster Confession of Faith* of 1647 was followed by an

[1] Vide, deed dated 9th March, 1825.

Independent revision in the *Savoy Declaration* of 1658, and a Particular Baptist version known as the *Assembly*, or *Second London Confession* of 1677 and 1689. Savoy added an appendix on *"The Institution of Churches, and the Order appointed for them by Jesus Christ."* which the Baptists transferred largely into the body of their Confession.[1] The *Savoy Declaration* can hardly be said to have replaced *Westminster* among the Independents, even though it was printed four times in 1659, and again in 1677 and 1688. While it was received as authoritative in its definition of Independent orthodoxy in their contemporary ecclesiastical setting, it was by no means authoritarian among the Independent churches where many took leave to dissent from it on one point or another. The *'Order of the Churches'* is modelled to some extent on the American *Cambridge Platform* of 1648, which in turn owes a great deal to the writings of John Cotton (1585-1652)—*The Keys of the Kingdom of Heaven* (1644), and *The Way of the Congregational Churches Cleared* (1648). R. W. Dale said of the Savoy *'Order'* that, "In its fulness and precision it is, perhaps, the most admirable statement of the ecclesiastical principles of English Congregationalism".

Against this general background, both historical and doctrinal, it is no surprise to find the *Ecclesiastica* constantly appealing to authority; it has its 'regulative principle', and is sensitive to it throughout.

> How beautiful . . . will Zion's assemblies be when . . . the Churches of Christ be thus constituted, and all the forms, ordinances and laws thereof to the utmost bounds and limits thereof . . . shall more exactly answer the rule of the great Lawgiver and the pattern shewed in the Mount (p.6).

1 The negative reason for this eagerness to be seen to be theologically at one with the much larger Presbyterian constituency was the rise of the Independents as a dominant party in the State under the Commonwealth, and the dislike they felt at the ill-odour that fell upon them by their being generally regarded as wild sectaries, as were the Ranters, the Quakers, the Levellers, the Fifth Monarchists, and the rest. So Thomas Goodwin was led to say publicly, "We desire to clear ourselves of that scandal which . . . some persons . . . have affixed upon us, viz. that Independentism (as they call it) is the sink of all Heresies and Schisms. We have therefore declared what hath been our common Faith and Order . . . And to shew our harmony with the most Orthodox at home and abroad." The Baptists in their turn smarted under the same malicious misrepresentation, and were eager to proclaim in their preface: "We, the Ministers and Messengers of . . . baptized congregations in England and Wales (denying Arminianism) . . . have thought meet (for the satisfaction of all other Christians that differ from us in the point of Baptism) to recommend to their perusal the confession of our faith . . ."

Ashwood is said to have been "very zealous for the pure instituted worship of Christ according to gospel rule and the order of the primitive Churches." (p.8). Even more explicitly is it said:—

> They were waiting for an opportunity and capacity to form themselves into a church of Christ according to gospel rule and the pure institution of the Lord Jesus Christ after the order of the primitive churches at the first publication of the gospel by the apostles of our Lord Jesus Christ, as far as they apprehended the mind of the Spirit of God therein. (p.8).

"Instituted worship", "pure instituted worship", "the pure institutions of the Lord Jesus" are the recurring phrases that express a constant ideal. When it came to dissenting from the "national ministry", this was held to be imperative because, "It is not keeping to the Word, to the rule, to the institution of the Lord Jesus Christ." (p.118). Most definitively, we are told, "Christ hath appointed congregational churches" (p.119), and "God hath instituted a gospel ministry, told us what qualifications it should be . . ." (p.119).

The Axminster church had inherited the mantle of those who had said:

> First, the supreme rule . . . was the Primitive patterne and example of the churches erected by the Apostles. Our consciences were possessed with the reverence and adoration of the fulnesse of the Scriptures, that there is therein a compleat sufficiencie, as to make the man of God perfect, so also to make the Churches of God perfect.[1]

That Scripture contained a fundamentally clear churchmanship they of Axminster were in no doubt. That the English reformers had gone some way to restoring it they also readily conceded. But that they who came after, who "are set upon their shoulders", must go the whole way in the return to primitive New Testament churchmanship, they were most fully persuaded. (pp.5f, 121).

1 *An Apologeticall Narration,* 1643. p.9. (A statement of Independent principles presented to Parliament by the five 'Dissenting Brethren' of the Westminster Assembly; viz. Thomas Goodwin, Philip Nye, Sidrach Simpson, Jeremiah Burroughes, and William Bridge).

Essence of a church "The matter of a visible church of Christ are visible saints; such as in the Judgement of rationall charity according to the revealed will of God, appeare to be saints", said Stephen Ford in his *Epistle to the Church of Christ in Chippin-Norton,* of which he was pastor (1657, p.33). With no such rule clearly spelled out in the *Ecclesiastica,* Axminster nevertheless set holiness of life as the standard of those who comprised their church.

Ashwood's ministry is said to have been used "to the awakening, enlightening, converting, and effectually drawing over some souls to close in with Jesus Christ, and whose hearts were engaged and made willing..." (p.8). They speak of "serious pious christians" (p.8), and "souls... whose hearts the Lord had wrought upon by His word and Spirit" (p.8) as comprising the church. In their embodying covenant they speak of "giving up ourselves to Him to walk... in all His holy commandments" (p.29). Their corporate life is described in retrospect thus:

> What liveliness! what zeal and forwardness in the work and ways of God, what spiritual edifying conversations, what fervent love and warm affections... ! What a blessedness was there seen and found amongst them! What an eminent presence of God in the midst of them, what a resemblance of heaven upon earth (p.11).

"The Judgement of rationall charity" would have to admit that these are the marks of positive holiness.

The negative side of holiness being separation, Ashwood counselled, "Keep at a distance from the corruptions of the times, both as to worship and conversation;... be 'A people dwelling alone' " (p.16). He echoes his fellow-Devonian, William Bartlett[1] who had said: "A visible segregation from the world, and a visible aggregation to Christ is necessary to church union and communion... a separation from sinful ways, and things, and persons... a separation of the precious from the vile." John Owen had arrived at the same view of the church when he drew up his rules: "Separation and sequestration from the world and men of the world, with all ways of false worship." He (Owen), proceeds: "Causeless separation from established churches walking according to the order of the Gospel... is no small sin; but separation from the sinful practises and disorderly walkings, and false unwarranted ways of

1 William Bartlett (1610-1681). Ejected rector of Bideford; Independent minister there. Author of *A Model of the Primitive Congregational Way,* 1647.

worship in any, is to fulfil the precept of not partaking in other men's sins ... He that will not be separate from the world and false worship, is separate from Christ."[1] The Axminster church was among "such as kept themselves faithful and separated from the corruptions of the day in matters of God's worship ..." (p.25).

Grounded in scriptures such as 2 Cor. 6.14-18; Eph. 5.11; 2 Tim. 3.5; Rev. 14.9 & 18.4, the theme is recurrent in the seventeenth century Independent tradition. Whenever Ashwood and Towgood lament decays in the life of the church, it is the decline of personal holiness that afflicts their pastoral hearts. The essence of a church is, "The power of godlinesse and the profession thereof, with difference from carnal, formal christians ..." in the judgment of the *Apologeticall Narration*.[2] A retrospective assessment arrives at the same thing: "Congregationalism is pre-eminently a spiritual polity. It is less than nothing and vanity if the power of a godly life be not behind it."[3]

Form of a church

> Mr. Ashwood, with the rest, endeavoured to incorporate themselves into one body . . . on a solemn day of prayer and supplication, voluntarily giving up themselves to the Lord and to each other by the will of God, solemnly covenanting and engaging to walk together in a due and faithful attendance upon the Lord Jesus Christ in all His ordinances and appointments, and in the faithful discharge of all those duties relating to the members of a church of Christ, so were embodied and constituted a church of Christ. (p.8ff).

Here is the essence of the 'gathered church' principle: God having gathered His people to Himself in grace and salvation, His people gather themselves to each other in His Name and fear. Savoy had put it like this:

> The Members of these Churches are Saints by Calling ... who ... do willingly consent to walk together according to the appointment of Christ, giving up themselves to the Lord, and to one another by the will of God in professed subjection to the Ordinances of the Gospel.[4]

[1] John Owen, *Eschol: ... Or, Rules of Direction for the walking of the saints in fellowship, according to the order of the Gospel.* (Works, Ed. W. H. Goold, XIII. 67-69).

[2] *An Apologeticall Narration,* 1643. p.4.

[3] H. M. Dexter, *The Congregationalism of the last Three Hundred Years*...1879. p.713,4.

[4] *Savoy Declaration of the Institution of Churches ... 1658.* VIII.

Voluntary consent in response to spiritual constraint is here explicit, and covenant commitment is implicit, though the Savoy divines were for some reason (possibly because of hesitancy concerning the Solemn League and Covenant) shy of the term 'covenant' in this context. Stephen Ford wrote:

> The formal cause of a visible Church of Christ, are Saints united in Gospell order: For a certaine number of true Believers walking at a distance from each other: and scattered up and down in a Towne or Parish, living as strangers to each other, doe not properly and formally make a visible Church: but only such as walke together according to Christ's appointment; so then that which gives being to a true visible Church of Christ is, when seaven or more Believers do freely and voluntarily give up themselves to each other...[1]

Many Independent and Baptist churches of this period had covenants committed to writing and subscribed by their members. The classical case is that of the church formed in London under Henry Jacob in 1616, when the members joined hands in a circle and, making a profession of their faith, "covenanted togeather to walk in all God's ways as he had revealed or should make them known to them."[2] Other early covenants still extant are those of churches at Yarmouth (1643), Norwich (1643), Wattisfield (1654), Taunton (1654), and Bideford (1658), to name but a few. For Scripture warrant they would point to the covenant theology of the Bible in general, and to 2 Corinthians 8.5 in particular—

1 *Epistle to the Church of Christ in Chippin-Norton*... 1657, p.34. On the smallest numbers of believers necessary to comprise a church, Ford evidently agreed with John Cotton:

> The first and lowest number of a church...is not expressly limited in the Word; only it is not so low as some have conceived... But the church must be a greater number than "two or three", seeing these two or three (Matt. 18.20) are to refer the person and the cause to a greater body than themselves. For though there might be a domesticall church in Adam and Eve at the beginning, yet such a church which Christ hath instituted in the New Testament consisteth of a greater number. The very officers of a church completely furnished, are no less than four—a pastor, a teacher, an elder, a deacon—and therefore the body had need to be of a greater number...And though the essence of a church may consist without the integrity of all her members—as a man that wanteth some of his members may have the essence of a man—yet under seven a church can hardly consist of so many members as do perform any part of a church body...(*The Way of the Churches of Christ in New England*...by Mr. John Cotton...London, 1645. pp.53-55).

2 Benjamin Hanbury, *Historical Memorials of the Independents*. 1839-45. I.292.

"They . . . first gave their own selves to the Lord, and unto us by the will of God." It is not putting matters too strongly to say that the covenant idea was the root principle of their church order; and from it, with due appeal to Scripture, flowed the related principles of membership and discipline.

In this contemporary setting the Axminster covenant is probably as well documented as any, and the prominence of the covenant in the church's on-going life is perhaps unmatched. The following analysis of references in the *Ecclesiastica* will assist the reader to pursue the matter further for himself.

	1660	Church formed by covenant	p.10
Embodying covenant	1660		29
Renewal		"several times renewed"	29
Renewal		"a re-giving up of themselves"	30
Revised form (1)	? 1666	"The manner of the church's covenanting"	31
Revised form (2)	? 1668	after addition of members	33
	1672	"Renew your covenant"	45
Revised form (3)	? 1672	during pastor's illness	48
Revised form (4)	? 1674	after discipline	54
Renewal	1678	after pastor's death	68
Renewal	1686	after conference on occasional conformity	123
Renewal	1686	preparatory to the Lord's Supper	123

Granting that not every revision or renewal of covenant may have been recorded, it is clear that its usage in the church's life was not fitful but regular, and its influence was not nominal but practical. Points of note are:

(i). *The solemnity with which the work of covenanting was undertaken.*

> The manner of this church's covenanting . . . was . . . on solemn days of humiliation and prayer. After the reading of the covenant deliberately and distinctly in the audience of the congregation, each and every individual member subscribed, or by their voluntary consent had their names subscribed to the covenant; or, which was more usually practised, solemnly lifted up their right hand to heaven in testification of their real assenting to this covenant, and then subscribed with the hand. (p.31).

Twenty years later the same seriousness of purpose prevailed:

> Now did they . . . once again pass themselves into a covenant with the Lord and with each other; with their right hands lifted up to heaven, solemnly and publicly declaring their purposes and resolutions to cleave to the Lord and unto each other . . . (p.123).

(ii) *The awe with which they viewed breaches of the covenant.* This is evident in each of the revisions, and most explicit in Ashwood's pastoral *Epistle to the Church* in 1672:

> . . . renew your covenant with God in Christ, and bind yourselves to Him again by a curse. You have broken the everlasting covenant, and God will smite you with breach on breach till that be made up . . . Solemnly, sincerely, sensibly renew your engagements to the Lord, . . . Do this in the shame of your former treacheries . . . (p.45).

(iii). *The successive revisions did not alter the substance of the embodying covenant,* but related it to the current state of the church's life, and so prevented its use becoming a ritual formality.

(iv). *The stress placed upon the God-ward aspect* is as great, if not greater, than that placed on the fellow-member aspect. Thus the covenant was never in danger of descending to the level of a human compact.

(v). *The sense of dependence on God for ability* in engaging, and in keeping covenanted engagements: "Do it in the sense of your own weakness and inability to fulfill it . . . Get Christ to be your Surety and to sign with you." (p.45).

Receiving members From an embodying membership of "but few, about twelve or thirteen" in 1660, the chronicler notes some, at least, of the occasions when new members were received:

(1661)	"The Lord adding to them and increasing their number"	p.11
(1662)	"The number increased . . . and more were added to the church"	18
(1663)	"Afterwards, the number of members increasing . . ."	24
(1669)	"Then was there an addition of members to the church . . ."	33
(1677)	"Several others were . . . added to this church"	56

(1679)	"This was the day in which Mr. Stephen Towgood was added"	p.72
(1679)	"of all their number ... being about one hundred persons"	72
(1681)	"the Lord adding to them such of whom there was ground of hope they should be saved"	75
(1685)	"There was this night a member more added to this church"	106
(1686)	"Some further addition being made to the church this day"	123

For all this information, however, we are told nothing except in the rather special case of the second pastor as to how the business was managed. "No person ought to be added to the church, but by the consent of the church itself", said the Savoy divines,[1] and Axminster would have found that a natural inference of its covenant concept of the Church already noted. But how was the 'consent of the church' to be obtained? Stephen Ford's rules may well be representative of contemporary practice:

> That when any persons are desirous to joyne themselves to the church; the said persons should first make known their desires to the Pastor or Elders ... That if the Pastor or Elder be satisfyed ... (he) is to propose the said persons to the Church at their next meeting. That all the members ... are upon Scripture grounds to be satisfyed in the fitnesse and worthiness of the person to be admitted; & also to give their free consent ... That such persons as through modesty, or want of the gift of utterance, cannot by word of mouth declare the dealings of God with them to the satisfaction of the Church, that then the said persons have liberty to give satisfaction to the Church in writing, or otherwise.[2]

Ford clearly reflected John Cotton in these points:

> They that desire to be added and joined to such a body ... make known their desires to the Elders; ... who take trial of their knowledge in the principles of religion, and of their experience in the ways of grace, and of their godly conversation among men, that . . . if found ignorant, etc., such may not be presently presented to the church. But when approved of the Elders, they are propounded by one of the Ruling Elders to the church; ... if no exception be heard of, they

[1] *Savoy Declaration of the Institution of Churches* ... 1658. XVII.
[2] *Epistle to the Church of Christ in Chippin-Norton* ... 1657. pp.35,36.

are called for before the church . . . and each one maketh confession of his sins, and profession of his faith . . . which done, the elder propoundeth to him the heads of the covenant which the Lord hath made with his church, what promises of grace he hath made to them; as also what duties he doth require of them,—as to take the Lord Jesus for their only Priest and atonement, their only Prophet and guide; their only King and lawgiver; and to walk in professed subjection to all His holy ordinances; as also to walk in brotherly love with the brethren of this church, unto mutual edification."[1]

Thomas Goodwin approached the matter from another angle:

Now to the manner how they must join. Three things they used in the primitive church, and long after. 1. Confession of their sins, Mat. 3.6. . . . 2. Profession of their faith . . . 3. By taking hold of the covenant. What covenant? Read Is. 56.6,7 . . . They may not receive into the church but those whom God receiveth in . . .[2]

Procedures in the reception of members at Axminster would be in harmony with her covenant concept of the church, and in general agreement with the gathered church principles of the Independents at large.

Membership Discipline The *Ecclesiastica* provides us with a classic picture of puritan church discipline in practice. Such discipline rested upon the accepted authority of (i) God's Word written, (ii) duly appointed church officers, and (iii) the obligation of church covenants freely entered into. It was not a matter of prying or petty interference with individual liberty; it was their view of the church which required these procedures. They saw themselves as a people who:

are constituted a church, and interested in the rights, power, and privileges of a gospel church, by the will, promises, authority, and law of Jesus Christ, upon their own voluntary consent and engagement to walk together in the due subjection of their souls and consciences to His authority, as their king, priest, and prophet, and in a holy observance of all His

1 *The Way of the Churches of Christ in New England . . . By Mr. John Cotton, teacher of the church at Boston in New England.* London, 1645. pp.53-55.

2 *The Government and Discipline of the Churches of Christ . . .* Works, (Nichol Series) XI.520.

commands, ordinances, and appointments. Mt. 18.20; 28.19,20; Ac. 2.41,42; Exod. 24.3; Dt. 5.27; Ps. 110.3; Is. 44.5, 59.21; Eph. 4.7-10; 2 Cor. 8.5."[1]

The objects of this discipline had a twofold bearing: (i) on the church, and, (ii) on the individual member. With reference to the church, discipline was designed to preserve the integrity of the gospel and of the church as its custodian; to preserve the holiness which is of the church's ultimate essence; and to preserve the church from scandal. With reference to the individual, discipline was first punitive, as a pledge of future judgement; then reformative, with a view to sanctification; and finally preventative by way of instruction and warning for the future.

The matter of discipline was (i) doctrinal error, and (ii) moral failure, and the application of discipline was always to begin with private admonition, after the failure of which, only, did the matter come under the jurisdiction of the church in an open way. As members must consent to the reception of new members, so must they give consent to the censure, suspension, or excommunication of a member. Nevertheless, the administration of public discipline was vested in the officers of the church. "All cannot exert and exercise that power that doth essentially reside in themselves as a church; neither can any private member, while such; and therefore it must be done by officers or one in office . . ."[2] "The Church is to labour to convince him, and to bring him to the sight of his sinne, and if possible to repentance."[3]

The following analysis of the cases of discipline recorded in the *Ecclesiastica* will assist the reader to trace out the application of the above general principles in the Axminster church practice.

	charge	*action*	*reaction*	
?1669 a sister	lying	admonition	—repentance & restoration	p.31
1673 R.B.	stealing & lying	admonition, lesser excommunication	—unrepentant — ?	52
?1675 J.T.	fraudulent dealing	admonition, excommunication	—unrepentant	55

[1] John Owen, *A Brief Instruction in the Worship of God* (the 'Independent's Catechism') 1667. (*Works*, Ed. W. H. Goold, XV.486).

[2] Stephen Ford, *A Gospel Church: or God's Holy Temple Opened.* 1675. p.77.

[3] Stephen Ford, *Epistle to the Church at Chippin-Norton* . . . 1657. p.37. See also *Savoy Declaration of the Institution of Churches* . . . 1658. XVIII-XXII.

?1675	A.B.	drunkenness	admonition, excommunication	—unrepentant	p.55
?1675	S.W.	disorderly walking	admonition, excommunication	—unrepentant	55
1678-9	H.P.	enthusiasm	admonition	—'a member out of joint', later restored	74
1679	M.M.	evil relationship	admonition	—withdrew	75
1680	J.D.	immodesty	admonition, greater excommunication	—unrepentant — ?	75
1687	C.B.	drunkenness	admonition, lesser excommunication	—unrepentant died	129
1687	A.B.	immodesty	admonition, excommunication?	—withdrew; 'a maimed member'	129
1687	P.S.	adultery		—failed to appear for admonition;	131
			lesser excommunication greater excommunication	—unrepentant	
1698	J.S.	drunkenness	admonition	—repentance & restoration	159
?	M.C.	?	lesser excommunication lesser excommunication	—restored	166

Granting that not all instances may have been recorded, we have here some thirteen cases in thirty eight years, distributed almost equally between the pastorates of Ashwood and Towgood. The following points should be considered:

(i). The solemnity, tenderness and grief with which each case was handled, both in private admonition, and all stages of the public dealing ('public' meaning here an open meeting of the church members only, except in the one case of 1673 when the meeting was open to all comers for the removal of scandal from the church). Accusations of vindictiveness and inquisitorial purges in later puritan church discipline will find no ground of support whatsoever in the Axminster record. It is a record that breathes a spirit of "great heaviness and continual sorrow" of heart.

(ii). It is stated or inferred in each case that private admonition did in fact precede each public proceeding. The rule of Matthew 18.15-17 was duly observed, either by offended parties, or by officers of the church in a pastoral way.

(iii). The *Ecclesiastica* does not always distinguish between the two forms of excommunication. The lesser was a suspension from church privileges while leaving membership intact; the greater was the termination of membership altogether. In three cases it is not clear which action was taken.

(iv). It is explicitly stated that the church "endeavoured to reclaim those that had gone aside amongst them, and to heal the disorders of offending members." In three such cases the discipline had its desired end in repentance and restoration to the full fellowship of the church.

Dismission of members

> If any member shall desire a dismissal from the said church; to joyn with another Church of Christ walking in Gospell order; and it shall upon tryall appeare to be for the advantage of his soule, or the conveniency of its habitation, as being nearer that church that he is to be a member of: that then the said person ought to have a free dismission.[1]

So said Stephen Ford of the church of which he was pastor. There are but two cases of dismission of members recorded in the *Ecclesiastica,* and the most notable is that of Henry Butler's dismission of Stephen Towgood from the church at Maiden Bradley upon his settlement as pastor at Axminster. Towgood had held the office of deacon under Butler, and Butler had had a hand in his introduction to Axminster; doubtless there was a close relationship between the two men.

> Then he (Butler) began first to give him a dismission from his membership, place and office in that church to which he was related, and to pass him over, or give him up as a member unto this church . . . So passing him over into a union

[1] *Epistle to the Church of Christ in Chippin-Norton . . .* 1657. p.44.

with this church, he added these words, 'Dear christians, I hope it is a blessed addition to your number'. (p.71).

The dismission of John Dunster, an Axminster member from Taunton, to join with a church in the place of his abode, as noted in the members roll, (p.167), indicates a cordial good will to other gospel churches, and that the Axminster church accepted the idea of "letters of commendation". (2 Cor. 3.1).

Withdrawal of members One of the questions proposed for consideration at a conference of three or four Independent churches, of which Axminster was one, in 1694, was: "What the church ought to do with respect to those members that withdraw themselves from church communion not being guilty of scandalous sins?" (p.152). The Savoy divines had said: "Persons who are joyned in church-fellowship ought not lightly or without just cause to withdraw themselves from the communion of the church whereunto they are so joined..."[1] And Stephen Ford, referring to Hebrews 10.24, 25 & 3.13, had said: "That no member withdraw communion from the said Church, until the said member hath given convincing reasons for his, or her withdrawing, why he cannot hold communion with the said Church."[2]

Withdrawal from membership was a breach of covenant undertaking, but it carried with it the practical difficulty that once a member had disavowed his connection, the church was powerless to apply effective discipline. The only thing left was the power of moral suasion, which was apparently the course followed at Axminster when one of the deacons found himself unable to concur in the election of Stephen Towgood to the pastorate, and withdrew—"quitted his station in this house of God." Thus Robert Batt was entreated by the elders and other male members to return, but without avail. (p.72). Another member withdrew after the death of Bartholomew Ashwood: "Carrettis Wyatt that had walked in fellowship for some years... left her place and returned no more." (p.73). There is no record of what steps the church took to reclaim her. These were withdrawals 'without scandal'. Alas the conclusions of the conference of 1694 on the subject went unrecorded.

Three cases of withdrawal under discipline are noted in the *Ecclesiastica.* Hannah Parker, "giving too much heed to voices,

1 *Savoy Declaration of the Institution of Churches*... 1658. XXVIII.
2 *Epistle to the Church of Christ in Chippin-Norton*... 1657. p.43.

visions and revelations", was admonished. "For some time she stood off from communion with this church, yet afterwards falling under great trouble of spirit, made her application to the church and was re-admitted into communion with them again." (p.73f). This happier ending was to a great extent the outcome of the diligent pastoral work of Stephen Towgood. M.M., however, on being admonished "... refused any further communion with this church ..." but there is no record of how the church dealt with her withdrawal. (p.75). A.B., on the other hand, was admonished and withdrew, and in spite of attempts at persuasion, "remained as a maimed member refusing to be healed." She was adjudged as "unfit for further communion with this body in those special privileges they did enjoy" and presumably excommunicated on those grounds. (p.129).

Church Officers That the said Church hath sufficient power to choose the Officers that Christ hath appointed, and ordained to teach, and Rule the said Church; for Jesus Christ hath appointed and given to his Church Pastors and Teachers, and other Officers for the well-being of his Church, & the said Church may call the said Officers to teach and rule her without the Officers or members of other Churches. Acts 6.3; Eph. 4.11-13; ... Acts 15.22; 13.1,2; 11.22; 2 Cor. 8.19; Matt. 16.18. The Officers that Jesus Christ hath appointed for, and given to his Churches are a Pastor, Teacher, Ruling Elders, Deacons, Eph. 4.11; 1 Tim. 5.17; Acts 6.3-6.[1]

The Officers appointed by Christ to be chosen and set apart by the Church so called, and gathered for the peculiar administration of Ordinances, and execution of Power or Duty which he intrusts them with, or calls them to, to be continued to the end of the world, are Pastors, Teachers, Elders, and Deacons.[2]

The Lord Jesus Christ hath ordained offices, and appointed officers to be established in the church, Eph. 4.11-15 ... Therefore unto the church right and power is granted by Christ to call, choose, appoint, and set apart, persons made meet

[1] Stephen Ford, *Epistle to the Church of Christ in Chippin-Norton* ... 1657. p.35.

[2] *Savoy Declaration of the Institution of Churches* ... 1658. IX.

for the work of the offices . . . Nor is there any other way whereby ordinary officers may be fixed in the church . . .[1]

	Pastors & Teachers	Elders		Deacons	
1660	B. Ashwood				
1662		J. Pinson	T. Lane		
1663				R. Bryant	R. Batt
1665		J. Hawker			
1670					
1678					
1679	S. Towgood				
1680					
1683					
1688					R. Hoar
1690					
1693		R. Bryant	M. Towgood M.D.	T. Miller	
1698					

[1] John Owen, *The True Nature of a Gospel Church*. 1689. (Works, Ed. W. H. Goold, XVI.37).

The *Ecclesiastica* illustrates how these widely held Independent church principles were applied at Axminster. The main points were: (i) the autonomy of the local church, and especially its power to appoint its own officers with no outside interference, and (ii) the officers actually appointed, were Pastors, Teachers, Elders and Deacons.

The foregoing comparative table summarizes information given in the *Ecclesiastica*. It will be noted that in Towgood's pastorate there was a ten year period when the church had but one elder, and another similar period when there was only one deacon. The number of elders participating in the discussion on occasional conformity in 1686 (pp.115-122) is carefully concealed, and could be regarded as an argument for Thomas Lane's compilership at that point.

Pastors & Teachers The essence of a minister lies in the consent of three wills; the will of God, the will of the people, and the will of the minister. The will of God is declared in the consent of the two latter, that is, when a people agree to elect, and the minister agrees to accept of the call of a people. Ordination is for order's sake.

So spake Thomas Lane, elder at Axminster, in 1686. (p.122).

Note, in the light of this the accounts of the settlements of Axminster's two pastors:

Mr. Bartholomew Ashwood was chosen by them to be their pastor, who immediately, by the consent of the church and his readily accepting their call . . . was ordained and set apart for the pastoral office. (p.11).

Mr. Stephen Towgood having received a call from this church to the pastoral office among them and likewise accepting and embracing the same . . . the church solemnly assembled together . . . ordaining him to the office and work of pastor among them. (p.69).

Here is the classic Independent view of the place of the ministry in the life of the church:

First the Spirit doth gift men, and qualify them for the work . . . Secondly . . . he doth stir up the hearts of men, to choose men, and to call them forth unto the works whom he hath gifted, and qualified for it; . . . Thirdly, there is yet something more, and that is persons being thus chosen, there is a sanction, and a stablishment from the Holy Ghost, that doth come upon them: ...[1]

Or, as Savoy puts the matter:

The way appointed by Christ for the calling of any person, fitted and gifted by the Holy Ghost, unto the office of Pastor, Teacher, or Elder in a Church, is, that he be chosen thereunto by the common suffrage of the Church itself, and solemnly set apart by Fasting and Prayer, with Imposition of Hands of the Eldership of that Church, if there be any before constituted therein: ...[2]

It appears that the laying on of hands was not practised in Ashwood's case. Formerly ordained to the parish of Bickleigh, and later removing to that of Axminster, Ashwood now submitted to the suffrage of the people ("but few, about twelve or thirteen"), and to the commendation of two fellow-pastors of Independent persuasion (William Benn and George Thorn). Towgood was ordained with prayer and the imposition of hands of the participating ministers (Robert Bartlett, Richard Downe, and Henry Butler). In neither case had there been any outside influence beyond what the church had sought by way of advice, help and fellowship.

Implicit in this view is the conviction that "The Church is before the Ministers, seeing the power of choosing Ministers is given by Christ to the Church."[3] Again: "There must be a Church of believers to choose a Minister lawfully... Therefore here is a Church before a Minister."[4] Nothing could be more opposed to the Roman Catholic view of the 'historic episcopate' and a sacerdotal ministry as constituting the essence of the church. But does the Independent view lead to a denigration of the pastoral office? On the contrary:

Though a Church without officers be a true Church in respect of the essence of it, when there is a society of visible saints, united into one body by mutual consent, in the profession of the faith of the Gospel, as appears Acts 6, there was a true church at Jerusalem before there were deacons; and a

1 William Strong, XXXI *Select Sermons,* 1656, Ed. Thomas Manton, pp.113f. The scripture ground for the statement is given by Strong as, 1 Cor. 12, 7-11; 1 Sam. 10.6,26; and Zech. 4.6.

2 *Savoy Declaration of the Institution of Churches*... 1658. XI.

3 Richard Mather, *Church Government and Church Covenant Discussed,* 1643.

4 Thomas Hooker, *Survey of the Summe of Church Discipline,* 1648.

church at Antioch before there were elders, Acts 14.23. But yet it is not a complete church in all the parts of it, as an organical body: therefore it hath officers superadded, and therefore as soon as the Apostle(s) had converted a people to the faith, first they did embody them, and then for their perfection they set officers over them.[1]

Members of the Axminster church who were ordained as pastors were John Ashwood and John Smith, of whose respective ordinations no trace has been found, and Samuel Baker. The latter's ordination at Bridport in 1696 in strict conformity with Independent principles by S. Towgood and J. Ashwood, led to a controversy between Independents and Presbyterians in the Exeter Assembly. See note, p.157.

One of the questions considered by the conference of Independent Churches in 1694 was: "What method is requisite for the church to take to continue a succession in the ministry?" The subject was crucial in a peculiar way at that time. The ejected ministers of 1662 were university men almost without exception, and the lapse of thirty years had considerably reduced their numbers. Some, like Matthew Towgood of Semly, had tutored their own sons, seeing that the universities were closed against nonconformists. Given a young man's fitness for, and call to the ministry, the urgent question was how to help him prepare for his task. To this the nonconformists responded with their version of the Old Testament 'schools of the prophets'. So the nonconformist academies came into being; whereby a number of younger men would reside with a minister of ability and maturity, share his life in home and church, and receive academic instruction in the overall context of the living church situation.

The question may have come home at Axminster by the fact that in 1693 their pastor had already received one of their own number, Samuel Baker, with a view to the ministry. (Note, p.147). Two years later, we learn from the Exeter Assembly minutes that some young men were being tutored with a view to the ministry by Stephen Towgood at Axminster and Matthew Warren at Taunton. Warren's academy was the original of the Western Academy which, after several locations, was placed at Axminster

[1] William Strong, XXXI *Select Sermons,* 1656, Ed. Thomas Manton, p.116.

under James Small from 1796 to 1828. The fascinating story of the nonconformist academies must however, be sought elsewhere.[1]

Ruling Elders The Church ... thought it expedient in order to its being rightly organized, to set apart two of the brethren whom they judged most fitly qualified for the work of ruling elders, to enquire after the state of the flock and be helpful to the church as to its edification, as the office of eldership required.

Thus runs the account of the initial appointment of elders at Axminster (p.18). Each subsequent appointment was regarded with similar solemnity and prayer, the weight of spiritual responsibility attaching to the office being regarded as but little less than that of the pastoral office. (pp.27f, 150f). Their careful designation as *ruling* elders indicates acceptance of the distinction implicit in 1 Timothy 5.17,[2] yet leaving full scope for their aptitude for teaching in matters of counselling, discipline, and conference.

Observation of the ruling elders at work at Axminster, as represented in the *Ecclesiastica,* suggests their basic harmony with John Owen:

> There is a work and duty of rule in the church distinct from the work and duty of pastoral feeding by the preaching of the word and administration of the sacraments ... A spiritual rule, by virtue of mutual voluntary confederation, for the preservation of peace, purity, and order in the church ... for to deny all rule and discipline in the church, with all administration of censures, in the exercise of the spiritual power internally inherent in the church, is to deny the church to be a spiritual, political society, overthrow its nature, and frustrate its institution, in direct opposition unto the Scripture. That there is such a rule in the Christian church, see Acts 20.28; Rom. 12.8; 1 Cor. 12.28; 1 Tim. 3.5; 5.17; Heb. 13.7,17; Rev. 2-3.[3]

1 Irene Parker, *Dissenting Academies in England.* 1914; H. McLachlan, *English Education under the Test Acts.* 1931; and J. W. Ashley Smith, *The Birth of Modern Education.* 1954.

2 "Let the elders that rule well be counted worthy of double honour, especially they who labour in the word and doctrine."

3 John Owen: *The True Nature of a Gospel Church.* 1689 (Works, Ed. W. H. Goold, XVI.108).

Deacons The church thought it meet that some of the brethren might be chosen for the office of deacons, to take care of the poor, and to minister in all other parts of the work belonging to the office of deacons, according to the institution in that primitive church. Acts Ch. 6. (p.24).

So Axminster appointed her first deacons in 1663, the last in the sequence of church offices to be filled, and grounded firmly in its special responsibility of care for the poor, concerning which John Owen says:

> This office of deacons is an office of service, which gives not any authority or power in the rule of the church; but being an office, it gives authority with respect unto the special work of it, under a general notion of authority . . . but this right is confined unto the particular church whereunto they do belong. Of the members of that church are they to make their collections, and unto the members of that church are they to administer.[1]

The diaconate being regarded as the lowest office in the church, the question of elevation from that to a higher office arose twice at Axminster. Stephen Towgood had been a deacon in Henry Butler's church at Maiden Bradley, and, like Philip the evangelist (Acts 6.5; 8.5-40) had also a gift of ministry which he exercised with the approval of his church, and with the eventual hearty commendation of his pastor to the pastoral office at Axminster. Robert Bryant, appointed deacon at Axminster in 1663, was, in 1693 proposed as a ruling elder. There was, however, some scruple as to whether he could be removed from his deaconship which some possibly felt he had assumed for life. But Bryant's spiritual calibre had already been demonstrated by his inclusion in the deputation to Tiverton in 1689, so the issue was "immediately resolved by the pastor from that Scripture, 1 Tim. 3.13, 'They that have used the office of deacon well purchase to themselves a good degree,'" (p.150; and see note, p.138). Moreover, in the event, Bryant was preferred before Matthew Towgood M.D., as elder.

Ordinances Baptism and the Lord's Supper, are God's Ordinances, and they are appointed to be sines and

[1] John Owen. *The True Nature of a Gospel Church.* 1689. (Works, Ed. W. H. Goold, XVI.147).

Seales of the Covenant of Grace between God the Father, Son, and Believers.

Thus, Stephen Ford in 1657.[1]

A Church furnished with Officers (according to the minde of Christ) hath full power to administer all his Ordinances . . . but where there are no teaching Officers, none may administer the Seals, nor can the Church authorize any so to do.[2]

The *Ecclesiastica* does not refer to the Ordinances collectively, except by way of their inclusion in the privileges of the Church.

Baptism The subject is mentioned but once in the *Ecclesiastica.* The church's doctrinal and practical position was governed by the *Westminster Shorter Catechism:*

Q.94. What is Baptism? A. Baptism is a sacrament, wherein the washing with water, in the name of the Father, and of the Son, and of the Holy Ghost, doth signify and seal our ingrafting into Christ, and partaking of the benefits of the covenant of grace, and our engagement to be the Lord's.

Q.95. To whom is baptism to be administered? A. Baptism is not to be administered to any that are out of the visible church, till they profess their faith in Christ, and obedience to Him; but the infants of such as are members of the visible church are to be baptized.

Stephen Ford was much more explicit:

That all such persons as are admitted members of the Church, their children also ought to be accounted and received members of the same church, and their Membership to be confirmed by Baptism . . . That all Children that shall be baptized in the Church are to be accounted members of the same Church; until they shall justly determine themselves by scandall or otherwise; for of such is the kingdom of God.[3]

Any adaptation of the classic federal theology of baptism was bound to conflict with the Independent 'gathered church' principle. It vitiated the central matter of the church covenant. They had already discovered this in pre-1662 parochial situations. How could the indispensable requisites of holiness, separation, and voluntary consent, be asked of infants? It was a contradiction

1 *Epistle to the Church of Christ in Chippin-Norton* . . . 1657, p.38.
2 *Savoy Declaration of the Institution of Churches* . . . 1658. XVI.
3 *Epistle to the Church of Christ at Chippin-Norton* . . . 1657. pp.37,45.

of both the essence and the form of the visible church, and made mockery of the notion of visible saints. Not all Independents, strangely enough, felt the difficulty, but many did. Almost certainly it was a problem at Axminster, for one of the questions for debate at the conference of Independent churches in 1694, was:

> What relation the church hath to those children of church members who are baptised by the pastor of the church, and what is the duty of the church towards them? (p.152).

Sadly, the resolutions of this conference are not on record, but clearly the subject was troublesome to more than one church. Nothing in the Axminster church roll suggests the presence of the names of infants.

The Lord's Supper The observance of the Lord's Supper is alluded to on eight occasions in the *Ecclesiastica.* (1) 1663, "in a lonesome place near a great wood", when the service was disturbed and no administration was possible. p.21. (2) 1678, at Weycroft, being Ashwood's last service. p.60. (3) 1683, "in a solitary wood" p.82. (4) 1684, in "a place remote" p.86. (5) 1685, p.92. (6) 1685, "in this desert place", the communion sermon being recorded, p.106. (7) 1686, preceded by a preparatory service of fasting and prayer, p.123. (8) 1693, the decision to observe regularly at six week intervals p.151.

Allowing once again, as we must, that many observances went unrecorded, some conclusions may be drawn from the passages referred to above:

(i). No regularity of observance was possible during times of severe persecution, and no statement as to frequency of observance appears before that of 1693.

(ii). In each recorded observance the ordinance was administered by the pastor.

(iii). Participation in the ordinance was limited to members of the church. There are references to the ordinance being administered "to the church", and a distinction is drawn between "hearers" (of the preaching) and "members" who received the ordinance. The practice of strict communion flowed directly from the gathered church principle, and was among the covenant privileges of those who were thus committed together to "walk together in a due and faithful attendance upon the Lord Jesus Christ in all His ordinances." Savoy, although with its eye on the pre-ejectment parochial position of the Independent ministers, had clearly said:

> They who are ingaged in the work of Publique Preaching, and enjoy the Publique Maintenance upon that account, are not thereby obliged to dispense the Seals to any other then such as (being Saints by Calling, and gathered according to the Order of the Gospel) they stand related to, as Pastors or Teachers . . ."[1]

The church's privileges were highly esteemed and jealously guarded, and it was the withdrawal of these which fell from time to time on members under discipline.

Much resentment, generally, had long since been caused by the refusal of the Independent ministers to open the Lord's table to all and sundry. Thomas Brooks, for example, laid down six conditions on his election to St. Margaret's, New Fish Street, London, in 1648, stipulating that when the people had fulfilled the first five, "then will I give you ye sacrament . . . and none else but ye body" (i.e. the church, which he had previously defined as "ye godlie partie").[2] The parishioners responded with a complaint to the Committee for Plundered Ministers: "The said Mr. Brooks refuseth to afford your petitioners the use of the ordinances of baptism and the Lord's supper . . ." In due course Brooks set out his position in a pamphlet:

> Though I do give the Lord's supper to those to whom of right it belongs, yet I cannot, I dare not give it to profane, ignorant, malignant, scandalous persons. I had, with Calvin, rather die, than that this hand of mine should give the things of God to the condemners of God. And with Chrysostom, I had rather give my life to a murderer, than Christ's body to an unworthy receiver; and had rather to suffer my own blood to be poured out like water, than to tender Christ's blood to any base liver . . .

On he goes with eight weighty arguments for his position, ending with this:

> Because the supper of the Lord is a feast instituted by Christ only for his friends and children, for those that have received spiritual life from him, and that have union and communion with him.

[1] *Savoy Declaration of the Institution of Churches* . . . 1658. XIV.
[2] A. G. Matthews, *Calamy Revised*. 1934. 79.

And such, Brooks feels, will join themselves to "ye godly partie (that) gather themselves together, and they owne one another's graces, in a way of conference."[1]

Similarly, Peter Ince, of Donhead St. Mary, Wilts, had it said of him in "an MS by no friendly hand (that) he was a rigid disciplinarian in the Independent way, so that he had a select number who were termed the church, to the exclusion of the rest, who, being hearers only, were left without the sacrament, or had to seek it elsewhere."[2]

(iv). Transient or occasional communion is not mentioned in the *Ecclesiastica.* However, in September 1691, just five months after the 'Happy Union' of the Presbyterian and Congregational ministers in London, the Axminster pastor attended a similar gathering in Taunton, which passed the following resolution:

> Resolved that members belonging to a congregation at a distance from the place where they live and ordinarily hear the word, are to be advised by their pastors to join occasionally in communion with the United Brother who is Pastor of that congregation where they hear."[3]

Long before this, Savoy had said:

> Churches gathered and walking according to the minde of Christ, judging other Churches (though less pure) to be true Churches, may receive unto occasional communion with them, such Members of those Churches as are credibly testified to be godly, and to live without offence.[4]

[1] Thomas Brooks, *Cases Considered and Resolved.* 1653. (Works, Ed. A. B. Grosart, Nichols Series, I. xxxviii, xli, xlix-li).

[2] H. Mayo Gunn, *A Memorial of the Nonconforming Clergy of Wilts. & East Somerset in 1662.* 1862. Debate between puritan writers on the subject of strict, restricted, and open communion had gone on from an early period. It was brought into prominence in 1652 by John Humfrey (Humphrey) of Frome, in his *An Humble Vindication of a Free Admission unto the Lord's Supper;* and by the prompt reply in the same year from Roger Drake of London, in *A Boundary to the Holy Mount, or a Barre against Free Admission to the Lord's Supper.* However, this debate was not concerned with the member/non-member distinction, but with the difference between the worthy member who should be admitted, and the unworthy member who should be excluded. Membership definition and interpretation was not always the same between the disputants. The concept of covenant membership settled the point at Axminster. See W. W. Biggs, *The Controversy concerning Free Admission to the Lord's Supper.* (Cong. Hist. Soc. Trans. XVI. 178-189).

[3] *Exeter Assembly Minutes,* p.9.

[4] *Savoy Declaration of the Institution of Churches*... 1658. XXX.

Church Meetings The church meetings of the Independents in the seventeenth century were essentially spiritual gatherings expressive of the covenant bond uniting the members of a local church. While a specific issue could give occasion for a meeting, there might well be preaching, prayer and fasting, either in anticipation, or in the meeting itself. The expression 'church meeting' occurs only two or three times in the *Ecclesiastica,* but phrases such as, "this church resolved", "it was determined by the church", "the church being assembled together", "then the church agreed", "this church thought it meet", "a solemn assembly", "they confer together about it", and "assembled to regulate things" all implying corporate church decision and action, occur some thirty times.

When better days arrived, and the eldership and diaconate had been strengthened in 1693, some review of past procedures and regularising of things for the future was undertaken (p.149ff). Only then was it recorded that from its first embodying the church had met once a fortnight on a weekday whenever possible, "for their mutual edification, sometimes more solemnly in fasting and prayer, sometimes in thanksgiving: ... sometimes by way of conference to regulate matters which did more peculiarly relate to the church" (p.151). There is, indeed, among Bartholomew Ashwood's dying sayings, a reflection on whether his impending departure may not be a judgement for the members' "lameness in coming to week day meetings" (p.61). Having now arranged for the Lord's Supper to be observed at regular six weekly intervals on a sabbath, provision is made for the fortnightly weekday meetings to continue in a (doubtless somewhat flexible) cycle of three: One was to precede the ordinance by way of preparation for it; a second was to "regulate matters respecting this church"; and a third in "resolving cases of conscience" (p.151). Three years later, in 1696, the church decided that their "church meeting days, being once in six weeks, should be spent by them in resolving cases of conscience, which practice was carried on for some space of time" (p.157).

> One of those weekday meetings once in six weeks should be spent... sometimes in resolving cases of conscience, in which each brother that would or had a capacity had liberty to bring in his sentiment to which case was then principally to be spoken unto or resolved (p.151).

The resolution of 'cases of conscience', or casuistry as it was sometimes called, was a distinctive feature of the Reformed and

Puritan tradition. A ministry learned in the Word and experiential in its application was bound to throw up questions, usually connected with the hearer's uncertainty as to his spiritual state. Some ministers had specialised in this kind of thing in their writings.[1] Many attempted to deal with it in their normal pulpit ministry. Had not Bartholomew Ashwood done so in his last sermon on October 20th 1678? He ended his discourse by answering:

> several doubts and objections of disconsolate, dejected souls, and endeavoured to satisfy and encourage the scrupulous and doubting christians (p.60).

Whether these doubts of the scrupulous had been notified in advance or arose out of the subject in hand we do not know. Certainly the advisability, doubtful in the eyes of some, of handling cases of conscience completely separately from the normal ministry of the Word, had been known in one way or another from the early days of the Reformation. Calvin and Zwingli fought shy of it, because of its abuse among some Anabaptists. John a Lasco held a weekly meeting of his congregation of Continental refugees in London in 1550 when, after a sermon and discussion by elders and others qualified, the ordinary member might submit his own question. John Knox introduced a modified version of this into Scotland in the Exercise in 1560.[2] Edmund Grindal's approval of the puritan prophesyings at Northampton in 1571-74 eventually cost him his archbishopric. The Religious Societies which flourished in London 1678-1730 had similar objects.[3] London ministers like Samuel Pike and Samuel Hayward collaborated in answering written questions in a series of public lectures.[4] In the Scottish highlands in the eighteenth century godly ministers received the questions of the scrupulous at regular congregational meetings, and with the assistance of their elders and other mature male members known simply as 'the Men', answered them. In its development the Scottish version came to centre on the Friday 'Question Meeting' which preceded the observance of the Lord's

[1] e.g. William Perkins, *A discourse of Conscience, wherein is set down the nature, properties, and differences thereof.* 1596; *The Whole Treatise of the Cases of Conscience.* 1606.

[2] *The First Book of Discipline,* 1560. The Ninth Head: For Prophecying or Interpreting of the Scriptures. G. D. Henderson, *The Burning Bush,* 1957, pp.42-60.

[3] Josiah Woodward, *An Account of the Religious Societies in the City of London, &c. and of their endeavours for the Reformation of Manners.* Ed.4. 1712.

[4] Pike & Hayward, *Cases of Conscience.* 1755.

Supper, when only 'the Men', venerated for their godliness, were privileged to 'speak to the question'.[1]

There is enough in the Axminster proposal of 1693 to set it firmly in line with the experience of others both before and since. Axminster, it seems, had great concern, because the following year one of the questions discussed by a conference of Independent churches was:

> What way the church ought to take for a mutual edification of itself in general, and of each particular member? (p.152).

At least the level of their church meetings ran higher than minutes, motions, and memoranda!

Synods & Councils The firmness of Independent opposition to the juridical powers of superior ecclesiastical assemblies was both the hall mark of its character and the stumbling block in its often uneasy relationship with the Presbyterians. But it was an opposition usually expressed in positive ways which excluded absolutely any spirit of isolationism.

> In Cases of Difficulties or Differences, either in point of Doctrine or in Administrations, wherein either the Churches in general are concerned, or any one Church in their Peace, Union, and Edification, or any Member or Members of any Church are injured in, or by any proceeding in Censures, not agreeable to Truth and Order: it is according to the minde of Christ, that many Churches holding communion together, do by their Messengers meet in a Synod or Councel, to consider and give their advice in, or about that matter in difference, to be reported to all the Churches concerned; Howbeit these Synods so assembled are not entrusted with any Church-Power, properly so called, or with any Jurisdiction over the Churches themselves, to exercise any Censures, either over any Churches or Persons, or to impose their determinations on the Churches or Officers.[2]
>
> The said Church may desire the assistance of other churches in difficult cases; which cannot be determined by the Church;

1 John MacInnes, *The Evangelical Movement in the Highlands of Scotland, 1688 to 1800*. 1951, pp.211-220. John Kennedy, *The Days of the Fathers in Ross-shire,* 1927. pp.78-109. Alexander Auld, *Ministers and Men in the Far North,* 1957, pp.96-216.

2 *Savoy Declaration of the Institution of Churches* . . . 1658. XXVI.

and the Church should submit to their determination if conformable to the minde of Christ.[1]

> As all Churches and all the Members of them are bound to pray continually for the good or prosperity of all the Churches of Christ in all places, and upon all occasions to further it... So the Churches themselves ... ought to hold communion amongst themselves for their peace, increase of love, and mutual edification.[2]

These guidelines seem to have been observed very well at Axminster. It is not clear whether Bartholomew Ashwood joined the original Exeter Assembly when it threw open its doors to the Independent ministers in 1656. When it came to the embodying of the Axminster Church in 1660, however, there was a "calling in the assistance of other churches, by the hands of Mr. Benn, pastor of a church of Christ at Dorchester, and Mr. Thorn, pastor of a church of Christ at Weymouth" (p.9). When, a few years later, there were both difficulties and differences at Axminster, the pastor did not hesitate "to call upon the pastors of other sister churches for their aid and advice in weighty cases, and those messengers of the churches have been very useful in composing of differences, repairing of breaches, and setting things in order again" (p.30). Nor was Axminster's independence breached when, prior to the settlement of Ashwood's successor, "Mr. Henry Butler came amongst them to give his advice and counsel in this case, that if possible all might be fully satisfied, and after conference with him, and at other times with Mr. Robert Bartlett, the brethren were more generally satisfied." (p.69).

The assistance was not all incoming. In 1689 the Axminster pastor, elder and deacon, formed part of a delegation to resolve difficulties in the church at Tiverton (note, p.138). Two years later the pastor was a member of the Exeter Assembly which sought closer union with the Presbyterians (note, p.144). In 1693 Towgood and others were sent to assist the church at Bideford (note, p.147), and in 1694 there was a conference of "the pastors and elders of three or four churches or congregations" at Exeter and at Weycroft, on matters affecting them all (p.151f).

[1] Stephen Ford, *Epistle to the Church of Christ at Chippin-Norton...* 1657. p.35.

[2] *Savoy Declaration of the Institution of Churches*... 1658. XXV.

All this made for good relations between the churches. The one glaringly irreconcilable difficulty was the refusal of the Independents to recognize the authority of the Exeter Assembly to approve and ordain men to the work of the ministry. In May 1694 it had been "agreed that no candidate be ordained by any of the United Brethren of this county but by order of the assembly." From that resolution Towgood and John Ashwood were unbending dissenters; hence the ordination controversy of 1696 (see note, p.157).

The Axminster Churchmanship here briefly surveyed is fairly representative of the Independent church polity of its period. Readers who wish to pursue this line of historical enquiry on a national scale may refer to G. F. Nuttall, *Visible Saints: The Congregational Way 1640-1660* (London, 1957), and, for the parallel development of these ideals in New England, to E. S. Morgan, *Visible Saints: The History of a Puritan Idea.* (New York, 1963).

Acknowledgements

It is a pleasure to acknowledge thankfully help received from many sources in the preparation of this book. I owe the initial incentive to the late Frank Leslie Rowell who, while visiting the Axminster area in 1971, stumbled on a tattered copy of the 1874 edition and was deeply moved by its content. Finding it spiritually profitable and historically stimulating he conceived the idea of reissuing the work, and invited me to undertake the research necessary to its republication in annotated form. The memory of his enthusiastic collaboration in the few months preceding his death in January 1973 is something I shall always cherish.

I am greatly indebted to the librarians and staffs of the British Library, the Congregational Library, the Evangelical Library, and Dr. Williams's Library in London, and also of Edinburgh University Library. In the alas unsuccessful quest for the manuscript of the *Ecclesiastica,* I have had the hearty co-operation of archivists radiating from the Public Record Office in London to most parts of the country.

To Allan Brockett, Esq., of Exeter University Library I owe, and gladly express my thanks for permission to quote from his edition of the *Minutes of the Exeter Assembly;* to East Devon Record Office for permission to quote from James Davidson's MS *Collections for Axminster;* and to Dr. Williams's Library, for permission to make use of a MS genealogy of the Towgood family.

Dr. G. F. Nuttall, Revd. C. E. Surman, Allan Brockett Esq. and Mrs. M. Rowe of the East Devon Record Office, have generously answered my queries, and made useful historical references and suggestions. I express to each my hearty thanks, though of course I must assume responsibility for the use made of their suggestions, and for the form in which the annotations and appendixes are cast.

I am grateful to Mr. Timothy Abbott for the symbolic chapter headings, and to Miss Ruth E. Rowell for the maps.

K.W.H.H.

INDEXES

INDEX OF PERSONS

Names in bold type were members of the Axminster Church at some period between 1660 and 1698. Names in italic are those of ejected ministers.

INDEX OF PLACES

Names in italic indicate the scene of an ejectment in 1662. Modern spelling is used in the Index; C.17th forms occur occasionally in the book. Do=Dorset; DV=Devon; So=Somerset; Wi=Wiltshire.

INDEX OF SCRIPTURE REFERENCES

GENERAL INDEX

Errata

p. 72n. For Appendix F read Appendix E.

pp. 264-8 *John Hodder, John Rowe, James Stevenson, Lewis Stucley,* and *Francis Whidden,* should be in *italic* type.

p. 266. **Samuel Rampson** (d. 1685) should be in **bold** type.

p. 270. *Stambourne,* should be in *italic* type.

p. 276. Foundation members, Likely - add: D. Lowring, p. 164.

The West Country-
all places mentioned in
"AXMINSTER ECCLESIASTICA"
Somerset
Devon
Glas
Bridgwater
Sedgemoor
Weston Zoyla
Lydeard St. Lawrence
Ash Priors
Kingston St. Mary
West Monkton
Dulverton
Taunton
Ruishton
Bishop's Hull
Wilton
Fivehead
Curry Mallet
Wellington
Angersleigh
Martoc
To Bideford
(17 miles)
Ashill
Loxbeare
Ilminster
Tiverton
Uffculme
Buckland St. Mary
Combe St. Nicholas
Cricket Malh
Newhouse
Whitestaunton
Cullompton
Upottery
Chard
Cricket
St. Thomas
Bickleigh
Luppitt
Haveland
Whatley
Winsham
Stockland
Chardstock
Ford
Abbey
Leigh House
Broadhembury
Thorncomb
Membury
Bu
Dalwood
Holditch
Wyld Court
Honiton
Coaxdon
Hawkchurch
Crediton
Cloakham
Westhay
Feniton
Loughwood
Weycroft
Bettisco
Kilmington
AXMINSTER
Poltimore
Shute
Ashe House
Whitchu
Ottery St. Mary
Musbury
Wootton Fitzpa
Colyton
EXETER
Sowton
Uplyme
Stanton
St. Gabrie
Seaton
Lyme Regis
Beer
To St. Breock (46 miles)
Topsham
Moreton Hampstead
Powderham
Littleham
Exmouth
Kingsteignton
Teignmouth
Newton Abbott
To Stoke Damerel (18 miles)
To Plymouth
(16 miles)
The following, now in Devon,
were in Dorset at the time
of this record:-
Chardstock, Dalwood,
Hawkchurch, Holditch,
Loughwood & Stockland
The followi
were in De
of this reco
Ford Abbey
Torbay
Paignton
To Modbury
(4 miles)
Dartmouth